The Turbulent Gulf

People, Politics and Power

Liesl Graz

I.B. TAURIS & Co Ltd
Publishers
London • New York

Published in association with
The Gulf Centre for Strategic Studies

First published in a revised
paperback edition in 1992 by
I.B. Tauris & Co Ltd
45 Bloomsbury Square
London WC1A 2HY

175 Fifth Avenue
New York
NY 10010

Published in association with
The Gulf Centre for Strategic Studies
5 Charterhouse Buildings Goswell Road
London EC1M 7AN

In the United States of America
and Canada distributed by
St Martin's Press
175 Fifth Avenue
New York
NY 10010

A full CIP record for this book is available from the British Library.

Library of Congress cataloging-in-publication card number: available
A full CIP record is available from the Library of Congress

ISBN 1-85043-557-X paperback

Photoset in North Wales by
Derek Doyle & Associates, Mold, Clwyd.
Printed and bound in Great Britain by
WBC Ltd, Bridgend, Mid-Glamorgan.

Contents

Foreword and Acknowledgements

This book has been in my mind for a long time, for almost as long as the period it is supposed to be concentrating on – the Gulf's turbulent decade. A great many people encouraged me to write it and even more helped along the way. I would like to thank all of them, particularly those in the countries concerned, many, even most, of them unconnected with the official information services. They were as generous with their time as with their knowledge and insights and they afforded me their confidence and, very often, more than that – their friendship. I will not name them all here. The list would be very long indeed and, besides, I know that many of them would prefer anonymity. It is not a question of fear, but of discretion, a highly-prized quality in the Gulf. In a recent issue of an American journal of Middle Eastern studies, a reviewer severely criticized an author for having used what the reviewer called 'the journalistic trick' of not identifying all his sources by name. I wondered whether the reviewer, considered an authority in his field, had ever physically set foot in the Arab Middle East. People there are ready to take a visitor into their confidence and are often far more open and spontaneous than Westerners would be in a comparable situation, but in return they expect absolute discretion. I plead guilty, not of indiscretion, but of what the American reviewer calls a 'journalistic trick'. I am a journalist and proud of it; I also pride myself on having never knowingly abused the trust that a friend or acquaintance may have accorded me. This said, each time that I have been able to do so and thought it useful, I *have* identified my sources.

The press offices of various ministries of information did help a great deal with everything from getting the requisite visas to obtaining appointments, finding written documentation, generally acting as fixers and providing a place to call home base. In some cases, our relationships went well beyond that of duty and we have become friends. I thank all of them, from ministers down to the last *faraj*, or coffee-server. But, and this hardly needs saying, this book is not in any way an official production. In some of the countries concerned, fortunately not in all, that fact alone was enough to make it – and me – slightly suspect. To give an idea of the difficulties that can surround the preparation of a book like this one, of which getting the necessary visas is the first and sometimes the most frustrating of all, I suggest the introduction to Jonathan Raban's excellent 'Arabia Through the Looking Glass' (London, Collins, 1979). Things are no easier now. And I took not just one long journey, like Raban, but have been in the Gulf and the Arabian Peninsula at least twice each year for well over a decade.

Trying to write a book like this with a minimum of prejudices and, I hope, no official bias also meant having to remain financially independent of all governments and official organizations. But I do thank Gulf Air and Air France for their help with some of the travel and especially the Banque Populaire Suisse which accorded me a research grant without which I would not have had the courage even to begin.

I would also like to thank Olivier Da Lage, Awad al-Jabry and Mauricette Gollut, who read all or part of the manuscript and helped tremendously with their comments.

A particular word of thanks goes to the editors of various sections of *The Economist*, and especially to Brian Beedham, for the extraordinary comprehension they have shown toward their wayward and monomaniac correspondent. And a final and particularly heartfelt one to my family, who have once again shown remarkable patience through the long birth-pangs of this book, even more difficult for them to survive than for me.

Foreword to the 1992 Paperback Edition

This book was originally written at a time when the Gulf was in a strange limbo, before and after the inconclusive cease-fire in the eight-year-long war between Iran and Iraq and the invasion of Kuwait by Iraq. When, between 1988 and early 1990, I wrote about the Gulf's turbulent decade there seemed to be a real chance that a period of greater tranquillity was in the offing. However, the storm warnings which were part of *The Turbulent Gulf*'s original premise were only too strongly confirmed in the momentous events of late 1990 and 1991. Politicians and polemicists who cared little for the Gulf before Saddam Hussein's great follies (what else were the successive invasions of Iran and Kuwait?) have multiplied their statements, their analyses – and their fantasies – since.

This new edition is being prepared in a very different atmosphere from that which reigned before what is now commonly, although with some over-simplification, called the Gulf War. The scars from that crisis will take a long time to heal. A brother Arab, one whom few people in the Gulf loved but whom they had helped during those eight long years of the Iran–Iraq War, viciously turned against the one of them who had helped most in those difficult times, and with whom, furthermore, he was linked by the general treaty of brotherhood and non-aggression that is the Arab League Charter. Since the modern Arab states began to emerge after the First World War there have been many quarrels between them, but never has one so blatantly invaded and tried to annhilate another. Memories are long in the Gulf. Although the physical scars even in Kuwait were quickly repaired, the psychological ones are deep, and not only in Kuwait. It will require much longer to find a climate of serenity, of self-assurance that, in the Gulf just as much as elsewhere, is an important ingredient of the pursuit of happiness.

Although it is perhaps foolhardy to continue my own fascination with a region of such enormous volatility, I feel I also owe it to the many friends there who have consistently tried to help me understand their way of looking at the world to try to pass on some of that effort. May this new edition contribute to a wider and deeper comprehension of a fascinating region that could all too easily once again be at the centre of the storm.

Epalinges, April 1992

CHAPTER 1

Introduction: In the Eye of the Storm

The Gulf: to English-speaking people, it was long known as 'the Persian Gulf'; then Arab nationalism got in the way and tried to promote 'the Arab Gulf'. There was even an attempt at 'the Islamic Gulf'. Ten years of boom, a decade of revolution and two successive wars have rendered this patch of salty water in the midst of sterile sands so familiar that by now 'the Gulf', *tout court*, unambiguously designates a steaming and shallow inlet lying between 48 and 56 degrees east of Greenwich and reaching from the 30th parallel almost to the Tropic of Cancer, stretched like an unbalanced boomerang between the mouth of the Shatt al-Arab and the Strait of Hormuz.

Once the improbable theatre of folly and fancy, the first Gulf war made it a disquietingly familiar term of Western geopolitical equations. In eight years of war between Iraq and Iran, its lovely turquoise waters saw more than a hundred ships in flames and some of the nastiest oil slicks on record; then the next war came along. The menace of ecological warfare was realized as bombs and deliberate sabotage brought a marine tragedy, and clouds of acrid smoke darkened the whole region. The Gulf, the northern inlet of the Sea of Oman, itself a subdivision of the Arabian Sea, has played a major role in two successive real-life tragedies. When Iraq invaded Iran in 1980 and precipitated a war that lingered on for eight years the other coastal states had only one hope: to stay out of the fray. The rest of the world by and large followed the same policy. When, on 2 August 1990, the Iraqi leader Saddam Hussein ordered his troops to attack once again

– this time his small, but very rich neighbour and fellow-member of the Arab League – the world did not remain indifferent.

Almost half the world's oil reserves are hidden beneath the sands of the countries bordering the Gulf or under its shallow waters: it is the easiest oil in the world to extract. Persian or Arab, Iranian or Arab, that oil remains vital to the West and not only to the West. In addition to the oil itself, for two decades the economies of all of the West (and of Japan) have been lubricated by the enormous amounts of money that the bordering countries spent, or invested in the outside world. We can no longer simply shrug our shoulders and say 'So what?' The destiny of the Gulf concerns us all.

By the end of 1987, not only the United States, but Britain, the Soviet Union, France, the Netherlands, Italy and Belgium had all sent warships to the Gulf. A year later, six months after the cease-fire went into effect, the majority of them were still there; only in the spring of 1989 did orders start coming for most of them to return to their home waters.

Even though it has become common parlance, it is still somewhat odd to hear the phrase 'the Gulf' used by itself. For centuries, the world's geographers called it the Persian Gulf, but by the 1970s, some Arabs, following the lead of the Iraqis, made such a vociferous fuss whenever a hapless outsider used the expression that, at least in Europe, it fell into disuse. The Americans continue to talk and to write about the Persian Gulf. On the other hand, few outsiders feel at ease with 'the Arab Gulf' which the Iraqi information services tried hard to introduce. The terminological confusion reflects something of the situation on the spot. For the Gulf, a true *mare nostrum* for its riparian peoples, has never known a period of indigenous political unity.[1] It has never in history been either a wholly Arab or an entirely Persian sea.[2]

Until very recently the local people hardly worried about such questions. They were only forced to think about it when the last Shah of Iran began to style himself 'the Gendarme of the Gulf'. Then Saddam Hussein started thinking along the same lines: before he became president of Iraq, long before he threw himself into the war, he was hoping to become the Gulf's Arab protector. In 1980, the war looked, from his point of view, like the perfect opportunity to realize his dream. The liberation of three tiny 'Arab' islands near the Strait of Hormuz,[3] claimed by the Shah in 1971, became the symbol of his ambition: to be recognized as the big Arab brother and protector of the Gulf monarchies against the louring menace of revolutionary Iran. This situation was not exempt from paradox. The Ba'ath Party, which had held power in Iraq since 1968, had execrated these same 'reactionary monarchies', stigmatizing them for corruption and reaction in terms hardly less violent than those used by the revolutionaries in Tehran. Iraqi agents were sent regularly to the Gulf to organize local Ba'athist movements whose task was to undermine the local monarchies just as they were beginning to behave like national, as opposed to purely tribal, governments. Iraq supported the Dhofar rebellion against the Sultan of Oman and all the subsequent incarnations of the Popular Front for the Liberation of Oman and the Arab Gulf. Its agents were at work in the United Arab Emirates, particularly in Ras al-Khaimah, at least up to 1982, still trying to stir up potential revolutionaries.

The removal of Egypt from the centre of the Arab stage in 1979 meant that Saddam Hussein was able to take upon himself the mantle of chief defender of all the Arabs. The Arab summits that ostracized Egypt were convened by Iraq and held in Baghdad; they were very much Saddam's show (see Chapter 2). At the time of the 1979 summit that finally excluded Egypt, he was still a few months away from the presidency of Iraq, but it was a high-water mark of his career: the whole Arab world seemed to lie open before him.

From the vantage point of Baghdad, the vulnerability of the Gulf states* was, in 1980, more important than their wealth. Before it sent hundreds of billions of dollars up in cannon smoke, Iraq did not need any more oil wells to do all it wanted to do. Ambition and pride were the motivations; greed came later. If things had gone according to Saddam's plan, Ba'athism, the Iraqi form of Ba'athism, would have been proved triumphant

* For the sake of simplicity the term 'Gulf States' is used here with no qualification to mean the six member states of the Gulf Co-operation Council: Kuwait, Saudi Arabia, Bahrain, Qatar, the United Arab Emirates and Oman.

and the ambitions of its master both gratified and reinforced. At the time, it all seemed possible.

After the outbreak of the war, the Gulf states felt, in fact, less threatened by Iran than they had during the previous year; the war, by keeping Iran busy, actually alleviated the danger of direct revolutionary interference in their eyes. And they feared Iraq just as much. That was the good thing about the war: it kept both the big powers of the neighbourhood occupied. When Saddam proclaimed that he, the champion of Arabism, was fighting to get back those three little islands, the ex-proprietors (Sharjah and Ras al-Khaimah, two of the United Arab Emirates) showed far less enthusiasm than he did.

The History

Before the oil boom which began in 1969 or 1970 (1973 saw the confirmation and the acceleration of the boom, not the beginning), the last time the Gulf had been anywhere near the centre of the world stage was around the year 1515. This was when the Portuguese, then at the height of their power, had managed to snatch a fragile supremacy from both the Safavid Persians and the Ottoman Turks, two dynasties enthusiastically building their rival empires.

The Portuguese were never colonizers in Arabia; all they wanted were safe havens along the route to the East Indies. They stayed in the Gulf just long enough to build a few handsome forts, and were expelled from Muscat, their last Arabian stronghold, in the middle of the seventeenth century. The two other empires left deeper marks. The Safavids were able to win control over the whole north-east coast of the Gulf; ever since, and with the sole exception of the British pretensions to the status of protecting power in the nineteenth and twentieth centuries, no doubt has ever been cast on the Iranian[4] sovereignty. The Ottomans pushed half-way down the other coast, but beyond Kuwait their authority was always fairly tenuous. The precariousness of the Ottoman control is reflected in some still-disputed borders, but few other tangible souvenirs of their presence remain.

The next few centuries were marked by tribal migrations.

Towards 1700, Bahrain had regained some of the lustre as a commercial centre it had enjoyed off and on for three thousand years. Its greatest attraction was its sweet-water springs which made it possible to sustain a relatively prosperous agricultural community. About the same time, the Al-Khalifa family and their followers, originally from the Nejd in the centre of the Arabian Peninsula, wandered east to Qatar, then north to Kuwait and back again to the Qatari peninsula where they established a pearling centre at Zubara. Bahrain and its tempting springs were just across the water and the Al-Khalifas established their rule over the islands in 1783. Repercussions of this conquest of what was until then a Shi'a island by a Sunni dynasty are still reverberating.

The eighteenth century also saw Kuwait emerge from anonymity. In 1764 the great German traveller Carsten Niebuhr wrote that Kuwait was 'a busy town of 10,000 souls who live from pearl fishing and commerce and own 800 ships'.[5] This is a perfect example of the standard eighteenth-century traveller's tale description and does not necessarily correspond to reality. Niebuhr never visited Kuwait and probably reported what a seaman told him. In fact, before 1775 Kuwait was no more than a tiny fishing hamlet like a dozen others. That year the Persians conquered Basrah and for the next four years the trading route by land from Constantinople to India passed west of the port, via Al-Zobair.[6] Kuwait replaced Basrah as a commercial relay and for the first time had to deal with both the Ottomans and the British. The British East India Company opened a small post near the bay and the Ottomans made political overtures to the local sheikh. So began an association with the Turks that was to become closer than any other in the Gulf when the sheikh of the time helped the governor of Basrah in one of his intermittent battles against the local potentates, and the region that makes up Kuwait today took up special status as a voluntary ally to the Ottoman *vilayet* of Basrah. To reward the Sheikh for this mark of confidence, in 1873 the Turkish governor, Midhat Pasha, presented him with a minor Turkish title and rich date gardens along the Shatt al-Arab, a practical gift because in any case Kuwait had to bring most of its fresh water from there to supplement the inadequate local wells. The water boats plied until 1950, when the first desalination plant went into service.

The co-operation between Ottomans and Kuwaitis was encouraged by their common fears of Wahhabi expansion. Wahhabism is a puritanical Islamic reform movement that was founded in the Nejd toward the middle of the eighteenth century by Muhammad ibn Abd al-Wahhab who soon allied himself with the Emir of Diriyya, Muhammad ibn Saud (see Chapter 5). For half a century, Wahhabi bands spread terror through the Gulf. At the peak of their expansion, they held the whole coast; only Kuwait and Muscat (which is not really part of the Gulf) held out. Their closest allies were the Qawasim who had made for themselves a considerable reputation as the masters of a small naval empire around Ras al-Khaimah, not far from the Strait of Hormuz. They were fierce rivals of the Sultans of Oman, themselves in the ascendant of their power, and relations oscillated between short periods of wary friendship and episodes of open warfare.

In the course of the nineteenth century, the cleavage between the north and the south (or more accurately, the northwest and the southeast) of the Gulf became more apparent. Once the general treaty of peace had been imposed in 1820, the sheikhdoms of the southern territories, or Pirate Coast, were incorporated into a system of British protectorates known collectively as Trucial Oman and then, until 1971, the Trucial States. Even though Kuwait formally also became a British protectorate after the collapse of the Ottoman Empire, it was never assimilated to the same degree. Saudi Arabia remained completely outside the system.

Until the eve of the First World War, the borders between these territories were, for all practical purposes, non-existent. An Anglo-Turkish Convention signed in 1913 tried, for the first time, to give the territories some legal definition. It was not an easy task in a world where the territory of one or the other tribe was defined more by loyalty to a sheikh than by lines on a map. The borders, as they were drawn in the 1913 Convention (which was never ratified) are deceptively precise. As Salem al-Jabir as-Sabah points out, when the Convention says that the northern border of Kuwait is at Khor al-Zobair, that means somewhere along the shore of a bay several kilometres long.[7]

Precise borders were, in any case, of only minor interest at the time; they became important only when oil was discovered under the sands, twenty years later.

The Turks and the British engaged in another map-drawing exercise two years later. The Treaty of Qatif officially recognized the existence of a Wahhabi state in Arabia and in return its emir (not yet king) Ibn Saud promised to respect the borders drawn up between his state, Kuwait and the other emirates of the Gulf. The idea was good, but it was practically impossible to apply with any degree of certainty, again because of the imprecision of the borders. The next attempt was at Ugayr in 1922, between representatives of Britain (which by then held the mandatory power over Iraq and the protecting power over Kuwait) and the kingdom of Nejd, as Ibn Saud had decided to call his domain. To this day, the Kuwaitis have not forgiven the British negotiator, Sir Percy Cox, for giving two-thirds of what they considered Kuwaiti territory to Ibn Saud on the pretext that the power of the As-Sabah of Kuwait was on the decline and that Ibn Saud, the rising star in the Arabian firmament, was better able to assure order. Sir Percy drew two big lozenges on the map, one of them the co-property of Kuwait and the Nejd and the other the co-property of Kuwait and Iraq. The bedouin were to be given the right to pass back and forth through them – as though a red line drawn on a map could stop a bedu – and any future riches were to be equably divided. By then, commercial quantities of oil had been discovered in both Iraq and Iran and drawers of maps were becoming warier. No administration at all was foreseen for these areas, the first example of a new concept called ‘neutral zones’.

In the lower Gulf, the Trucial Coast, sometimes called Trucial Oman, experienced a completely different history. At the end of the eighteenth century, when the British began to call it the Pirate Coast, the appellation was only partially justified. According to recent research, this seems to have been an early application of the classic technique of disinformation, a way of justifying intervention at a key point on the route to India, which became particularly important once the French began to show signs of interest. The sheikh-historian Sultan Muhammad al-Qasimi, emir of Sharjah, goes rather far in trying to defend his ancestors against all charge of piracy,[8] but his arguments showing the motivation of the British East India Company and its methods (especially the use of the pirate motif as *ex post facto* justification for the intervention) are convincing. Once the general treaty of peace had been imposed in 1820, the Pirate Coast was renamed: for the next century and a half, it would be known as the Trucial Coast.

When the Qawasim[9] of Ras al-Khaimah accepted Wahhabism and became faithful allies of the Diriyya sheikhs, an already complicated situation turned to chaos. One of the Qawasim turned against the rest of the family and declared himself the sheikh of Sharjah, helped in his dissidence by the Sultan of Muscat. At the same time, the hostility between rival clans of the Bani Yas tribe took on territorial aspects: the An-Nahayan tried to cement their claims to Abu Dhabi while their rivals, the followers of Maktoum bin Buti retreated to Dubai where they quickly learned the fine art of alternating alliances with one or other of their neighbours. The confusion was general, but in its midst alliances began to take shape. From the middle of the last century, by looking carefully at who is where and who is friendly with whom, one can see the contours of the political map of the 1980s emerging. There is nothing of modern nationhood, neither a whisper of governmental organization nor the hint of a modern nation-state. But the network of loyalties grounded in a double foundation of family and of trust is discernible. The web is held together by a system of protection and exchange: the bounty of desert raiding or the fruits of the oases were little by little replaced by subsidies and cash gifts. The exchanges and the gifts, whether in the old style or the modern, had no need to be mathematically equal; they must, however, be in conformity with a minimum of justice. Otherwise the whole system of loyalty will break down. The sheikhs know these facts very well.

Within this context, the fact of belonging to a social group is far more important than the attachment to any particular territory. This idea had, at least until the early part of the present century, a corollary: the economic space to which an individual or a family belongs is more important than the physical one. Thus, the Ottoman influence in Kuwait actually extended as far as the ports of Al-Hasa, Ahsa being the most important, and turned its back on the territories under British protection. Even while the India Office was busy parcelling the authority of the individual sheikhs it considered the whole Gulf as one larger entity;[10] the British Residence was established in Bushire, on the Persian shore, in 1778 and only transferred to Bahrain in 1946, by which time British influence in Iran had been strongly eroded in favour of the Americans. In any case, Indian independence the following year made the Gulf far less important to Britain.

The period between the two world wars was marked by two phenomena whose key importance would become apparent only later. The first was the consolidation of power in Arabia by the Al Saud; the decisive step in that consolidation was the conquest of the Hijaz, which extended their power to the Red Sea coast. More important, it made them masters of the holy cities of Mecca and Medina. In the 1920s and 1930s the pilgrimage taxes were a welcome source of income for the impoverished Saudi state. Far more significant, the Al Saud knew how to use their guardianship of the holiest places of Islam as sources of prestige, power and finally legitimacy, as important, if not more so, as the wealth yet to come.

The other major event of the inter-war period was the discovery of commercially exploitable oil. Before 1914, large fields were known to exist in Iraq and Iran. Between 1911 and 1923, Britain signed agreements with all the local rulers from Bahrain to Muscat assuring it the exclusive right to any future oil rights. Only the emerging Saudi state was excluded from the system. In 1923 Bahrain was the first of the small states to sign an actual concession. The first commercial shipment left the island in December 1933. Kuwait signed its first contract in 1934, but the Second World War stopped exploration efforts and exports began only in 1946. The rest followed: Qatar's first shipment left port in 1949, Abu Dhabi's in 1962, followed by Dubai, Sharjah and Ras al-Khaimah; finally Oman, where the first laden tanker left Muscat in 1969. During the First World War, oil was still less important than coal. By 1939 things had changed, and yet the war period did not give the Gulf any particularly important role. The oil wells that counted were further north, in Iran and Iraq, in the Soviet Union and in Romania.

The end of the war brought with it a resurgence of fervent nationalism, but this far corner of the Arab world did not catch fire as quickly as the rest. When the Egyptian monarchy was overthrown, the excitement was far away and Gamal Abdul Nasser's passionate appeals for the Arabs to rise up in revolt had fewer repercussions here than in North Africa or the Fertile Crescent. They did not, however, go completely unheard. One can consider what happened in the Yemens, where the situation in the 1950s was really not very different from that of the Gulf.

The paradox was that after the independence of India and the Suez debacle of 1956, the Gulf became for the British a last point of support for the defence of Aden, which had originally been occupied because of its position on the route to India. It was only after the withdrawal from Aden that the British Government announced that it would also leave the Gulf within three years, budget restrictions being given as the justification. The decision was debated again in London after the Conservatives were returned to power in 1970, but was upheld despite the discreet offers made by several of the sheikhs to contribute to the cost of maintaining the British troops, estimated at £25 million sterling per year. The British Defence Minister declared that such an offer was unacceptable because 'it would make mercenaries of Her Majesty's subjects'.[11] The sheikhs may have been nervous; their subjects not at all. Those who thought about such things were happy to see the British go.

The madness and after

This brief introduction to the history of the Gulf seems indispensable if one is to understand what has happened since: the years of oil-boom madness and the difficult adjustments that have been taking place since 1982. Contrary to what many people in the West have thought, the Gulf did not simply emerge out of the sands in 1973 like Venus rising from the waves. As for 1982, this date is deliberately chosen rather than 1980 as the year when things began to change. The latter date may have marked the beginning of the Iran-Iraq war, but for the states of the Gulf Co-operation Council it was far less important than 1982 when the war first began to affect them directly. By 1982, the GCC had been founded in direct response to the war, and the first serious discussions were being held with a view to finding a common attitude towards the belligerents. It was also the year of the great stock-market crash in Kuwait and of the first big subsidies to Iraq – officially $31 billion between 1981 and 1984, mostly allocated by the three richest countries, Saudi Arabia, Kuwait and the United Arab Emirates.[12] Thereafter the UAE practically stopped their subsidies and the others diminished theirs. There was some compensation via oil transactions: both Saudi Arabia and Kuwait sold oil on Iraq's account to make up at least some of the deficit in its exports. Nobody dares to guess at the amount of the subsidies given to Iran by the same Gulf countries, but they did exist, in lesser amounts and in various forms. After the attacks on Kuwait and the riots in Mecca during the 1987 pilgrimage, they were probably cut off, except perhaps from the UAE.

The point of this introduction is also to avoid boring repetitions in the chapters which follow, which are devoted to the eight coastal states of the Gulf, the six members of the Gulf Co-operation Council,[13] and their neighbours, Iran and Iraq, particularly in their relations with the Gulf as they fought for eight years and as they began the search for peace. This rapid historical survey should also make it easier to understand what all or several of these states and their inhabitants have in common and what is specific to one or the other. Going on from there, it should also help to discern the elements of unity and those of diversity, the first as important as the second. To think and speak of the Gulf, as many Westerners do, as one homogenous mass peopled by a particular species of *homo arabicus* is not enough; it is even, in my view, incorrect.

Of course there are common traits. For the six member countries of the GCC, the first of these is a common social structure that remains strongly marked by the double influence of tribal traditions and of the old merchant families. Both are necessary to a general consensus surrounding the monarchies and to the idea of monarchy as such; they are accepted even among those who would like to see some changes and updating.

The traditional structure must find some way of accommodating the new elites who are a product of the major advances in education which begin with literacy programmes and go on to grants in the world's great universities. The fact that many of the first generation of the educated elites are scions of the great merchant families is no guarantee of docility.

The second common trait is a profound attachment to Islam, which means that the discussions of 'Islamic fundamentalism' as it appeared in the northern parts of the Arab world are simply not relevant. The populations of the Gulf states are made up of a majority of Sunni Muslims, with the exception of Bahrain, where the majority is Shi'a, and Oman, which is strongly marked by Ibadhism.[14] The Islamic revolution in Iran (most people in the Gulf dislike the use of the name, considering it a usurpation) made such a storm that it often hid the existence of an Islam where faith runs strong and deep without being either revolutionary or even 'Islamist'.[15]

At the beginning of the Iranian revolution there were demonstrations of greater or lesser violence in all the cities of the eastern part of the Arabian Peninsula, with the exception of Muscat. Not surprisingly, the most violent were in Manama (Bahrain) and Dammam, in eastern Saudi Arabia; the province of Al-Hasa has a Shi'a population of at least a quarter of a million. The most important of all the demonstrations was, of course, the occupation of the great mosque in Mecca in 1979, which had very particular characteristics completely different from the 1987 *hajj* riots (see Chapter 5). Yet in general in the Gulf countries, Islam remains such an integral part of normal life that there is far less fertile ground for the zealots to plant their seeds of discord. There is no need to let one's beard grow and cut off one's *dishdasha* to show that one is a good Muslim; despite the inevitable personal failings here and there, being a good Muslim is the normal thing to be. Public prayers for rain mark the beginning of each winter. A discussion on agriculture, say, can easily turn to theology and no one thinks anything odd about it. Islam is such a natural part of life that many interlocutors are astonished that one can manifest an interest in them and in Islam without being a Muslim oneself.

Another constant has become an unavoidable cliché: the

boom. All of these countries became very rich in a very short period of time. This holds true also for pre-war Iran and Iraq although there, with their far larger populations and differences in structure, the manifestations were different. There are varying degrees to this wealth, but its benefits were felt everywhere, not necessarily by every individual in each country, although among the citizens of the GCC countries it would be difficult to find one who had not enjoyed some advantages. The fisherman along the desert coast north of Salalah, the bedouin wandering on the borders of the Rub al-Khali, the 'empty quarter', even the Bahraini villager – all have seen their lives fundamentally transformed. The problem is that many of those who have had the fewest benefits can make comparisons with others who have had far more.

In 1982, the boom peaked; it was also when the first signs appeared that the madness would some day come to an end. Of course, sensible people had been saying so for years, they all knew it, but there had been little evidence to support such common sense. By 1982 the hard facts began to appear; some of the signs were linked to the pursuance of the war (which had, of course, not been expected to last so long) and others were absolutely independent of it. That year the combined oil revenues of the three major exporting countries, Saudi Arabia, Kuwait and the UAE together reached $186 billion. By 1985, they were down to $57.6 billion and by 1986, $36.9 billion. What marked the boom period even more than the money itself was the feverish rhythm that went with it, a rhythm absolutely uncharacteristic of the region; the 'I want it all, and I want it now' syndrome was applicable to whole countries. Whatever judgement may eventually be made of the authoritarian, paternalist systems of the local monarchs, it is only fair to remember that they understood that their enlightened self-interest was *also* to use the enormous riches to give their countries the basic institutions of modern social life: schools and teachers, hospitals complete with doctors and nurses, roads, air-conditioned houses, power plants, irrigation channels and factories and much more.

Almost everywhere, the process of development began from scratch or so close to it as to make little difference. The hardest task of all, when so much wanted doing, was to define priorities. A still unresolved dilemma was to decide just how far development should be pushed to include new socio-political concepts that might be more easily compatible with modern life than with the traditional structures. One example among hundreds: should medical care continue to be free (the state as the head of the enlarged tribal structure taking care of its people) or should at least token payment be demanded?[16] And what about personal taxes? This question moved beyond theory into painful practice in Saudi Arabia. Or again, in the schools and the new universities, are students supposed to learn to ask questions or should they just learn facts? (see Chapter 5)

As the boom ended, the most difficult problem of all was learning to make choices, both in the field of political adjustments and in those where, for a time, simple riches had made it possible to obfuscate the problem. Oil revenues, as we have seen, have dropped considerably and yet, despite all the efforts at diversification, their influence remains preponderant. Even after the price falls of 1986, they represented 45 per cent of Kuwait's gross national product, 85 per cent in the UAE, 60 per cent in Oman and 55 per cent in Saudi Arabia.[17] Even taking into account the dramatic drop in income, none of the Gulf countries has rejoined the ranks of the impoverished and the least rich among them, Bahrain and Oman, are still among the world's privileged. Growth in all of them had been exponential; and it fell almost as fast. Yet the fall brought neither the countries nor the populations back to their starting point. For the first time in their history, these countries are in a situation that one could describe, for want of a better term, as 'normal'.

No longer among the poor of the world, these once forgotten populations have not lost all their collective memory of what life was once like on the shores of the Gulf. What it was like to live in Qatar after the only real source of income, pearling, was ruined by Mr Mikimoto's discovery of the art of encouraging oysters to produce pearls on demand. Or to be Omani after the empire fell apart and the maritime trade was reduced to virtually nothing by the competition of steam. How long will people really remember what it was like to be a bedouin in the centre of the peninsula, burnt by the sun and the stinging sand, pushing from one well to another at the rhythm of the animals, seeing children suffer and die, knowing no certainty but the absolute presence of God?

Not long ago, the common picture of all these countries was as the spoiled darlings of God and fate. Up until August 1990, some individuals lived as though that glorious moment could last forever. In one night, that illusion was shattered. Some individuals had amassed enormous private fortunes and invested them wisely enough to continue living in high style. But even before the shock of the invasion of Kuwait by its northern neighbour, governments had realized that the time of euphoria was over and that hard questions would soon have to be faced: how to balance a budget – or even how to draw up a budget – and how to run a country when means are no longer infinitely expendable. Above all, governments are now faced with the issue of how best to run a country when the transition from patriarchal, even feudal, society to a modern society is not yet complete. These countries are not looking for a return to 'normality' (and I use that word knowing that it is indefinable). They are discovering what it is to live in a whole new world whose questions and problems, albeit with a special Gulf cast, are increasingly those that the rest of the world also faces.

It is a mistake to fall into the trap of those who say that the end of the boom and the drop in oil revenues is an excellent thing, that finally the people of the Gulf will have to learn self-reliance and to work for themselves. It is more apposite to ask whether the citizens of the Gulf are ready to take on the jobs that need to be done if or when all the immigrant workers are sent home. Kuwait and Saudi Arabia are both, in different contexts and with different types of labour, facing that question directly as a result of the Gulf crisis; neither has resolved it. (In fact, Kuwait expelled, or failed to renew visas for a large proportion of the 400,000 Palestinians who lived in the Emirate before August 1990. Saudi Arabia did the same for some 800,000 Yemenis.) With or without a drop in oil prices and even without the Iraqi invasion and the consequent shocks, a slowdown was inevitable and the question had to be faced sooner or later. Before the invasion, Kuwait was the best example of a Gulf country that had finished the long process of building its infrastructure; it had done such a thorough job that even though the invasion and the occupation dented it badly, it was not destroyed. In the huge spaces of Saudi Arabia and in Oman there is still work to be done, but elsewhere only details remain to be fussed over and, more importantly, the entirely new concept of maintenance is gradually emerging.

Before the invasion of Kuwait, the Gulf was just beginning to think about living at a cruising speed, to work at continuing whatever had been established with innovations as they were needed – repairing, maintaining, planning carefully, becoming accustomed to a completely new rhythm. That, literally as well as figuratively, a whole society has moved directly from the camel to the jet, may prove the most difficult factor of all.

The world of the Gulf is much like those wonderful old-fashioned papers whose marbled designs mix forms and colours, sidle up to one another, cross and interpenetrate, but never melt into uniformity. It is easy to be fooled by an outward veneer of Occidental gadgets. All the latest inventions of Western (including Japanese) technicians and engineers appear in the Gulf as if by magic. I saw my first home video programmer in Qatar and, at a time when only ministers' cars in Europe had mobile telephones, Kuwaitis routinely handed out cards listing at least three numbers: home, office and car telephone.

And yet, despite first impressions, there is very little desire for a complete imitation of the Western style of life. It is instructive to go to the home of a fairly well-off city dweller, say a member of the technical elites who studied in the West or, when it was possible, at the American University in Beirut. You will be shown into a large living room where opulent 'Western'-style armchairs (a major Egyptian export) are lined up along the walls interspersed with small rectangular tables for glasses of tea and boxes of Kleenex. The strictly rectilinear arrangement is an odd reflection of what a 'modern' room should be: Western building-blocks, so to speak, in the spatial idiom of the traditional reception room. Nobody is really at ease there, neither host nor guest. For the host and his family, it does not really matter; in any case this is not the real centre of the house.

Behind the formal living room there is another, the real *majlis*, where you take off your shoes before sitting down on a carpet, propped against cushions; tea and trays of fruit are set on the ground; so are the huge platters from which everyone eats together, using fingers in accordance with the strict rules of etiquette. This is where one can feel at ease, and where a guest can finally learn to understand the Gulf. The societies are much like their houses. One could, in fact, go one step further, through the next door – if, that is, you are fortunate enough to be invited. In many houses it is only there, in the third room, that one can meet the women and begin to understand the structure of the family.

Of all the factors separating Westerners from the people of the Gulf – those that can lead to an abyss of incomprehension but must be taken into account – the most difficult to apprehend is the difference in the sense of time. By that, I do not in the least mean the old jokes about '*Boukra, incha'Allah*' – tomorrow, God willing.

Keeping or not keeping appointments, being or not being punctual, is only a small part of the question. In any case habits and behaviour can be very different in different parts of the Gulf; in Kuwait and Muscat, a quasi-Swiss exactitude is normal behaviour, and I have been chided for being fifteen minutes late for an interview. No, what is far more important is the different relationship between the individual and time as an abstract, the passage of time as such. A distinguished French scholar[18] considers an indeterminate relationship with time to be characteristic of Islam, or rather of Muslims. It would be the natural result of a lunar calendar by which all feasts are movable through the seasons (in a normal lifespan, a Muslim will probably see Ramadhan twice in winter, twice in summer) and where the determining moments of the day, the five prayer times, vary with its length. Only the Day of Judgement is pre-determined, and no man knows when it will come.

Applied to the Gulf, this theoretical analysis can be used to throw light on empirical realities. Until very recently, the rhythm of life was a function either of the hazards of navigation where uncertainty was as much a reality for the merchants awaiting their ships as for the sailors at sea, or of nomadic pastoralism in a hostile environment. The first of these factors, that of uncertain maritime transport, was not unique to Arabia; Antonio, Shakespeare's merchant of Venice, knew it well. Nevertheless, in Arabia it was probably exacerbated by the other factors of basic temporal mobility. Settled farmers live according to the rhythm of the seasons.[19] The bedouin could never know with certainty where they would be able to find fodder for their animals, or if the next water-hole had gone dry. Even today, when one arrives at a camp in the open desert, one of the first questions in the long liturgy of greeting is 'Has there been rain anywhere?' Nothing in the bedouin's world was certain.

It is still difficult to make appointments for a week in advance, but when something has been decided, it is expected to be accomplished immediately, whether it be a meeting with a minister, an invitation to lunch, the signing of a contract or the departure on a journey. This generalized practice of the concept of immediacy can be extremely disconcerting to an outsider, just as it can provide pleasant surprises. Its interiorization can also help to explain how the populations of the Gulf have been able, on the whole, to accommodate the enormous changes that they have seen and lived through in a very short period without falling into an immense collective schizophrenia.

This sense of the immediate, and even more the expectation of immediate results, also has its reverse side. It is very difficult in the Gulf to make long-term commitments and to keep them step by step. For example, when an organization like the Gulf Co-operation Council is set up, the ordinary citizens – and even many of the elite who should know better – expect to see results instantly; plans, projects and promises are not enough to avoid an almost inevitable disappointment, however objectively unjustified it may be.

The period that began with the end of the short and bitter conflict between Iraq, the invader, and Kuwait, Saudi Arabia and the other Gulf countries, together with the coalition of states under the military leadership of the United States, working under a United Nations mandate, is not yet over. For the people of the Gulf, the victory was bitter, because Saddam Hussein was still in power and they could not, they said, ever feel safe so long as he was. The formal map of the area had not changed although there was some talk of shaving off a bit of Iraqi territory to give to Kuwait in the framework of a border settlement. But the political climate had changed completely. A year after the end of the conflict, there was little joy in the Gulf and much bitterness.

The chapters that follow, one each per country, are not mini-guides. On the contrary, I have tried to single out one or two salient aspects, which give each one its personality and its savour. This deliberate choice was not made from a desire to divide them, but in an attempt to go beyond the clichés of over-simplifying generalities.

CHAPTER 2

Iraq: The Long Shadow

When the first Gulf War between Iran and Iraq ended, all the ambiguity surrounding Iraq's relations with its neighbours, the six countries of the Gulf Co-operation Council, who hated seeing the word 'Gulf' applied to a war that was never theirs, returned in force. Arab solidarity had given Iraq the support it needed to hold out and then, to all intents and purposes, to win against a far larger Iran. As the war ended, and during the long negotiating process that began with the cease-fire in August 1988, the positions began subtly to shift. Iraq, understandably heady with what was presented to its own people as a great victory, quickly began to flex its muscles: towards the rebellious Kurds of the North and, what is more germane to our subject but was then less obvious, towards the Gulf States.

Iraq touches on the Gulf directly for less than 50 kilometres of swampy coast, most of it on the Faw peninsula, a place few people had heard of or cared about before it became one of the most celebrated battlegrounds of the war, conquered by the Iranians in January 1986 and retaken by the Iraqis in a lightning offensive in April 1988. In conquering Faw, the Iranians – who during the first years of the war had used steam-roller tactics rather than finesse – accomplished such a sophisticated river crossing with rapidly constructed mobile bridges that rumours were flying around the Arab world that they could never have done it alone but had had outside help, possibly from the Israelis. There seems to have been no basis to the rumours, a new variation on the ordinary conspiracy theories. More to the point, the newly sophisticated Iranian strategists were far more frightening as a serious threat to Basrah and the whole southern third of Iraq. The period after the Faw offensive of 1986, when not a great deal really happened on the front, was probably the low point of the whole war from the Iraqi point of view. The surprisingly easy reconquest of the peninsula, just after the 'war of the cities' rocket duels in February and March 1988, was the real signal that the tide had turned. From then on, Iraq seemed to go from victory to surprising victory until, in July, Iran accepted the cease-fire resolution proposed by the United Nations a year earlier, which Iraq had accepted almost immediately, at a time when it was in a far less favourable position.

The Iraqi ports were useless from the very beginning of the war. Basrah, 100 kilometres upstream from the mouth of the Shatt al-Arab,[1] was bottled up long before it was shelled and Umm Qasr, primarily a military port and further west, was blockaded from the very first day. Even in peacetime Iraq never really turned towards the Gulf. True, this is its only direct access to the sea, but emotionally, sentimentally and even intellectually, it has always looked toward the Mediterranean with a few sidelong glances in the direction of Iran. Even at the time of the Crusades, the caliphs, sultans and emirs of Baghdad and Mosul were constantly being called upon for help by their cousins and peers in the Levant and considered that they had a legitimate interest there.[2] In contrast the Iraqis have always tended to look down on the Gulf and the whole Arabian Peninsula.

And yet, Iraq's shadow inevitably looms over the Gulf all the way to Hormuz. Iraq is such a complex subject that it merits far more than one chapter – and more attention than most authors have given it in recent years.[3] This chapter cannot be an exhaustive study.[4] It has no pretensions to anything more than presenting a few signposts to help make the recent evolution of the country slightly more intelligible, particularly in its relations with the countries of the Gulf and the Peninsula.

Considered from almost any angle, Iraq is very different from all the other countries touching on the Gulf.[5] Rather than list all the differences in history, politics, social organization, demography, ethnic composition and even religious make-up, it is easier to list the points of convergence. Three of these are important: the community of Arab language and culture – a factor that should not be underestimated, a sense of belonging to the Arab Middle East, an elastic but very real concept, and, finally, the oil factor. Islam is not included for two reasons. First, because of the avowed secularism of Ba'athist Iraq, even though Islamic references have returned and multiplied under the onslaught of the Iranian revolution. Secondly because, in contrast to the countries of the Peninsula, there are not only the Shi'a (well over half the population) to be taken into account, but the other heterodox groups as well. Before many of them fled the country in 1991, perhaps 8 or 9 per cent of the native Iraqi population was made up of Christians of a dozen sects, not to mention such religious curiosities as the Yazidis and Mandeans.[6]

Iraq is the only country of the Arab Middle East which fuses the three elements nowadays considered essential for long-term success in the region: oil, water and a relatively numerous native population. France recognised this fact almost twenty years ago and therefore chose Iraq as a privileged ally at a time when the country had a particularly nasty reputation for bloody revolutions followed by brutal repression. The war helped to change this image to that of a bastion against the Islamic wave symbolized by the Ayatollahs' republic. But the underlying fear remained, and the Iraqis' actions at the end of the war, particularly as regards their own Kurdish population, did nothing to dispel lingering doubts either in the West or among fellow-Arabs, whatever faithful lipservice the latter may have paid at the time.

An Egyptian diplomat, Tahsin Bashir, has been quoted as saying 'Outside of Egypt, there are no states in the Arab Middle East; the others are nothing more than tribes with a flag'.[7] With no disrespect, it would seem that he forgot about Iraq in his too-clever aphorism. Iraq enjoys all the attributes that he considered the indispensable marks of a nation-state: real historical roots, a sense of identity and a coherent native population, which is not necessarily the same thing as a homogeneous one.[8] Over the centuries, or millennia, the names have changed, but it is difficult to deny the reality of the civilizations that have flourished in Mesopotamia from Sumer to the Abbasid Caliphate. They were organized states; just as in Egypt, they had to be in order to provide the necessary management of large-scale irrigation. For the same millennia, Mesopotamia, whatever its name, has also been the only serious rival to the Nile Valley for supremacy in the Arab Middle East. The Iraqi population today, some 16 million people, is varied, but the war showed that it is far less fragmented than many observers thought. Otherwise, the Arab population, Shi'a as well as Sunni, would not have held out as well as they did against the repeated onslaughts of propaganda, and the incitements to revolt launched against them from the time of the revolution in Teheran in 1979. The Kurds are different but even then one might venture to say that until the sad days of August 1988, a majority felt themselves to be loyal Iraqis, admittedly in search of autonomy, but opposed to the regime rather than to the country itself.

Towards war with Iran

From the first months after the proclamation of the Islamic Republic in 1979 the cross-border vilifications had reached a degree of violence unthinkable in Europe outside a state of declared hostilities. From the outset, Iran tried to strike at the internal cohesion of Iraq by seeking to seduce and suborn the heterodox parts of the population, the Shi'a Arabs, to begin with, the Kurds of course, and even, surprisingly, to some extent the Christians.

Seen through the prism of the Iranian revolution, Iraq offered a prime target for three main reasons. The first was a function of the dynamics of the Islamic revolution itself. There were similarities here with many other ideological movements at the time when they combine a high degree of internal energy with nascent internal friction: both the French and Chinese revolutions could serve as comparative examples. Iran, for whom the war with Iraq was considered a veritable blessing, was no exception. A hereditary enemy next door can be very useful to revolutionary leaders. As Chubin and Tripp put it, 'the war was used to consolidate the regime, unite and divert the people, repress the opposition and provide a platform for the regime on which to perform.'[9] This judgement could also be applied to the other side, of course, for slightly different reasons.

The second cause for animosity towards Iraq grew directly from the idea that the Islamic Republic of Iran has a mission to restore the honour of Shi'a Muslims and Shi'ism everywhere, redressing the real and imagined wrongs done to the Shi'a minority over the centuries. Shi'a are at most 10 per cent of all Muslims and Iran is the only country where Shi'a Islam is the state religion. In the two other countries where the Shi'a form a majority – Bahrain and Iraq – the reins of government are held by Sunnis. According to the best estimates,[10] approximately 60 per cent of the total population of Iraq are Shi'a. Furthermore, for the Iranian theologians, the indignity of Sunni rule is compounded in Iraq by the fact that the principal Shi'a shrines – of Ali, Hassan, Hussein, Abbas – are situated there. The effort made by the Iraqi Ba'athists since their rise to power to blur the line between Sunnis and Shi'a changed none of the Iranian resentment – on the contrary – and the excellent care that has been given to the shrines, before the war and since, did nothing to mollify the zealots. An eternal minority had finally become a fearsome power; centuries of real and imagined injustice added more kindling to the flames of fervour.

Thirdly, it was unthinkable for the triumphant Islamic revolution to accept that a Muslim country (in the sense of a country where the majority of the population are Muslim) should be governed by a regime that calls itself secular. This point also led to friction with Turkey,[11] which holds to its secular status even more firmly than Iraq. The idea of non-interference in the domestic affairs of another country does not enter into the equation because the *umma*, the community of the Muslim faithful, is perceived as indivisible. The opposition to Arab nationalism among Iranian and other theologians is rooted in the fact that it is considered a negation of the universality and indivisibility of the Islamic community. One of the basic tenets of Ba'athism is its theory of Arab nationalism, based on the idea that Arabism as such is an absolute value. The incompatibility is patent.

The Iranian revolutionaries were convinced that their fellow Shi'a in Iraq (and in Bahrain and eastern Saudi Arabia) would be only too happy to rise up against their Sunni-dominated governments. But the revolt did not come; there was no uprising, not even the intimation of a rebellion, despite continued appeals for almost a decade. That seems the best of all possible proofs of the internal cohesion of Iraq. Coercion and repression were indeed practised by the government, with the expulsion of tens of thousands of Iranian citizens and Iraqi citizens of Iranian origin, most of them resident in the holy cities of Kerbala and Najaf, the arrest of Shi'a religious-political leaders, executions and intimidations. Nevertheless, if the majority of the Shi'a population had wanted to rise in revolt – and they make up more than half the inhabitants of the country and far more than half the Arabs – such measures would not have sufficed.[12]

Conversely, if the incitements to revolt had so little effect, one can infer that, for the Iraqi population, the war was considered something other than a religious conflict. The Iraqi government information service did a brilliant job of presenting the theme of the war as an age-old opposition between the Arabs and the hereditary enemy, the Persians (and of the Iraqis as the defenders of all the Arabs). But the theme was not constructed out of nothing, and the seed did not fall on sterile ground. The Iraqis had used the same theme in the summer of 1980 and at the outbreak of the war in the hope of provoking the Arab-speaking population of Khuzistan (called Arabistan in Iraq) to rise up against the Iranians and return to the Arab fold with the help of the Iraqis, who expected to be welcomed as liberators. The analysis was wrong, in both cases, of course. The failure of both campaigns was costly proof of the unexpected power of nationalism inside the borders drawn on the map.

All of that would change in 1991; the strain and constant internal repression so corroded the equilibrium that had held against outside attacks that it snapped. For both the Kurds and the Shi'a Arabs of southern Iraq, the fateful days of March and April 1991 when they rose up were to turn the tide of history. Not immediately, as they had hoped, but ultimately their relations with any central authority in Baghdad would never again – or not for a very long time – be the same.

The Kurds

The victory of Iraqi nationalism over ethnicity had ceased to apply to the Kurds well before March 1991. Four million or so, they form the second largest group of the Iraqi population, approximately one quarter of the total; their problems are many. They not surprisingly became the objects of Iranian blandishments after 1979, despite the fact that with minor exceptions they are Sunni Muslims. For revolutionary Iran, they represented the 'downtrodden' and, more importantly, seemed an easy element to exploit against the Iraqi regime. The Kurds have been in intermittent revolt for half a century. At the end of the 1970s the situation was comparatively calm, but the war provided the Kurds with an excellent opportunity to rise in revolt once again.

The Iraqi response was as harsh as might have been expected. From the spring of 1987, reports began to filter through of the demolition of hundreds of hamlets in northern Iraq. These 'strategic destructions' were supposed to help the army control a difficult terrain where the Iranians had enlisted the help of Iraqi Kurds.[13] The inhabitants had only one alternative: either to go to the new towns built with little thought for anything but minimum shelter, or drift into the cities. Their arrival in Mosul made it the country's second-biggest city after considerable numbers of the population left Basrah under shelling. Iraq was short of labour during the war years, but it was still difficult to integrate these fiercely independent mountain farmers into an urban economy. They were highly receptive to the appeals of the leaders of the rebellious Kurds who were often camped only a few kilometres from Mosul, Kirkuk or Sulaimaniyya.

The Kurdish rebels were a real thorn in the northern flank of Iraq at war. The Iranians had managed the considerable feat of reconciling the two main leaders into a tactical alliance which lasted until the spring of 1988. The 'traditionalists', or Barzanists, followers of Masud Barzani who inherited the mantle of his father, the quasi-legendary Mullah Mustafa, managed to put aside their traditional rivalry with the 'progressives', the Democratic Party of Iraqi Kurdistan led by

Jalal Talabani, an ex-protégé of Syria. At a time when Iran seemed a likely winner, it promised them, in return for their help, the establishment of a Kurdish state in northern Iraq more or less under Iranian protection. Those who believed in such an idea seemed to have completely forgotten the absolute hostility of Turkey, which would not, under any circumstances, have tolerated the establishment of a Kurdish state on its borders, whatever its degree of real independence. In the summer of 1987, a few influential voices in Ankara were talking about mobilization and the possibility of marching into northern Iraq, if necessary, to prevent such an eventuality.[14]

The Iraqi Kurds who entered into some form of collaboration with Iran were far more numerous and important than the small group of Iranian Kurds who rallied to Baghdad. Kurdistan has always been difficult territory for regular troops and, like all guerrilla forces on their home terrain, the Kurds kept a disproportionate part of the Iraqi army busy. When an army helicopter carrying a posse of Iraqi generals crashed in the mountains north of Sulaimaniyya in January 1988, the official communiqué blamed the accident on bad weather. That did not stop persistent rumours, and in the chaotic situation then prevailing in north-eastern Iraq, there was no way of knowing whether the Iranians or their Iraqi Kurdish friends might have been involved.

The great Iranian offensive of the winter of 1987-8 never materialized, but military analysts think that the continued low-intensity warfare in Kurdistan was one of the triggers of the resumption of the 'war of the cities' in February, which itself led to the final acceptance of the cease-fire by Iran in July. Iraqi policy took a new turn in March with the chemical bombing of Halabja, a small Kurdish town just inside Iraq, which had been captured by the Iranians a few days earlier. After the bombing, there were reports of at least 1,000 and then of 5,000 victims. The Iraqis denied the figures, but not the use of chemical weapons.[15] On the other hand, they did consistently deny the use of chemical weapons on Kurdish hamlets at the end of the war. Leaving aside the context, in other words, the fact that Iraq had admitted to using chemical weapons on the war front since 1983,[16] an examination of what happened at the end of August

1988 is in order, particularly since the events gave rise to a furious polemic and a good deal of distortion of the facts.

As soon as the cease-fire went into effect on 20th August, President Saddam Hussein apparently decided that it was safe and necessary to clean up the resistance in Kurdistan and punish those who had collaborated with Iran. During the next five days the Iraqi army sent some of its best troops to Kurdistan, in particular occupying positions along the major roads. On the morning of 25 August, the day the foreign ministers of Iran and Iraq were to meet for the first time in Geneva, the Iraqi air force bombed a number of villages. It is impossible to know the exact number attacked; at least thirty names have been seriously documented, but there may have been more in the three districts of Zakho, Dohuk and Amadiyyah, all very close to the Turkish border, from where the overwhelming majority of the more than 50,000 refugees who arrived in Turkey between 25 August and 1 September came. The descriptions of what happened are not identical, but similar enough to be considered consistent, taking into account the fact that they were mostly given by panic-stricken people whose one thought at the time was to flee for their lives. They knew the Iraqi government had used chemical weapons against the Iranian army and probably against civilian settlements, they had all heard what happened in Halabja in March (the Kurdish rebel radio station took care of that) and of the attacks against pockets of Iranians after the acceptance of the cease-fire in July.

Among the many Iraqi Kurds with whom I talked in Turkey when I was in the refugee camps in October 1988[17] one of the most articulate was a doctor. He had seen the effects of chemical attacks before, in May 1987, on a village near which his group of *peshmerga*[18] were camped, and knew exactly what he was talking about when he described the events of August 1988.

> On the morning of 25 August, I was in the Amadiyya area, between two hamlets called Kanibaref and Warmele. I saw the attack on Kanibaref. The planes came, throwing down bombs, which made very little noise when they fell, but gave off smoke and a smell like putrefied fruit. We had already told people that when they saw something like that they should leave as quickly as possible and go uphill, because the smoke is heavier than air. We

> also told them to take wet cloths and put them on their faces as they fled and that they should in any case stay away for several hours, if possible overnight, before going back.
>
> Two days after the attack, I went to Warmele. There I saw the animals, cows, mules, poultry – all dead. I also saw four people dead in the street; their skin had turned black and there were no signs of injury on their bodies. They had vomited and bled from noses and ears and there were boil-like spots on their skins. I did not touch them and left the place quickly.

The doctor said calmly that he could not say what kind of gas had been used ('In the mountains we have no laboratories') but that the injuries he had seen were consistent with the use of several types of gases, including mustard gas. Besides the symptoms mentioned above, he had seen pain in the joints, blood in the urine and painful irritation of all the mucus membranes, sometimes to the point of bleeding and, of course, burns. As with the informants of the US Senate commission which very quickly produced a report,[19] my interlocutors all repeated that only the least injured could walk through the mountains to the Turkish border. And that, by the fourth or fifth day of the attack, the Iraqi army had advanced far enough to seal off the passes and the roads, making it impossible for more people to leave.

The figure of over 100,000 Iraqi Kurds fleeing to Turkey was slightly exaggerated. Just over 51,000 were registered by the Turkish authorities during September and given food ration cards. Another estimated 15,000, at most, crossed the Turkish border and continued straight on into Iran, and perhaps twice that number went directly to Iran, where 30,000 Iraqi Kurds had already fled before the end of the war. In other words, 100,000-odd is the total for the Kurds who fled, which is still a fairly small percentage of the 4 million Iraqi Kurds. At the time of writing, no outsider has been allowed to travel freely in Iraqi Kurdistan since the end of the war – or even during the previous years. The members of the United Nations Iran-Iraq Military Observer Group (UNIIMOG) have only limited access to the border areas. But by putting together all the available evidence – including a confirmation that the Americans did indeed intercept Iraqi radio communications which specifically talked about the use of chemical weapons during those fateful August days[20] – the conclusion seems inescapable. With a very high degree of probability, chemical bombardment was used in the Kurdish mountains during two or three days after 25 August, though it was probably not as widespread as was later reported, nor an attempt at systematic genocide of all the Kurds. However, used even in relatively few places, together with the memories of Halabja and other less well known attacks (like the May 1987 one seen by the doctor quoted earlier), it was enough to provoke panic and flight.

The Iraqis were furious about the furore over what they insisted was a matter of internal policy – which, strictly speaking, it was. Emerging from eight hard years of war, they considered themselves entirely within their rights in taking advantage of the brand-new cease-fire to clean out the pockets of resistance and at the same time punish those whom the regime considered to be traitors. The eyes of the world, or at least that part of it that cared about what happened in Iraq, were glued to the Palais des Nations in Geneva, where the long peace talks were beginning and the Iraqi government realized that it had perhaps a unique opportunity.

What was more difficult to understand was the position of Turkey, which seemed at the time very ambiguous. But then Turkey was in a highly ambiguous situation. Bitterly opposed to any separatist tendencies on the part of its own Kurds,[21] Turkey was trying to keep on good terms with both Iran and Iraq for multiple political and economic reasons, and it was both courted and feared by Iraq. Iraq badly needed Turkey in order to export its oil and Turkey needed the gentlemen's agreement concluded in 1983 giving it the right to pursue the Kurdish guerrillas as Iraq abandoned control over the extreme northern areas. Certainly the last thing the Turks wanted was to have tens of thousands of armed Kurdish guerrillas appearing on their border asking for asylum. Conversely, since the *peshmerga* were well aware of the situation of their fellow-Kurds in Turkey, one can safely assume that only a mortal danger would have pushed these seasoned fighters to seek refuge there. However, partly because of their desire to show a humanitarian face in Europe and, to be fair, also out of real humanitarian concern, the Turks did let those who appeared at the border cross, after disarming the men.

The Iraqis made much of a statement by a Turkish medical team that they had seen no sure evidence of the use of chemical weapons on the refugees[22] in Turkey. A high-ranking Turkish diplomat told me that the statement had been slightly misused by not being quoted in full: 'We did not say that Iraq had not used chemical weapons.'[23] He then corroborated what both the doctor quoted earlier and the American investigating team had pointed out: within a relatively short time, light injuries either disappear by themselves or can be mistaken for those due to other causes and nothing more can be proved; those who were most seriously injured simply did not make it to the Turkish border.

Ba'athism and Iraqi nationalism

Like all other major oil producers, Iraq enjoyed a tremendous boom in the 1970s. The Ba'ath party had seized power for the second time in 1968, and managed to hang on to it. As a result, the country has experienced its longest period of political stability since the collapse of the Ottoman empire, under a regime of quasi-Stalinist centralism. Fuzzy Marxist economic theory was combined with a leaden party structure hardly enlivened by a bureaucracy that was a double heritage of the Ottomans and the India Office, as revised by Bulgarian advisers.

Politically, Ba'athism is basically a doctrine of Arab nationalism pushed to the nth degree, with Arabism as such taken as the supreme value. The ruling Ba'ath Party is called the 'regional direction', in accordance with the postulate that the Arab nation is a single whole. In consequence, it was logical that a citizen of any Arab country could arrive in Iraq without any border formalities and from the day of his arrival be considered *de facto* a citizen.[24] He had all the rights of an Iraqi, such as being able to take up employment with no particular permits, but also the obligations, which explains the presence of most of the Egyptians who found themselves enrolled in the Iraqi Army. Not all, because some were volunteers, as were nationals of a dozen other countries, from Tunisia to Kuwait.

In practise, the Ba'athists' supranational Arab idealism never supplanted all national feeling nor personal rivalries. The interpersonal battles for influence are, of course, nowhere more in evidence than in the stormy relations between the two Ba'ath regimes of Syria and Iraq. Ba'athism was founded by two Syrian students in Paris in the 1930s, Michel Aflak and Salah Eddine Bittar.[25] They were much influenced both by the ideas of Arab nationalism that had begun to circulate in Damascus and Cairo and by the very Western philosophical strain embodied in the *personnalisme* of Emmanuel Mounier. A complete theoretical and historical discussion of Ba'athism would be out of place here, but remembering the two ideas that presided at its founding is basic to any understanding of Iraq. The profound belief in Arabism, in the reality of the Arabs as such, remains very much alive, despite all the distortions and manipulations it has undergone. And the personalist strain also remains. It is most unusual in the Middle East to regard an individual as having a right to a personal relation with God or the absolute in any form whatsoever. Even more than the much older notion of the hereditary enemy, this is one of the main elements of the naked hatred displayed by Ayatollah Khomeini and the other theoreticians of the Islamic revolution. The idea that there could be a separation between state and 'church' is fundamentally contrary to all Islamic political doctrine and, *a fortiori*, anathema to the Islamic Republic in Iran. The idea that man is a responsible individual who can choose for himself the form of his relationship with God, believe or not believe, practise or not practise, is heresy. Such ideas are, it must be said, hardly more acceptable in the conservative Gulf states or, for that matter, in most other (non-Ba'athist) Muslim countries. In Iraq, personal liberty hardly extends beyond the field of religion, but there it really does exist.

Arab nationalism never completely eclipsed the narrower sense of belonging to a particular region, whether a nation-state or not. The rivalry between the Valley of the Nile and the Valley of the Twin rivers for primacy in the Middle East has existed for millennia and clothing it in new language did not make it disappear. In 1978 Saddam Hussein was not yet president but he had secured his place as obvious successor to his uncle, the aging President Ahmed Hassan al-Bakr, and for several years had been considered the real power in Iraq. He was also preparing himself for a role on the wider stage of the Middle East. In 1977, the Egyptian President Anwar as-Sadat went to Jerusalem and, in 1978, the Camp David Agreements were signed, followed by the peace treaty between Egypt and Israel. It seems clear, with hindsight, that the two Arab summits in Baghdad in 1978 and 1979 in which Egypt was first warned and then effectively banished from the Arab stage were at least partially motivated by the ambitions of Saddam Hussein. The indignation provoked in many Arab leaders and their populations by what was described as the treachery of Egypt was certainly not feigned. But there was a certain element of manipulation in it and the removal of Egypt from the centre of the Arab scene was a necessary step for anyone who hoped to become the new master of the Arab world.[26]

The next year, the Gulf war began. It was supposed to confirm Saddam as the new master of the Gulf, the protector of the Arabian Peninsula, the veritable bulwark against the Shi'a revolution and the Arabs' paladin against the 'Persian hordes'. After a lightning victory over the Persians, he should have been triumphantly hailed as chief of all the Arabs – that, at least, is how it was supposed to work out.

To defend and illustrate these theses, the Iraqis rediscovered the battle of Qadissiya, presented as the crucial turning-point in the great saga of the spread of Islam. In 637, an army of 30,000 Arabs of the peninsula under the command of Saad ibn Abu Waqqas crushed an army of 120,000 Persians (and their northern Arab allies, whom the modern Iraqis were conveniently able to equate with Syria) fighting under the orders of Rostam the Sassanid. For the Iranians, Qadissiya is only one battle among many, but even before the beginning of the war, the Iraqis made a seminal patriotic reference of it, a theme to be exploited with ingenuity and imagination. Towards 1985, the intelligent Iraqi propagandists recognized the danger of boredom, and began to vary the themes, without entirely forgetting Qadissiya. The particular advantage of Qadissiya as a symbol was its flexibility. The first super-production of the Iraqi film industry was a film called 'Qadissiya' on which production began in 1979.[27] The war was officially called 'Saddam's Qadissiya' or 'the second Qadissiya'; the president was often called, officially, 'Saddam of the Qadissiya'; innumerable painters used the theme in every imaginable style from neo-realist posters to modern, just barely recognisable, abstractions, as seen in many an exhibition in the Baghdad galleries. Sometimes Saddam appeared in a medallion or, Chagall-like, as a benign celestial observer; sometimes the battle was used as a backdrop for a presidential portrait. A huge diorama was built on the presumed site of the original battle; it became a favoured spot for school outings and families in search of new picnic grounds.

Iraq and the Gulf

During the Iranian revolution and then during the Iran-Iraq war, the GCC countries did not ask Iraq for protection. Despite their apprehension when they looked across the Gulf at Iran, they had almost as much reason to be fearful of Iraq, whose political and economic system was diametrically opposed to their own. They did not like Iraq's socialist and revolutionary positions nor even its consistently hard-line stances within OPEC. Several of the Gulf countries had been victims of Iraqi attempts at subversion, either in the hope of furthering its own version of Ba'athist revolution or, before 1975, as a Soviet proxy. Even in 1980, Iraq's verbal menaces directed at the petro-monarchies were only faintly veiled.

At the end of the Iran–Iraq war, after eight years of more or less actively supporting Iraq (which itself had apparently changed), the Gulf countries were still wary. They certainly were not ready to entertain the idea of admitting Iraq as a member of the GCC. Steps were taken, boldly and openly by Iraq, flushed with its claims of victory. One of the odder moves in that interim between two wars was the signing of a non-aggression pact with Saudi Arabia when King Fahd made his surprising visit to Baghdad in March 1989. This was the first by a reigning Saudi monarch in thirty years. At the time, it was difficult to imagine that Iraq would attack Saudi Arabia, its main financier over the previous decade; the idea of Saudi Arabia attacking Iraq seemed even more absurd. Besides, the Arab League was supposed to be a mutual non-aggression treaty between all its members. With hindsight one can only conclude that the Saudi-Iraqi treaty was designed to lull Saudi apprehension in the wake of the newly-constituted Arab Cooperation Council. The Council had been touted, like all such treaties, as a purely economic agreement, but was nevertheless made up of countries that ringed Saudi Arabia: Iraq as chief organizer after being spurned for GCC membership, Jordan, Egypt and Yemen.

The question of who really began the Iraq–Iran war was whipped into a major international issue by Iraq. With the invasion of Kuwait, the question became largely academic – though not for Iran, which never renounced its pretensions to compensation. Who did begin the war? It is worth recalling the basic facts.

First, the situation as it was in September 1980. For months, the brand-new Islamic revolutionary government and all its organs had been hurling insults at the Iraqi government and inciting the Iraqi population to rise in revolt. Furthermore, skirmishes, euphemistically called border incidents, were taking place almost daily, punctuated by mutual violations of air space. The Iraqis say that Iranian shelling of the towns of Khanaqin, Qata Mandali, Munsatiya, Zorbatiya and Mustafa Luand on 4 September marked the beginning of the war. For the Iranians, these were simply further incidents in a long series with no more reason to single them out as a *casus belli* than many others – again on both sides.[29] On 27 August, the official Iranian news agency, IRNA, had announced the lobbing of Iraqi ground missiles into the Qasr-e-Shirin area; on 21 August, according to the Iraqi agency, there had been 'a general bombardment of Iraqi villages, ports and oil installations' by Iran. Abdel-Magid Zemzemi, whom Paul Balta describes as 'reflecting the Iranian point of view,' kept track of all the attacks announced by both parties in the five months between 11 April and 11 September 1980, amounting to 172 by Iran and 352 by Iraq.[30]

On 17 September, Saddam Hussein denounced the 1975 Algiers agreement with Iran, literally tearing it up in a dramatic television performance. His speech made no specific reference to the incidents of 4 September; perhaps at the time they were not considered more significant than many others. The Algiers agreement, which Saddam himself had negotiated with the Shah, was supposed to resolve all the border problems between the two states, especially the question of the Shatt al-Arab: the Iraqis accepted that the border should be the *thalweg*, the line marking the deepest point of the river, rather than – as they had previously claimed – the Iranian bank. This issue was to become the main sticking point in the negotiations at the end of the war, when the Iraqis insisted on renegotiating the border. In 1975, the *quid pro quo* had been that the Shah stop supporting the rebellious Iraqi Kurds; the revolt promptly collapsed.

One of the clauses of the Algiers agreement[31] states that disputes between the two countries 'should be resolved primarily by negotiation.' In 1980, Iraq tried, several times, to take some diplomatic action in reference to the agreement; Tehran denounced each step as 'hypocritical'. On 22 September, the Iraqi army crossed the border into Khuzistan, or Arabistan, where the Iraqis expected to be welcomed by an Arab-speaking population only too happy to return to the fold. It was perfectly logical Ba'athist reasoning.

In the summer of 1980, Iran was not an easy place. There was indeed some effervescence in Khuzistan, but it was much milder than what was happening in the north, in Kurdistan and Azerbaijan, or in Baluchistan far to the south; there, it was said, nationalist stirrings had been stimulated by the Soviet invasion of Afghanistan. The Baluchis were reported to be ready to rally to the Soviet Union and give the Russians their long-desired access to the warm seas. All summer the news from Tehran had been nothing but conspiracies, bombs exploding, internecine fighting among the various currents of the revolution. And the American hostages were still held prisoner in their own embassy.

The Iraqi attack

On the day that Saddam Hussein denounced the Algiers agreement an important meeting was held in Baghdad. Members of the Iraqi Revolutionary Command Council (RCC) sat down with several Iranian generals in exile and Shapur Bakhtiar, the Shah's last prime minister, who had been the victim of an attempted murder at his house near Paris in June.[32]

Why did Saddam Hussein and the members of the RCC give the order to attack on 22 September? Unless Saddam writes his memoirs – and even in that unlikely eventuality it would be difficult to unravel fact from *ex post facto* justification – it will probably never be possible to progress far beyond the realm of informed speculation. Three factors at least should be taken into account. First, the influence of those exiled Iranian generals and the others who were living in Baghdad or who had come to give their advice. They were convinced that without them, without the thousand pilots imprisoned by the revolutionary regime and without the American spare parts, what had once been the strongest army in the Middle East had fallen to pieces. It was only natural that a taste for revenge should have coloured their judgement; while the facts on which it was based were largely correct, it took no account of the dynamic that can be generated by a revolution in which, at least for a time, faith can move mountains.

Secondly, it seems likely that the Americans influenced the decision.[33] The Middle East is rife with conspiracy theories, one of which holds that the Americans pushed the war – the theory hardly distinguishes between who was encouraged – in order to weaken the Arabs or, in a variant, the Muslims. While not subscribing to that theory, I do believe, much more simply, that the Americans thought that a quick Iraqi victory was possible over a weakened, divided Iran and that the first fruit of that victory would have been freedom for the 52 American hostages. The hostages were an obsession with the Americans, including the President, Jimmy Carter, who was standing for re-election. In what seemed a desperate situation after the disaster in April of the Tabas raid,[34] they probably saw the Iraqi initiative as a ray of hope. At the time, of course, the Americans had even less direct knowledge of the way the Iranians were thinking and how they were likely to react than they had had before the revolution.

The third reason for Iraq to attack at that moment was the belief that the Arab-speaking Iranians of Khuzistan were in just the right state of rebellion: ready to open their hearts and their towns to the liberators who would permit them to 'return to the Arab nation', but not so far advanced in their revolt that the Iranians, who had other worries and priorities at that time, would begin to do something about it. The imprecations spewed forth from Tehran month after month were intolerable to the pride of Saddam Hussein, champion of the Arab cause and at that time at the height of his power. Sub-consciously, the Iraqi people also resented the scurrility, despite the fact that, calculated as it was to hasten a revolt, it always distinguished carefully between the people and their government.[35] By September, the flashpoint had been reached, and the 'objective advice' from well-meaning sources provided the spark. With hindsight, one can argue that if Saddam Hussein had had the patience to shrug off the Iranian provocations for a few more months, Iran would probably have fallen into an anarchy deep enough to obviate the need for a war. The Iraqi attack, it now seems evident, had the classic effect of promoting internal cohesion at a time when it was very feeble indeed.

Iraq at war with Iran

The war changed many things in Baghdad, but not in the classic way of wars. Never, not even during the episodes called the 'wars of the cities', when missiles were flying back and forth between the two capitals, did Baghdad take on the air of a besieged capital. During the war years enormous building projects were undertaken, and completed. Some, like the congress centre built for the non-aligned conference of 1982,[36] were planned before the war at a time when there was plenty of money to spend on prestige construction. Others, like the gigantic new housing blocks along Haifa Street, on the right bank of the Tigris, have not only remodeled whole sections of the city, but changed the way Baghdadis live. Until 1980, it was so difficult to persuade Iraqis to live in flats rather than houses that Baghdad sprawled over an area larger than greater London. The enormous influx of population during the war (many from Basrah and quite a large number from the small towns in the north) was temporarily absorbed by their families and, in some of the poorer neighbourhoods, led to increased crowding. But since morale-building measures, particularly in the early years of the war, were supposed to ensure that the civilian population felt as few privations as possible, a supply of new housing was imperative. And so Iraqis began to live in flats, not only in Baghdad, but elsewhere too. The plans for the reconstruction of Basrah included a good deal of multiple housing, which even the newly urbanized could not but consider an improvement over the nauseous pre-war slums.

In the latter years of the war Iraq also underwent a complete turn-about of economic policy. The Arab Ba'ath Socialist Party abandoned much of its socialism and by the winter of 1986–7 an increasingly brisk wind of economic liberalism was sweeping over the country. Before the war Iraq had been the Middle East's third largest oil producer after Saudi Arabia and Iran. Beginning in 1982, its principal policy goal in the economic sphere was to keep production equal to that of Iran, a country three times bigger, with three times the population and no rich friends to help pay its war bills. The battle for quotas was bitterly fought within OPEC and the more demand fell, the sharper the quarrels. It remains a mystery that none of the oil experts ever managed to explain satisfactorily why the other members of OPEC continued to accept the Iraqi demand to stay outside the quota system. It was fairly easy to understand during the first years of the war when export capability had been sharply reduced. The sea route through the Gulf was closed immediately by the Iranian blockade of the Iraqi ports and when Syria sealed off the pipeline from Kirkuk to Tartus in April 1982 it was felt as an even greater blow. But by late 1987 the second pipeline through Turkey and the first pipeline through Saudi Arabia were functioning; and the 'rolling pipelines' of tankers through Aqaba and Turkey were capable of carrying close to another million barrels each day. Total exports of oil came to more than the Iranian quota, without even going into comparisons of production. At the June 1988 OPEC meeting in Vienna, several countries wanted to end the Iraqi privilege; but Iraq continued to claim it as its due until the end of the war because, it argued, it was willing to make peace and continuation of the war was imposed upon it. The Iraqis went on exporting outside any quotas, going up to 2.6 million barrels and even, for a time, 2.8 million barrels per day, more than the average daily production of any previous year with the exception of 1979. In December 1988, they returned to the OPEC fold, but with a privileged status giving them production parity with Iran; the latter, with its far larger land area and population, consumes much more for its domestic needs.

As long as Iraq was riding the crest of the economic wave in the Middle East, and its own political wave, too, it could afford a few major mistakes in planning, equipment and working methods and still offer its citizens probably the most equitable income distribution of any of the oil-producing countries. The land reform had made it possible by 1986 for many smallholders to experience the beginnings of a decent life. What was not a success was the public agricultural sector; the state farms on the *kolkhoz* model soon proved a complete disaster but the party was opposed to their dismantling on purely ideological grounds. Finally, after 1985, the reform was completed and the land reverted quietly to farmers' co-operatives or private farms.

Before the war, the private sector had been hemmed about with severe restrictions. Practically all productive activity was forbidden it, with the exception of very small family enterprises, and stringent import regulations effectively hampered any real initiative even in retail commerce. Everything that had made and reflected the fortunes of the Gulf merchants – the flashy shopping centres and luxury shops, the agencies and sponsorships – was banished. On the other hand, major corruption was practically unknown. With the constraints of war and the simultaneous liberalization, it was probably inevitable that it should make its re-appearance. In 1987, two high-ranking officials, Abdul Wahhab al-Mufti, the mayor of Baghdad and a close associate of the President, and Abdul Muneim as-Samurrai, the vice-minister of oil, were arrested, tried and condemned for crimes of corruption; both were hanged. The severe punishment was no doubt meant as a warning. On the other hand, the long years of frustration and the dinar's unrealistic exchange rate[37] now favoured the black market and petty graft, which were unknown before the war.

Unleashing the economy

Even during the opulent pre-war years, shopping in Baghdad was about as exciting as in Sofia and inexplicable shortages were the norm. Spare parts for cars were in chronically short supply: the coppersmiths whose work had been one of the glories of Baghdad were very clever at hand-hammering silencers to order. Then, in the spring of 1987 came the great change in policy. At a time when the war was not going at all well a new set of regulations was published almost every month to illustrate the decision by the Revolutionary Command Council[38] to lift yet another restriction on the economy. Those businessmen whose ambitions had survived nineteen years of numbing bureaucracy suddenly found new horizons opening before them as they were increasingly allowed to deal directly with foreign suppliers. Until then, practically all imports had been handled by the state. By the end of the war, the businessmen were complaining more about restrictions on travel abroad than about problems of permits and licences; an illegal but tolerated parallel exchange system which worked through compensatory payments to foreign creditors was useful. A single yearly trip abroad was barely enough to keep the system functioning smoothly unless there was a cousin in Frankfurt or London to help out.

Retail businesses were returned to the private sector at breathtaking speed; signpainters were making small fortunes in Baghdad. In the late 1980s, practically nothing remained taboo, except arms and the oil sector. According to the Ministry of Planning, once oil was removed from the equation, 60 per cent of the gross commercial product, half the industrial product and 90 per cent of agricultural production were in private hands. There was even a proposal to sell off half of Iraqi Airways, but that idea has been temporarily shelved. The Rafidain bank, the only commercial bank in the country until it was split to stimulate competition, has been given the job of selling shares of other national companies, but not its own.

A law inviting foreign investment was passed with promises that at least part of the operating profits could be exported, along with all the profits of a later sale of the capital investment. One restriction was that the investors must be Arabs; something does remain of the Ba'athist ideals. The Iraqis were rather disappointed with the lack of enthusiasm shown by their rich neighbours, even though special symposia were organized for potential Kuwaiti and Saudi investors.

One of the surest signs of the changing times is the reappearance of the agent, after twenty years of anathema. As the representative of foreign companies, he is allowed to deal with both the private sector and the government. The role of an agent in Iraq is not the same as in the Gulf; it is far more like that of his European namesake than of an Emirati sponsor. After two decades of Ba'athism, it may require a little time before the rules become absolutely clear and there may be some difficulty in delineating the fine line between legitimate work and illicit currying of favour. If the fight against corruption goes on, few people may be tempted to test the limits of the rules.

The only economic sector apart from oil that the RCC wants to remain completely state-owned is the arms industry. Only months after the cease-fire went into effect, an arms show was staged in Baghdad which was clearly designed to show off to the population what the home-grown industry had been able to do. In April 1989 the Government staged a fully-fledged arms fair to attract potential buyers. The message was now clear. By giving a high priority to its arms industry, Iraq had managed to produce or at least assemble and transform an amazing range of military hardware from transmission equipment to the Hussein and Abbas rockets (modified Soviet SCUD-Bs) used to such devastating effect against Iran during the spring of 1988. The end of the war most emphatically did not change those priorities. In November 1989, an anti-missile missile called the Babylon was tested in a controlled launch.

One secret not unveiled was what had happened to the Iraqi nuclear reactor called Osirak by the French who delivered most of it, and Tammuz II by the Iraqis, which had been destroyed by the Israelis in a daring raid in 1981 before it could be put into service. The whole sector where the reactor/research facility is located was out of bounds to most foreigners and many Iraqis, but according to Western diplomats in Baghdad, one quarter of all Iraqi anti-aircraft defences were deployed in the Baghdad suburb of Ishtar, that is, around the reactor. The neighbourhood, where industrial plants and low-cost housing subsist practically side by side, is approximately 25 kilometres from the centre of Baghdad and was the apparent target of a high proportion of the Iranian rockets in 1987 and 1988. Persistent rumours of nuclear cooperation between Iraq and Brazil, with a sprinkling of Argentinian technical advisers, were confirmed in 1990. But it was only with the International Atomic Energy Agency inspections in 1991 and 1992 that the extent of Iraq's nuclear programme was revealed. Even in defeat, the Iraqi government continued trying to hide what it could: the Iraqis tried every form of deception and the IAEA inspection teams were subject to continued harassment. On one memorable occasion in October 1991 they were kept prisoners in their vehicle in Baghdad for two days and, although by March 1992 the IAEA was putting out soothing communiqués saying that Iraq no longer had the nuclear capability to do real harm, nagging doubts lingered. Those doubts were also one of the major reasons that the UN Security Council remained deaf to Iraqi pleas that the economic sanctions imposed against it after the invasion of Kuwait be lifted. Few people doubted that so long as Saddam Hussein remained in power, and as soon as he was able to get his hands on large sums of oil revenue, he would reactivate Iraq's nuclear programme.

In the arms field, the most lasting impact of the war will probably prove to be the re-introduction of chemical weapons into the normal arsenal of regional conflicts. Despite all Iraqi protests, a United Nations mission of enquiry concluded that as early as 1983 Iraq had repeatedly used chemical weapons.[40] By the spring of 1988, Iraq was no longer denying this but, according to the Defence Minister, Mr Adnan Khairallah, was ready 'to use any and all means to defend Iraqi territory'.[41] Most, if not all, of the chemicals were produced in Iraq. In the last years of the war, foreign diplomats in Baghdad were concerned about the very real danger that Iraq, if pushed to the wall, was – both technically and morally – capable of also using biological weapons: anthrax virus bombs, for example, are easy to manufacture. The undoubted Iraqi use of chemical weapons, both on the battle-field against Iran and then in the operations in Kurdistan at the end of the war, showed the whole world, and particularly the Third World, how easy it was for a country with average technological capabilities to make them without too many risks. The raw materials can be fairly simple and the whole operation easily disguised as a fertilizer factory or a paint plant, particularly when carried out in a society ridden by secret police and hemmed about by restrictions of all kinds.[42]

Worst of all in the long run will probably be the conventionalization of chemical weapons. The exceptional circumstances of the Iran-Iraq war, in which so much was forgiven Iraq because its adversary was considered, by most Western and Arab circles, as the incarnation of evil, helped. Little by little, Iraq was able to accustom the world to the use of what has, inaccurately, been called 'the poor man's nuclear bomb'.[43] Only at the end of the war, when gas was used in Kurdistan, was there a real outcry. And then the political circumstances were such that Iraq managed to rally most of the Arab countries to its side, to support it loyally in its cries of a 'Zionist plot'.

Iraq had a long war, but Saddam Hussein had a very good one. He was the rallying point for the Iraqis through some very hard years. Whether he achieved this through fear or through love is not really the question: the point is that he managed to ensure a position for himself where the line between his person and the nation became blurred. Holding out – which the Iraqis did, and it would be unfair not to give them the credit they deserve – became almost synonymous with preserving the person of Saddam. It would have been unseemly to pray particularly for the safety of the President; there is no Muslim equivalent of 'God Save the Queen', but everything was done to make the people feel that their survival as Iraqis was linked to the survival of the regime, itself linked to that of Saddam. During the dark days of 1983 and 1984, when the Iranians were saying that removal of Saddam was the non-negotiable condition for peace talks, some soundings were apparently taken by Saudi emissaries to see whether it might be possible to persuade Saddam to retire or go abroad for medical treatment. The answer was always no, from Saddam himself. But probably at the time, if such a thing as a plebiscite had existed in Iraq, a majority of the people would have agreed with him.

No one knows how many victims there were of the war, on either side. In 1987 an American military expert, A.H. Cordesman, estimated a total of 3 million dead and wounded,[44] but other experts think that figure is exaggerated. The conventional wisdom – based on nothing but pure guesswork – used one million dead as a base for discussion. Arnold Hottinger[45] is more conservative in his reckoning: he thinks perhaps 200,000 soldiers died in combat, two thirds of them Iranian, one third Iraqis, and that, as a general rule, three men are wounded in combat for each man killed. If we take his figures and add the victims in the last six months of the war, when there were no more major offensives nor, despite the 'war of the cities', mass bombings of civilian targets (the most murderous of the whole war was Halabja), the total is about 1 million victims. The population of the two countries is 60 million. Cordesman made a sad but pertinent remark about the extreme difficulty of even trying to approach statistical or, for that matter, any other accuracy: 'In Iranian and Iraqi reportage, the truth was dead long before the war started.'

The war had another serious consequence for the Iraqi population. In wartime, and in an ideological war that inevitably undermined some of the government's confidence, the small taste of personal freedom that Iraqis had just begun to enjoy during the late 1970s was again denied them. In the name of security, the heavy hand of state control came down once again. Many, particularly among the educated elites, resented it but they were ready to accept the situation as long as the war lasted.

They hardly had a choice, because the slightest deviation from the prescribed path was severely punished. Any criticism of the government, any remark that could be construed as insulting to the President, carried a prison sentence of eighteen years even if uttered in private; informers were so prevalent that few people risked comments of a kind that would have seemed mild in almost any other country – including Iran.[46] Criticism expressed in public was punishable by death and that was no idle threat.

Private contacts with foreigners were discouraged and unfortunately the security services were ubiquitous enough to dampen the Iraqis' natural sense of spontaneous hospitality.

Even high government officials and old friends hesitated before talking alone with foreigners; a witness was almost always present to be able to answer questions in case of later accusations.

There were at least three more or less secret services at work. The best known is the *mukhabarat*, the ordinary run-of-the-mill secret police; it is also the least feared because its members are fairly well trained and disciplined. Far more random brutality and sheer nastiness were ascribed to the Ba'ath party's own security service; many of its members are ordinary neighbourhood bullies who have found in the party a good place to work out their frustrations. The Ba'ath used to be an elitist organization, but in the last years of the war it tried to widen its base by more open recruitment, and in the process it seems have lost something of the strict discipline that was once its hallmark. The two secret police groups are quite often rivals, each trying to show itself the more assiduous in rooting out the enemies of the state and, as long as the war lasted, to justify the presence in mufti of so many healthy young men.

The third secret force is the much-feared counter-intelligence service. A number of foreigners have fallen foul of their extraordinary faculty of seeing spies at work in fortuitously misinterpreted situations. No member of the Iraqi CID could imagine that an engineer from one of the Nordic countries working in Iraq for a central European company could be anything but a spy, especially when the censor discovers that the lonely and homesick engineer has written a letter saying that 'life in Iraq is getting harder and harder'. Another group of censors is charged with listening to overseas telephone calls. Their job is difficult, particularly when the conversation is in a relatively rare language like Schwyzerdütsch or Swedish. In that case, they have been known to break into the conversation and politely ask that the speakers switch to a better-known language. For those who fall foul of counter-intelligence, or one of the other services, the interrogation period can be very hard. Even for foreigners, diplomatic intervention is useless, whether it is to protest against the use of torture, to ask for less arduous conditions of detention, or in trying to seek a pardon or reduction of the prison sentence. The contempt for any rule of law became wholesale when Saddam declared that almost all foreigners caught in Iraq and Kuwait on 2 August 1990 were now 'guests of the state', in other words hostages. The transfer of several dozen – mostly Britons and Americans – to strategic sites was an added fillip.

Year after year, accusations of major displacements of population, of torture and of mass executions were presented by Amnesty International to bodies like the United Nations Human Rights Commission. The problem was that the international community did not want to hear them, and took refuge behind the lack of corroborative evidence. In Iraq even careful observers always found it difficult to know exactly what was happening. The story of the President's son, Uday, is a case in point.

It is a sad tale indeed. On 21 November 1988, an official announcement was made in Baghdad that the President had ordered his eldest son, Uday Saddam Hussein, to be tried for murder. Twenty-four-year-old Uday had, in a rage, beaten to death one of his father's guards, Kamel Hanna Jaijo. The date given was 18 October; at the time not a hint filtered from behind the thick walls of the Presidential palace. In Baghdad people knew that Uday was quite obviously being groomed for high office. The Iraqi youth and sports establishment had been given to him as his fief: he was president of the National Olympic Committee (where one of his first acts had been to get himself awarded an Olympic medal), head of the football association, editor-in-chief of the sports daily. He was also said to be a helicopter pilot and during the war had been incorporated into the air force just long enough to be much photographed in uniform, although no one could remember when he had gone through the long training period. Despite or perhaps because of all this, Uday still appeared to the public as an arrogant young man and his occasional wild rampages (unreported in the papers, but well known all the same) went down badly with the basically puritanical Iraqis. So did the huge new palace which was being built for him, at government expense, on the Tigris dam in one of the best districts of Baghdad. In the fairly spartan world of high Iraqi politics, particularly in wartime, Uday was an anomaly and, months before his fall, he was described to me as 'his father's dangerous blind spot'. It is impossible to know exactly what Saddam's plans for Uday were, but in the last year of the war, and even more so in the flush of victory, the President began to show odd dynastic proclivities. Even though a large number of important posts in the government were given to members of the Takriti clan, direct inheritance à la Kim Il Soong is practically unimaginable. Ba'athism is not democracy, but it is indissolubly linked to a republican form of government. That is why a small incident in the late summer of 1988 provoked such a shock. When King Hussein of Jordan was in Baghdad, the President accompanied him on a solemn visit to the tomb of his cousin, the last Hashemite king of Iraq, Faisal II, who was savagely killed in the first revolution on 14 July 1958. The pomp and publicity given to the occasion were more than was called for out of simple courtesy to his guest.

After the trial, at which Uday was acquitted 'because of mitigating circumstances', he was sent off to Geneva, with his uncle, ex-head of Military Intelligence and half-brother of the president, Barzan al-Takriti,[47] who was appointed ambassador to the United Nations European Office. Uday was at first sent as a student; then he was supposed to become first secretary in his uncle's mission. To the intense embarrassment of the professional diplomats (and Iraq has some very competent ones), the son continued to behave like a spoiled playboy. When he again physically abused one of the mission drivers (this time without serious consequences) he was sent home. In the spring of 1991, Uday emerged again as the 'editor' of a new daily paper called, significantly, *Babil* (Babylon). There was a shortage of newsprint for every other publication but not for *Babil*, showing yet again that the family won out over army, party and even the Revolutionary Command Council.

This rather sorry tale would belong only in the tabloid press had it not had consequences beyond those in an ordinary family. The power structure of immediate postwar Iraq still rested on the tripod of army, party and *mukhabarat*, with Al-Takriti family members strategically placed in all three branches. Even before the war ended, Saddam realized that stability on three legs was risky; if one buckled the whole edifice could crumble. But trouble came where it was least expected: in the family. The

Uday affair brought on a crisis which was difficult to cover up completely. Saddam's wife, who was beginning to be given some public exposure, apparently sided with those who were in favour of covering up the son's scandal, including some of her close relatives. When Uday was banished to Geneva, she accompanied him. At that time, to the great surprise of the Iraqis, Saddam produced a second wife in public, together with a very young son. Those who were wondering about shattered dynastic dreams began to muse about whether the four-year-old son might be considered a long-shot successor. The shock was heightened because Iraq had practically abandoned polygamy before the war and only recently re-introduced it, to the dismay of many educated women. Now the example came from on high.

In 1989, Saddam seemed to have seriously considered introducing some reforms to the tripod structure. The promises for multiparty elections and a free press came to nothing. And yet after the Iran–Iraq war, he could just possibly have managed to base his own legitimacy on the popularity he enjoyed in 1988 and 1989. There had been real changes in the late 1980s. Saddam had made sure that his unconditionally faithful henchmen retained key posts, but had also brought in sophisticated technocrats, chosen for their ability rather than their political credentials. Membership of the Ba'ath party no longer guaranteed a smooth career.

Between 1980 and 1985 a real effort had been made to offer women a role in society. Compared to most other places in the Middle East they were emancipated, with access to education and employment and even, some say, in their choice of marriage partners. In 1986 there was a sharp reversal of policy. Women once encouraged to work outside the home and given responsible jobs were suddenly passed over for promotion and pushed into ridiculously early retirement. Seven or eight children were promoted as the ideal family, and contraceptives, once freely available, became subject to distribution restrictions. Polygamy, which had been practically abolished, was re-introduced – with the president himself setting the example. The official explanation was that so many men had been killed in war that the country urgently needed more children. Some Iraqis thought that the real reason was that capable women were beginning to make men feel threatened in their supremacy.

Most observers regarded the attack on Iran in 1980 as a grievous miscalculation. But what about the invasion of Kuwait on August 2 1990? The Arab propensity to conspiracy theories was particularly active after that invasion. The most widespread of these put all the blame on the USA, accusing the superpower of luring Saddam into a trap in order to break the might of a great new Arab leader. Some Americans, including many in the academic community, have also gone to great lengths to support all or part of this theory. It has often been said that there is an absence of understanding between the Arab world and the American government. Rarely has it been demonstrated to such dramatic effect. Apparently, in the days just preceding the event, the State Department chose both to ignore the CIA predictions of an Iraqi invasion[48] and continued sending Saddam Hussein 'signals' that he could interpret (although they may indeed not have been meant that way) as an American green light, or at least a yellow one.

The strangest event of all was the conversation on 25 July (the day the OPEC meeting held under the Iraqis' diktat opened in Geneva) between April Glaspie, the American ambassador to Iraq, and President Saddam Hussein. Glaspie was summoned to the presidential palace with almost no notice, certainly not enough time to ask for instructions from Washington. According to a transcript communicated much later by Iraq to the *Washington Post*, Glaspie told Saddam – who had been attacking Kuwait verbally for months – that 'the United States does not take sides in a dispute between Arab countries, like yours with Kuwait'.[49] In another version, she is reported to have said: 'We have no opinion on the Arab–Arab conflicts, like your border disagreement with Kuwait' and to have 'emphasized that this position would be stated publicly in Washington'.[50] April Glaspie is no novice in diplomacy, nor in the Middle East. But apparently neither she nor John Kelly, an Assistant Secretary of State, realized how much could be read between the lines of what, in good American fashion, was the simple, naked truth.

It came out in hearings after the war[51] that Ambassador Glaspie's remarks had been edited, for propaganda purposes, by Iraq before release. Why the Americans did not immediately react by publishing their own version remains difficult to understand. The embarrassed explanations that they did not want to demean themselves by sinking to the Iraqis' level, or that a release would have distracted attention from the main issue, are not entirely satisfactory. The question remains open, especially in the light of the enormous impact of the Iraqi transcript on Arab and European public opinion. John Kelly, on 31 July, told the House Foreign Affairs Committee which was holding public hearings on Iraq's increasingly bellicose behaviour (in order to decide whether to recommend sanctions against it) that the United States had no treaty commitment to protect Kuwait from an attack by Iraq.[52] Strictly speaking, that was true. After the event, it is easy to criticise such statements and the messages that can be read into them. But most importantly, they provide two examples of cultural differences that have often confused American relations with the Arab Middle East. Americans, even American diplomats, usually like to speak plainly; Arabs, by and large, see much importance in what is left unsaid, implied, hidden between the lines. And Iraqi propagandists are masters at exploiting that difference.

Two wars have not eradicated the extreme identification of Saddam Hussein with the regime and of the regime with the country. In 1988, the celebrations at the end of the fighting in Baghdad were not feigned; the majority of Iraqis believed that they had achieved a great victory under Saddam. As Shahram Chubin put it, one could say that for Iran not to win the war was in a sense to lose it, so for Iraq just holding out in the face of an enemy three times larger was in itself victory.[53] The same reasoning was used to explain that it was Iraq, not the coalition, that was victorious in the six-week war of 1991; after all, had Iraq alone not faced a coalition of 30 countries ranged against it? And was not Saddam the master, indeed the hero whom all feared and none could touch? Such explanations can only be used in the tightly controlled world of Iraq under the Ba'ath Party, but there they work. More surprising perhaps is that a not inconsiderable number of non-Iraqis from Algiers to Sana'a and beyond were touched by such reasoning.

Even while the propaganda tide was still high, at least in the central Iraqi heartland, there was occasional talk of reform. Talk of reform never went as far as it had in 1989 when timetables were given for democratization, even though they were never kept. On the other hand, in 1990 and 1991, new themes were introduced into the regime's rhetoric. The most striking was that of Saddam as an Islamic leader, culminating in the decree to add the words 'Allahu Akbar' (God is most great) to the Iraqi flag in the final days of the ultimatum to retreat from Kuwait. It was so blatant an attempt to assure popular support in the wider Muslim community as to seem laughable. But many people believed that Saddam really had been touched by the grace of God.

With defeat, all pretense at a broad national representation was abandoned, particularly as it became evident that neither the Shi'a population of the south nor the Kurds in the north were entirely recuperable. For almost a year after the end of the fighting, discussions were carried on with diminishing enthusiasm, between leaders of the two main Kurdish factions and Saddam's regime. Jalal Talabani gave up first; Massud Barzani was only a little longer in losing hope of finding an autonomy arrangement within the existing Iraqi state. Successive ministerial changes concentrated more and more posts in the hands of the Takriti clan with very few outsiders remaining (The ex-foreign minister, Tariq Aziz, who became a world figure during the 1990–91 crisis, was stripped of whatever effective power he may have had (and it was little enough). Always the faithful servant, Tariq Aziz was considered the acceptable face of Iraq: a Greek Orthodox Christian who spoke fluent English. After months of eclipse, he was trotted out to plead for the lifting of sanctions in front of the UN Security Council in March 1992, but even his undeniable skills were not enough.)

A year after the end of the second Gulf war, the future of Iraq remained problematic. The idea of a dismemberment of the country, considered unthinkable a year earlier, was no longer quite as unthinkable. Iraq, as a state, had been created from three distinct Ottoman provinces. The Iraqi opposition abroad remained fragmented and unable to organize a serious rebellion. Saudi Arabia, which in early 1991 had apparently been one of the leading voices in opposing the idea of a possible breakup, was reported as no longer opposed: it had, in the meantime, found a *modus vivendi* with Iran. Apparently giving some power to the Shi'a majority of southern Iraq, almost inevitably friendly to Iran, but not necessarily ready to be annexed, was less distasteful than the continuing presence of Saddam at the head of a resurgent Iraq. Even Turkey, busy with its new-found role as protector and/or arbiter in the southern republics of the former Soviet Union, was less adamantly opposed to the Iraqi Kurdish aspirations.

Saddam's sabre-rattling in the spring of 1990 should have given warning that trouble was brewing. Even if the invasion of Kuwait was difficult to predict (unless one credits the conspiracy theory entirely) the international community should have opened its eyes earlier. After the Bazoft affair and that of the smuggled capacitators (vital to the nuclear programme) in March, came news of the 'super gun', which most Arabs and many others refused to credit. That the arms programme was not just propaganda was, of course, amply proven both during and after the 1991 war. Saddam's insulting behaviour towards several of his guests at the Baghdad Arab summit in May should have set off warning bells. Even less attention was paid to some significant civilian innovations. In March 1990, a decree was promulgated that a man who killed his wife or any female relative, on suspicion of adultery, was not liable to prosecution. This decree goes far beyond the rules of *Sharia*, Muslim canon law; it was presented as a return to the law of Hammurabi, the Amurite King who was the founder of the first Babylonian empire. His reign, which lasted for over forty years, beginning around 1730 BC, saw the extension of Babylonian power over all of Assyria, Sumer and as far as Mari, now in Syria.

Two years later an unrepentant Saddam Hussein was still master in Baghdad. The new Hammurabi, as he continued to style himself, had had only a temporary setback – and that, according to Iraqi theory, had been hardly his fault. His appetite for power apparently unabated, Saddam continued to defy the United Nations, playing deadly games of cat and mouse with the inspectors sent to find and destroy his weapons of mass destruction, and cynically exploiting the theme of the starving children of Iraq, because he refused to accept the United

Nations' terms for selling oil and the international community refused to dig into its pockets for a rich country.

No one knew quite what to do about Saddam, nor what would be the immediate future for his country and for a terrorized population that had been dragged through two devastating wars. Only one thing was sure, the Gulf countries would not make their peace with Iraq so long as Saddam remained in power.

CHAPTER 3

Iran: Neighbours are still Neighbours

One October day in 1978, as I was returning home from Baghdad, the Iraqi Airways flight was very late. For once, the passengers were given an explanation for the delay other than the usual 'technical reasons': we were waiting for a VIP. Only when we were back in Europe did I discover that I had travelled on the plane that carried Ayatollah Ruhollah Khomeini to his short exile in France. True, at the time it still required a conscious effort to remember the full name of this extraordinary person but I have often wondered whether, had I broken through my natural reluctance to push myself forward, had I been a bit more resourceful and – with luck – been able to talk with the Ayatollah on that five-hour shared journey, would I have a different perception today of revolutionary Iran?

The extraordinary complexity of revolutionary (and post-revolutionary) Iran has become a constant feature of our political landscape over the past decade, causing shock waves all over the Middle East and beyond. At the time of writing the seemingly endless war with Iraq has technically ended, with not much more logic than it began. Just as most people thought that the revolution had calmed down, came the affair of the anathema called down upon the writer Salman Rushdie (see below). The names of organizations more or less linked to Iranian Islamic revolutionaries – and some who claimed links that existed only in their own imaginations – have become familiar symbols of exotic terror. 'Islamic Jihad', for example, whose name has become shorthand for a whole movement in much of the Western press and television, may not be an organized body at all, but a catch-all label for a rabble of small groups who have little or nothing to do with one another. It is all gain for them: the name alone suffices to strike terror.[1]

Hezbollah or the 'Party of God', the 'Organization of Revolutionary Justice' or the 'Organization of the Oppressed of the World' are odd names indeed. The spectre of international terrorism is carefully kept floating before us; international hostage-takers become key figures of European – particularly French – domestic policy and an American government puts itself in an untenable position by trying to sell arms to a government it stigmatizes as 'terrorist' and 'outlaw'. Name-calling works both ways. The American public would probably have been less tolerant of the misdeeds of its own government in the Iran-Contra affair, had the insults hurled westwards from Tehran been even slightly less violent. 'America' *per se* has become a dirty word in Iran, as in 'the American brand of Islam', considered the worst of all calumnies with which to charge Saudi Arabia.

As Iran became a terrifying spectre in the Western imagination, it became increasingly difficult to distinguish fact from fantasy. The official language in Tehran ranted on about greater and lesser Satans: the United States was consistently given the first place in this hellish hierarchy, but, depending on the situation at any given moment, the Soviet Union, France, Britain and eventually West Germany joined the list. Under the circumstances, it was probably inevitable that Iran should be demonized in the eyes of the West. Much of the information coming out of the country was manipulated, though not always consciously. It was not difficult to do: the gross incoherence of words and deeds in the early years of the revolution provided the material for an elaborate mythology of 'mad mullahs', which once planted, grew in the imagination of the West – and not only in the West.[2]

Nevertheless, dispassionate examination shows that even during the height of the revolutionary fever in 1979, the main lines of Iranian policy remained entirely consistent with its internal logic. The shock and the confusion arose because the basic principles were and remain absolutely different from those considered the norm in the West and more or less universally adopted. Furthermore, there has often been a hiatus between the principles enunciated and the actions as they were carried out. The handling of the hostage crisis at the American embassy in 1979–81 is just one example. Six years after the event, an American expert wrote:

> Khomeini demonstrated a cool and calculated ability to manipulate events for his own benefit and to function purposefully in the midst of political and economic tumult. The leadership in Tehran also displayed an appreciation for damage limitation, as when it quietly squelched calls for a hostage trial and expelled a hostage who was seriously ill in order to avoid probable U.S. retaliation.[3]

The paradox is more apparent than real. With time it has become increasingly evident that power in Tehran is not monolithic, even though those who talked or wrote about conflict between 'radicals' and 'moderates' oversimplified the issue. Neither of these words really applies; even less so now that the war seems to be over. It has become clear that a debate went on for close to a year within Iran between the group in favour of perpetuating the war, at whatever cost, and those who wanted to negotiate, and that the latter managed to get the upper hand. The quarrel continues between the dogmatic purists, those who wanted to fight to the bitter end and who subsequently preached against all contact with the corrupted West, and those who believe that contact is necessary to rebuild and advance the country.

The victory of those whom it seems more realistic to call the 'pragmatists' was all the more extraordinary because, in fact, the war was extremely useful in the exercise of domestic policy in a highly unstable revolutionary state. In the summer of 1980, internal ethnic tensions threatened not only the regime but the cohesion of the state itself. The war helped to legitimize a foreign policy that flouted all the rules of conventional diplomacy. By its final year, the only good reasons to continue it were domestic; its prolongation could only harm Iran on the international scene. It was extremely difficult to stop without provoking new and unpredictable domestic upheavals – until, somehow, a favourable diplomatic situation could be presented to the population. As peace came in the second half of 1988, it was fascinating to watch what appeared at the time to be a clever, if sometimes bloody, handling of the internal transition. Reports from Tehran spoke of hundreds, then thousands, of executions of opponents. Many were members of the Mujaheddin Khalq, the political organization whose exiled armed wing, the 'Mujaheddins' National Liberation Army', fought alongside the Iraqis in the final phases of the war.

Iran's growing sense of international isolation almost certainly helped towards the acceptance of UN Security Council Resolution No. 598 in July 1988, which had been rejected a year earlier when the circumstances would in fact have been much more favourable. During the early excitement of the honeymoon period of the Islamic Republic, the Iranians were sufficiently infatuated with their revolution to have little need of the outside world. Indeed, they flaunted its rejection. Even in the conduct of the war itself they wanted as little interference as possible. While one of the principal objects of Iraqi policy had been to internationalize the war, to involve as many outside elements as possible, Iran was constantly concerned to circumscribe it.[4] This runs counter to the accepted wisdom that Iran's principal objective was exporting its revolution. Although export of the revolution had indeed been an important element of doctrine between 1979 and 1984, in subsequent years the theme practically disappeared from official speeches and documents. In response to this shift, the Gulf states returned, insofar as they had ever departed from it, to their traditional policy of seeking (and usually finding) a *modus vivendi* with Iran, whatever its politics of the moment. Saudi Arabia, by its very nature, always had more difficulty in subscribing to such a policy. When it broke off diplomatic relations with Iran in April 1988, it did so for reasons having to do with its guardianship of the Holy Places rather than because of any specific changes in the political situation – if, indeed, one can in this context separate religion and politics. None of the other Gulf states followed Saudi Arabia's lead, not even, or perhaps particularly not, Kuwait, which at the time had at least as many reasons to mistrust Iran.

Relations between Iran and the Gulf states are complex,

interwoven with historical, ideological, economic and psychological considerations that cannot be treated schematically. Looking at even a few of the salient points may help to understand what happened on both sides both during the war and in the post-war period.

As the preceding chapter tried to show, it is difficult to doubt that Iraq physically began hostilities when it crossed the border on 22 September 1980; it is also clear that it did so in response to a series of serious provocations. The whole argument about who began the war turns on the question of when a provocation becomes an act of war. However, it is equally true that once the war had begun, it was Iran that set the rules and the limits. Iraq wanted to get out of the war almost as soon as it got in and declared the fact openly; Iran proclaimed that its one non-negotiable aim was to end the rule of the Ba'ath Party in Iraq, or at the very minimum, obtain the departure of Saddam Hussein. In the end, in July 1988, Iran abandoned that apparently irreducible demand in circumstances that were revealing of both the strengths and the weaknesses of the Islamic Republic.

The oil factor

Iran is the real heavyweight of the Gulf, far more so than Iraq, and certainly more than Saudi Arabia. Besides the size of its area and population, there is the undeniable fact of its position at the vital geo-political junction of the Middle East with South Asia. Iran covers the whole north-eastern shore of the Gulf, from the mouth of the Shatt al-Arab to Hormuz and beyond along the Baluchi coast. Its population of 50 million is almost double that of all the Arab Gulf states (including Iraq) put together. A major oil producer, its proven reserves are the third largest in the Middle East, after Saudi Arabia and Iraq.[5] In 1974, Iran exported an average of 6 million barrels a day; in 1987, the average daily figure was down to 2.3 million barrels. Like its Gulf neighbours, Iran is almost entirely dependent on oil revenues to finance indispensable imports, from foodstuffs to arms and machinery. A thriving export trade in pistachio nuts and the excellent fresh fruits and vegetables which have become staples in the markets of the UAE and Oman is not enough, nor is the trade in carpets, many of which are smuggled out. Even though Iraq was buying more expensive weaponry, the war cost Iran far more dearly than Iraq. Under the Shah, Iranian military equipment was almost entirely American and that door was slammed shut immediately after the revolution. There were always ways of getting round the embargo, including help from Israel beginning in 1981[6] and through the international arms dealers' fraternity. However, the prices charged to Iran got higher and higher as the war dragged on. And bereft of wealthy allies, it had to meet its bills.

Nevertheless, Iran emerged from the war with relatively little foreign debt, compared to an estimated $70 billion owed by Iraq. The revolutionary government paid off most of the $6.5 billion external debt left by the Shah; paying interest is un-Islamic. It has short-term debts of $6–8 billion, mostly in letters of credit (usually paid up as they fall due), but these are practically covered by its liquid overseas assets.[7] As the time for reconstruction appeared on the horizon, Iran was considered by most Europeans as presenting excellent investment opportunities. By early January 1989, Peugeot had signed a joint venture to produce half a million cars over the next eight years.

Iranian defence expenditures for 1986/7 were estimated at $5.9 billion and for 1987/8 at $8.96 billion to which should be added almost $1 billion diverted from the development fund and $3 million in foreign exchange already abroad.[8] Oil revenues for 1986, the year of the great oil market collapse, were $5.6 billion; in 1987 they were up to $10 billion[9], despite the difficulties Iran had in exporting any oil at all. Years of bombing of the main oil terminal at Kharg Island never put it completely out of action. The Iraqis began to attack Kharg in earnest after France lent them five Super-Etendard fighter-bombers in 1983, and the escalation in the attacks on Kharg can be linked, point by point, to the arrival of increasingly fancy French technology. In 1984, it was AS-3 laser-guided missiles and in October 1985 the even more sophisticated ARMAT. The Iranians did not miss the correlation, and declared that it put France in a 'state of co-belligerency'.[10]

The Iranian riposte was a shuttle of tankers plying between

Kharg and hastily-furbished terminals on the islands of Sirri, Lavan and Larak, ever nearer to the Strait of Hormuz. In turn, that pushed the Iraqis to polish their air attack tactics. Once they had mastered in-flight re-fuelling, even the terminals nearest the mouth of the Gulf were no longer inaccessible. In May 1988 the most spectacular of the raids made a hit on the world's largest tanker, the Liberian-registered *Seawise Giant*, used as a floating storage tank off Larak – a direct blow to the Iranian jugular.

The idea repeatedly floated both before and during the war that the Strait of Hormuz could be blocked by sinking a ship across it was always nonsense.[11] Such a feat is physically impossible. The Strait is 23 maritime miles across at its narrowest point, which means that there are no international seas between the territorial waters of Oman and Iran, both of whom, like most other coastal countries, have declared a 12 mile limit. The shipping lanes pass through Omani waters; they are well marked and nowhere less than 100 metres deep. Even the biggest tanker draws only thirty metres, so three at least would have to be sunk exactly one on top of the other to block a single lane of the separation scheme. Accidents, even in wartime, are extremely rare. Radio guidance and other navigational aids are all excellent in the Strait; the weather is usually good and on most days one can see across with the naked eye. There are obviously other ways to block navigation, including shooting from one or the other shore. But when alarmist cries went up about the danger of the Chinese Silkworm missiles,[12] a whiff of either disinformation or naïvety was in the air. It does not require very sophisticated weaponry to fire 20 miles across the water.

A far more important factor was that no one had more interest in keeping navigation open through the Strait than Iran. As the war went on, Iraq was able to ensure exports of well over 2 million barrels of oil per day – practically all it could pump over and above its domestic needs – overland, bypassing the Gulf altogether. Iran, on the other hand, remained entirely dependent on maritime transport through the Gulf. There was a flurry of talk in 1986 and 1987 about refurbishing the old gas pipeline through Baku towards the western Soviet Union;

refitted, it could theoretically take 700,000 barrels a day. It would not, however, have been ready for commissioning before 1990. Even before the end of the war, the idea had simmered down, more likely because of possible political complications than because of any technical difficulties. The Russians, in any case, were keen to keep talking about it, whether the project was in fact realistic or not, as one more way to keep up some kind of dialogue with Iran.[13] The project for a new oil pipeline that would bypass Hormuz completely and feed a terminal at Jask on the Baluchi coast off the Gulf of Oman was slowed down, presumably because of the cost. With the end of the war, it will probably be scrapped altogether as Iran returns to its normal export terminals centred on Kharg.

The export of the revolution

It is never easy to live next door to a revolution, even less so when that revolution comes by surprise (it is easy to say 'you should have been warned', but then not even the American intelligence services foresaw what was coming) and in the middle of a euphoric boom period. But the revolution did not change the geographical facts of life, and first among them is the fact that for the Arab states on the other side of the Gulf Iran is a neighbour. By this I mean not just a contiguous but largely ignored territory, as has usually been the case, war or no war, between Iran and Iraq. In the newspapers of Qatar or the UAE, Iran is often included on the pages of local and Gulf news; traders have been plying back and forth for centuries and have sometimes come to rest on the opposite shore from where they started. The Shah was not much loved on the Arab side of the Gulf. Whatever fellow-feeling there might have been for another monarch was more than cancelled out by a dislike of his arrogance, of his propensity to imitate what were considered the most perverse aspects of Western civilization, from secret police methods to topless bathing on the beaches, all part of his lurching race towards the modern world.

The tiny pockets of vaguely progressive society in Bahrain or in Kuwait had contacts with the Iranian opposition in Europe and the United States. They were familiar with the reforming ideas of intellectuals like the future (and now former) president Abdolhassan Bani Sadr; they may even have admired them. But where they, just as much as Iran-watchers further afield, miscalculated was in gauging the force of the religious opposition and its power to marshal an impressive part of the population behind it.

Practically all Westerners and most Arabs have found it difficult to come to grips with the idea that Iran lived through a genuine revolution in 1979 – not a coup like the government upsets that like to give themselves the glorious name of revolution in the Third World, but a profound upheaval in the social structure of the country. Like any other revolution, it had its supporters and its detractors (and victims) among 50 million Iranians. During the first year after Ayatollah Khomeini's triumphant return to Tehran there were incipient revolts among the Kurds and the Azeris in the north, and the Baluchis in the far south. Oddly, there were hardly any serious signs of revolt among the 2 million Arabic-speaking inhabitants of Khuzistan, called Arabistan by the Iraqis, despite persistent Ba'athist appeals to rise up and return to the Arab fold. There were not even moves in that direction after the Iraqis crossed the border on 22 September 1980, into Khuzistan, where they sincerely expected to be welcomed as liberators. True, at the beginning of the war the Iranians did carry out mass displacements of the Arabic-speaking population. The movement could be called evacuation from a war zone or deportation to avoid an uprising. When asked for clarification, a high-ranking Iranian official refused to go any further than 'Appropriate measures were taken'.[14]

The Iranian revolutionary leaders welcomed the war, which was presented as an imposed, but nevertheless holy, conflict. To them it was literally a God-send: in the name of the war against the 'infidel' next door, Iranian nationalism could eclipse the stirrings of non-Persian particularisms. Persia and Iran are not synonyms. Persia is the area inhabited by the Persians, the Farsi-speaking majority within the larger national space that the first Pahlavi Shah, father of Mohammed Reza Pahlavi, decided should once again, as in pre-Islamic times, be called Iran, a name derived from the same root as 'Aryan'. Farsi is an

Indo-European language, with many Arabic admixtures and written in Arabic script.

In point of fact, such nationalist sentiment is in contradiction to the doctrine of the unity of the *umma*, the community of the faithful, and Iranian internal propaganda encouraging support for the war had to be carefully balanced so as not to give too much prominence to national as opposed to religious arguments. In reality, however, the idea of belonging to a nation is strong in Iran and its clear manifestation was one of the surprises, on both sides, of the war. In late July and early August 1988, when Iran had declared its acceptance of the cease-fire resolution and it was Iraq's turn to dither while trying to gain last-minute territorial advantages, there was a sudden influx of Iranian exiles from Europe and America, most of them staunch opponents of the regime, flocking back when they thought the homeland was in real danger. After the death of Ayatollah Khomeini in June 1989, Persian nationalism gained ground very quickly, references to 'Persia' increased in official speech and writing; renewed insistance on the 'Persian Gulf' completely eclipsed the idea, put about during the war, of calling it the 'Islamic Gulf'; Persian, as opposed to Islamic, historical monuments were pushed up the list for restoration and maintenance.

What made Iran so frightening to its Gulf neighbours and, less understandably, to the West, was its loudly-trumpeted intention of exporting its revolution. As soon as the Islamic Republic was proclaimed, its expansion or, more accurately, its replication, became an essential goal. Similar missionary zeal has existed in other revolutions; most lose much of their ardour as the years go by. The reasons for abandoning expansionist policies can sometimes be found in a modification of the ideological doctrine. They may also, as seems to have been the case with Iran, reflect a change in tactics as the flame of the zealots encounters hard reality on the ground. Iran has redefined rather than abandoned its theory of exporting the revolution: the Iranian experience should, says the newer version of the doctrine, serve as an example to be willingly imitated, not to be imposed by an outside force. Just how such imitation could be encouraged in the post-war period was an important question to be faced. Hints appeared in Lebanon, where Iranian support to its friends did not slacken – on the contrary. The Rushdie affair was another, surprisingly effective intimation.

According to strict Muslim doctrine, the *umma* is one and indivisible – a tenet that transcends even the Sunni-Shi'a schism. In modern times, at least, this doctrine has never been taken so seriously as a basis for action as by the Iranian theocracy. According to their strict interpretation, the division of the *umma* into national states is absurd, false and evil. Those who have been able to found a state based on righteousness, even in one small territory of the *umma*, have the right, are in fact duty-bound, to take an interest or a hand in what is happening anywhere and everywhere within the *umma*, in any territory where Muslims are or could conceivably be in a majority. Following this line of reasoning, the notion of non-interference in the internal affairs of another country has no meaning within the *umma*. Iraq, a neighbouring territory governed, according to current Iranian cosmogony, by men who defy the will of God is as worthy of their attention as the city of Isfahan. Lebanon has, in the Iranian perspective, long been subject to an illegitimate form of government in which Muslims in general, and Shi'a Muslims in particular, are ill-used. Turkey is another flagrant example of what Tehran considers an iniquitous government: the Kemalist abolition of the Caliphate still rankles even though, strictly speaking, this should not concern the Shi'a.[15] In fact, the minority position of the Shi'a requires some fine tuning of the relationship with the *umma*. There was much official rejoicing in Tehran when the Islamic candidates gained a near-majority in Jordan's first free parliamentary elections in November 1989. However, a similar victory in one of the large Arab and Sunni countries, Algeria, say, or Egypt, would be far more difficult for the Iranian revolutionaries to deal with, because it would inevitably rob them of the leadership of the Islamic movement.

Afghanistan, as long as the Soviet invasion lasted, was another patent case in which the Iranian revolutionaries considered they had a right to intervene. This right was, in fact, left unexercised except for some aid given to the Shi'a resistance groups based in

Iran. One might add that such solicitude for the welfare of the *umma* should logically mean that there is no need to worry about an Islamic revolutionary onslaught on Europe. Even the intensive missionary work among Muslim immigrants should be of concern only to their home countries or to rival Sunni missionaries. Despite occasional firebrand proclamations that the whole world is interdependent and therefore ready for mass conversion, there seems little risk that Europe could become part of the *umma* in the near future; the fears of the French far right seem unfounded.

In this context, revolutionary Iran's interest in its Gulf neighbours was inevitable. These countries were obviously prime targets for the export of the revolution. First of all, Iran remains the only country in the world where Shi'a Islam is the official creed. Only about 10 per cent of the Muslims in the world are Shi'a and they have often, not entirely without reason, felt themselves to be a discriminated minority. It was perfectly natural for a theocratic government that suddenly acceded to the helm of a regional power to become a rectifier of old wrongs. The fervour of its own citizens could only be reinforced by promises to ensure respect and power for the Shi'a in other countries. Bahrain, where Shi'a are a majority under a Sunni ruling dynasty, would naturally be high on the list; so would the eastern province of Saudi Arabia.

The Iranian revolutionaries inevitably applied their analysis of the Pahlavi monarchy to the sheikhdoms and kingdoms of the Gulf. In doing so they made a serious error. The Arab rulers are not and cannot be autocrats in the style of the Shah. Furthermore, none of them has attempted to force his subjects into the mould of the modern world on the ruins of Muslim precepts as the Shah tried to do; if anything, the monarchs have fostered a reverse movement. The very different relations that Shi'a and Sunnis entertain with what, for lack of a better term, we must call temporal as opposed to spiritual power, is another factor. The general rule in Islam is that there is no separation between the spiritual and the temporal and that all power derives from God. However, while Shi'a Islam admits the existence of a clerical hierarchy organized into a quasi-autonomous network of power parallel to the state, in Sunni

Islam, the preachers and even the *ulama*, or jurisconsults, are usually affiliated, if not subordinate, to the secular power with which they interact in a symbiotic relationship. In that sense, the Islamic fundamentalists who, in several Sunni Muslim countries (but not in the Gulf states, with the exception of those who occupied the Great Mosque of Mecca in 1979) have called on their followers to revolt against their governments could, strictly speaking, be considered heretics.[16]

Finally, Iran, whether imperial or revolutionary, remains Iran (and its ethnic majority, the Persians, remain Persians) and mutual suspicions and recriminations between them and the Arabs subsist. The Persians continue to look down on all those fishermen and bedouin, as they invariably consider the inhabitants of the opposite coast. Although they may now be rich, thanks to luck and the gifts God has given them, that does not entirely compensate for their lesser culture, in the eyes of the Iranians who barely trouble to hide their feelings. The Iranian scholar, Shahram Chubin, speaks of traditional Persian arrogance.[17] His use of the word arrogance is particularly interesting when set alongside the language of the revolution, which consistently castigated arrogance as one of the deadliest sins: Saddam Hussein must be punished for his arrogance; the nations of the world are divided between the arrogant, deserving of the most scathing punishments of man and God, and the meek, whose destiny is to be as blessed as in the New Testament.

Iraq worked hard to exploit the theme of the Arab-Persian opposition among its would-be allies. Its success was almost in inverse proportion to the geographic distance from the scene of the conflict. In the Gulf, neither governments nor public let themselves be drawn into what they considered a dangerous game whose premises they did not, in fact, basically share. Persian-Arab opposition was never used as a theme for official Iranian propaganda; after all, Arabs and Persians are both part of the *umma*. Instead, repeated vociferations against reactionary or benighted regimes alternated with assurances that the Gulf would come to no harm, that Iran was ready to ensure its security. This apparent contradiction can be explained in part by real changes in the political perspective as seen from Tehran and in part by the hyperbole that seems to be an integral part of the revolutionary vocabulary. But above all, the contradiction probably stems from real differences within the Iranian power structure, which is far more multicentric than foreign analysts realized for years.

Quite often, and this was true even at the beginning of the revolution, decisions were taken on several levels, independent of and sometimes contradicting each other. Pronouncements were made by individuals who effectively held a parcel of power, or held it for a time. Nobody, not even Ayatollah Khomeini, held it all. Such multiplicity inevitably perplexed all those who were used to the absolute and centralized power structures common to the Middle East. When Saddam Hussein speaks, it is tantamount to giving orders to be carried out immediately with no hint of internal discussion nor contradiction. In Iran, things do not work that way. The Guide of the Revolution, Ayatollah Khomeini, never really regulated all the details of daily life; even during the first years of the revolution, his pre-revolutionary writings on day-to-day conduct were quoted more than his direct contemporary interventions. As the years went by, he increasingly appeared as the supreme arbiter whose moral authority guaranteed that major decisions did not transgress the laws of Islam as he interpreted them. Such a role implies that differences exist and are known and allowed (if not encouraged) to exist; it does not necessarily imply a Western-style pluralism. The public airing of the differences can lead to an apparent incoherence which becomes terribly confusing as seen from the outside. In July 1988, the Iranian Government officially announced that it would accept the cease-fire with Iraq as set out in the UN resolution of almost a year before. The next day, Ayatollah Khomeini was widely quoted as having said that accepting the cease-fire was 'like taking poison'. Did that mean that the Ayatollah had lost his authority and was, in a sense, buried in his own lifetime? Not really; it meant that, however reluctantly, he had given his blessing to an act which he hated; just how far he was in a position to appreciate the basic internal economic and political difficulties that pushed the different centres of power to take that decision is a question that has plagued the analysts. But when there was an important point that needed clarification, the Ayatollah, like a phoenix rising from the ashes, was always present, however aged and ill he might have been.

Mutations of the revolution

From the vantage point of the Gulf, post-revolutionary Iran has passed through several mutations; each of them corresponded in time, if not necessarily in essence, to distinct phases of the war with Iraq. The first was the pre-war period between the departure of the Shah, at the end of January 1979, and the outbreak of the war in September 1980: it was then that Iran was most frightening to its Gulf neighbours, particularly to the smaller states.

The idea of revolution, whether or not applicable to the local situation, was in the air; people who had no real reason to be dissatisfied were caught up in a wave of enthusiasm that swept over the whole of the Muslim world. More or less violent demonstrations broke out in all the cities in the eastern part of the Arabian peninsular, with the sole exception of Muscat. It was easy to blame them on Iranian provocateurs, but they could just as likely have been spontaneous popular outbreaks, signs of the times, however uncharacteristic of the local *mores*. In the Gulf, there was an unspoken but real (although, of course, never publicly avowed) satisfaction when the war began. The two powerful neighbours, the regional bullies, were going to keep each other busy for a while and the smaller states would be able to get on with their real business, getting richer and hauling themselves (as distinct from being pushed) into the comfort of the modern world.

The second period, which can be broken down into several stages, ran from the outbreak of the war up to early 1987. Probably the most important event of those years – as seen from the western side of the Gulf – was the establishment of the Gulf Co-operation Council, the GCC (see Chapter 10).

These were also the years when the political fact of terrorism was injected into what had until then been the remarkably peaceful life of the Gulf states. Even then, although a good number of individual actions were carried out, they never added up to a state of sustained terrorism. Iran was certainly behind many of these acts (although not all those ascribed to it). They were one more expression of Iranian disappointment with the reaction, or lack of reaction, of 'the people' in the Gulf. The disappointment stemmed from another error of appreciation. The theoreticians in Tehran, like others before them, missed the point: a majority of 'the people' had drawn far too many benefits from the oil boom to go beyond a little ritual grumbling.

Most of the acts of violence were accompanied by verbal threats, which alternated oddly with soothing words that no harm would come to Iran's neighbours – on condition that they themselves stayed calm. Kuwait, at least until 1987, was particularly adept at dealing with these changing moods. Its usual tactic was to ignore them.

Newspapers, magazines, radio and television, both in the West and in the Arab world, constantly painted Iran as an outlaw state. Even academic circles, where a better perspective might have been expected, joined in. The picture was so consistent that it was easy to forget that, from the beginning of the war, Iraq was responsible for far more hostile acts towards the Gulf countries than Iran, and that the longer the war went on, the more impunity it enjoyed. It was Iraq that began the attacks on neutral shipping and that attacked the Abu Bakuch oil rig off Abu Dhabi in November 1986. It was an Iraqi missile that hit the American frigate *Stark* in the spring of 1987. The attack, in which 37 sailors were killed, was officially a mistake and the Iraqis presented their excuses to the United States in due diplomatic form.[18] Each time Iraq managed to turn what looked like an act of aggression to its advantage.

The Iranians considered this a profound injustice. Despite appearances, Iran, particularly after 1986, was not indifferent to world opinion and especially not to that of its immediate neighbours. What looked like cynicism was often the outward sign of a defence mechanism: the more the proud Iranians were (from their point of view, unjustly) pushed into a psychological corner, the more they defended themselves. When that defence looked even faintly like a ruse, the world called it perfidy.

The final months of the second phase were marked by the arrival of foreign warships in the Gulf and surrounding waters.

First, came those of the Soviet Union and the Americans, invited in by Kuwait, followed by the Europeans, France, Italy, Britain, Belgium – all of them much more discreet about their activities.[19] The Iranians called it the 'NATO armada', but the co-ordination was minimal, completely *ad hoc*, and with no sign of a single command.

In the early months of 1987 the attitude towards Iran among the GCC states once again showed some differentiation. In contrast to what had happened in 1982, Saudi Arabia was no longer alone in its position against all the smaller states; Kuwait had come to almost the same conclusions. Wittingly or not, they had both drawn ever closer to Iraq, or at least to a position where strict neutrality had been abandoned for one distanced further from Iran. The states of the lower Gulf, the UAE and Oman, and to some degree, Qatar, defined their neutrality as definitely keeping on speaking terms and sometimes more with Iran. Bahrain tried to keep the lowest profile possible.

The beginning of the third phase can be dated precisely: 31 July 1987. On the last Friday of that year's pilgrimage to Mecca, violent clashes broke out, first in all probability among the pilgrims and then between worshippers and the Saudi security forces. At the end of that fateful day, over 400 were dead, most of them Iranians. Some impartial observers – they were few – thought that the reaction of the Saudi police might have been over-harsh; the police were understandably nervous after the repeated threats and incidents of previous years. Relations between Iran and Saudi Arabia deteriorated rapidly, leading to a complete break in April of the following year. One reason for the break was to make it more difficult for Iranian pilgrims to obtain visas for the *hajj*; this became obvious when Saudi Arabia simply ignored Turkish offers to represent the Kingdom in Tehran, as it represented Iran and Iraq in their respective capitals. One month before the 1988 pilgrimage, Iran announced that it would send no official delegation to the pilgrimage at all, but Saudi Arabia took no chances. The whole Kingdom was in a state of alert throughout the *hajj* season, which passed without incident. Admittedly, in January, Ayatollah Khomeini had taken the precaution of announcing that, in case of need, reasons of state could, at least temporarily, supersede the obligation of pilgrimage for the true believer – an announcement that created an uproar among Sunni theologians.

As the Iranian revolution matured, aggressiveness towards the monarchies on the other side of the Gulf had begun to alternate with a mellower tone that verged on blandishment: there seemed to be a need to seek at least a minimum of understanding in the absence of real sympathy or of allies. Once Iran understood that the Arabs, and the rest of the world, would not let Iraq be defeated, the message directed towards the neighbours across the Gulf began to be one of encouraging them to take care of their own security concerns, i.e., not to get too close to the Americans. A formal message had been sent to the Gulf states in 1986, proposing a mutual security pact as the chief guarantee of that security. The idea did not get very far at that time, but even before the cease-fire negotiations were complete, Iran was again proposing it, and this time it was given a more sympathetic hearing. Iran had consistently denied participation in terrorist attacks on the Gulf states, particularly in the attempted assassination of the Emir of Kuwait in 1985 and the Riyadh explosions of the same summer. Who might have inspired these attacks was something else, as difficult to deny as to prove.

It was harder to plead complete innocence in the two hijackings of Kuwaiti aircraft, the first in 1984 and the second in April 1988. The full story of the second hijacking has not come out, but there are strong and convergent indications of some Iranian involvement, although it may have been peripheral and partial. Without some collusion it is difficult to understand how the plane was able to overfly Iran, in wartime, from Hormuz to Mashhad without being officially reported by the radar system; there is also a strong probability that the hijackers received arms and reinforcements during the plane's first stop in Mashhad, before it continued to Cyprus.

During this period, there was growing recognition inside Iran that such violent, irresponsible and often contradictory acts were becoming increasingly counterproductive. They had led to virtual international isolation and made it possible for Iraq to get away with almost anything. Iraq had consistently managed to show itself as the international 'good guy', reasonable, officially accepting the peace initiatives even though its conciliatory words were not always followed by corresponding deeds. The truces in the 'war of the cities' in the spring of 1988 were an example. Two truces were announced, not negotiated. The first announcement said that no rockets would be fired during the celebrations of the Iranian (and Kurdish) feast of Nowruz, which marks the spring equinox and, although of pre-Islamic origin, is still the big holiday of the Iranian year. The second was to mark the visit of Turgut Ozal, then Turkish Prime Minister, to the two capitals. Iraq announced that its participation in the truce was conditional on its right to fire the last rocket. The proclamation went straight into the international press, as though such a demand were normal; it is not difficult to imagine the outcry had it been Iran that issued the ultimatum. Iran held its fire while Ozal was in Baghdad; Iraq did not when he went to Tehran.

Even stranger, the repeated use by Iraq of chemical weapons caused only limited international indignation so long as the war lasted. The use was documented by the United Nations and implicitly admitted by, among others, Tariq Aziz, the Iraqi Foreign Minister. Again, one can imagine the outcry had it been Iran that was accused of using gas; Iraq tried to launch countercharges, but the use by Iran was never proven. Only at the end of the war, when the Iraqis were accused of using chemical weapons against their own Kurdish population, was there an international uproar.

Iraq brilliantly managed its campaign to internationalize the war. There were only two real naval battles in the course of the conflict, on 18 April and 3 July 1988, and both were between Iran and the United States. The immediate result of the first was that Iraq attacked not only Iranian tankers but an increasing number of neutral vessels – all with impunity. Ten days later, the United States announced that henceforth it would extend its protection to other ships in the Gulf, whether or not they flew the US flag. The Iranians took this as a blatantly partisan act, despite pious American protests. The US warships had orders to go to the assistance of any neutral vessel being attacked, on condition that it was not dealing with either of the belligerent parties and was not in a war zone. But Iraq's ports were out of commission, and so could not be a port-of-call; in addition, Baghdad had declared the whole of the Iranian coast an 'exclusion zone'. In other words, ships having anything to do with Iran or near the Iranian coast were to be considered free game for the Iraqis.

The second battle was the one in which an Iran Airbus was caught in the fighting and shot down by the *USS Vincennes*, with the loss of all 296 on board. The official American version was that the Airbus had been mistaken for an Iranian F-14 in the attack position. The ensuing inquiry at one point incriminated the electronic surveillance equipment and then talked about human error. In May 1989, Iran lodged a complaint with the International Court of Justice in The Hague. This in itself could be considered a sign that the time when Tehran refused all credit to the international community was over – at least within the foreign ministry.

The Syrian alliance

By 1988, Iran had only one more-or-less ally left: Syria. After the fall of the Shah and at the beginning of the war, three other members of the 'Steadfastness Front', Libya, South Yemen and the PLO – but not Algeria – had rallied to it with enthusiasm on the strength of the young Islamic Republic's hostile declarations towards Israel and its avowed support for all the oppressed peoples of the earth. Algeria tried hard to stay neutral in order to attempt mediation; its foreign minister paid for the venture with his life. In 1982, as Muhammad Saddik Benyahya, with a delegation of a dozen other diplomats, was on his way to Tehran for one more attempt at conciliation, his plane was shot down near the border where Turkey meets Iran and Iraq. As with several other incidents since 1980, no verifiable proof has ever been made available to researchers, but indications are that the plane was hit by Iraqi fire and not that of Kurdish guerrillas as claimed by Iraq. Thereafter, Algeria stopped practically all its efforts at mediation, even though it felt a special responsibility because of its association with the Algiers agreement. Other Arab friends withdrew their support one after the other. The PLO was happy to find a way out of the alliance when the

Iranian attitude towards the inter-Palestinian squabbles in Lebanon and Syria became unacceptable: a senior PLO official told me privately that as early as the summer of 1981 they were uncomfortable with the Iranian friendship and subsequently drew closer to Baghdad. South Yemen declared its neutrality after Iran repeatedly refused proposals for a negotiated peace, Libya finally turned a somersault and rediscovered its Arab and Sunni connections after the 1987 incidents in Mecca. Only Syria remained.

The Irano-Syrian alliance was frankly bizarre: most of the reasons for animosity between revolutionary Iran and Ba'athist Iraq could apply just as well to Iran's relationship with Syria. Syria is just as Ba'athist as Iraq (despite their diverging ways of interpreting Ba'athism) and probably even more thoroughly secular. Admittedly, there are fewer Shi'a in Syria, but the large Alawite minority, who are in fact Shi'a heretics, should logically arouse the missionary zeal of the orthodox Shi'a clergy just as much as the 'liberation' of the Iraqi Shi'a did. There is one difference; the Alawis may be heretics, but they do happen to hold most of the reins of power.

There were only two real points of convergence: the shared historical opposition to Iraq and the virulent hatred of the Iraqi president, Saddam Hussein, shown by the leaders of both countries. Never mind ideology; this was a case of my enemy's enemy being my friend. The far-from-holy alliance was not impregnable, however, and one of its weakest links was (but here we are far from the Gulf) in Lebanon. There was an ever-widening rift between Hezbollah, the Party of God, with strong links to the Iranian Shi'a hierarchy and AMAL[20] which is just as Shi'a, but – at least in 1988 and 1989 – was an important link in the pro-Syrian alliance in Lebanon. By late 1989, while the war between Iran and Iraq was over along their common border, it was still being continued by proxy in Lebanon. Iraq began shipping arms to the Lebanese Maronites almost as soon as the cease-fire with Iran was signed. In the peculiar logic of the Lebanon, the Maronites, as enemies of the Syrians, had become Iraq's friends.

The Irano-Syrian alliance was, however, extraordinarily useful to both sides. For Syria, the advantages were mostly practical and financial: oil deliveries at preferential prices and some even free (made as gifts to the 'front line army' – that is, against Israel). There were also some diplomatic gains. Friendship with the much-feared Iran gave Syria more importance than it might otherwise have had, especially at times of negotiations to try to free Western hostages. However, on balance the friendship may have brought Syria more problems than benefits: the cost of being branded 'a terrorist country' or 'the friend of terrorists' is not negligible. The stigma of terrorism-cum-friends-of-Iran stuck in Britain long after the United States had either forgotten or forgiven it.[21] The cost in terms of being considered an outlaw among the Arabs was probably mitigated by the fact that financial support kept coming anyway, especially from Saudi Arabia.

For Iran, the advantages of the Syrian alliance were overwhelming. As long as the war lasted, it meant that Iraq had to keep one eye – and a few troops – on its western flank, just to be sure. It opened another avenue for arms procurement from countries like North Korea or Czechoslovakia. But the most important advantage was that Syria is a quintessentially Arab country; having it for an ally should have proved to the world, whatever the Iraqis were saying, that the war was not simply a war between the Arabs and the Persians. Other Arab countries did not see it that way and tried various means of persuasion on Syria: none really worked. At the Arab summit in Amman, in November 1987, Syria's President Hafez el-Assad did consent to sign the resolutions which included a fairly stiff condemnation of Iran for not having accepted the UN cease-fire resolution of the previous summer. The Syrian President, at the head of a country in dire economic straits, could not afford to ignore the sweetener offered by Saudi Arabia to ensure unanimity, rumoured to be $2 billion. For a short period, there was the possibility that Syria would switch alliances, or at least join the ranks of the neutrals. It did not happen. And when, the following July, Iran did accept the cease-fire proposals, the Syrians were bitter about not having been informed in advance so that they could have performed a face-saving switch just before the public announcement.

Up to the end of the war, Syria remained Iran's only real ally;

Pakistan may have tiptoed around it but never came out into the open. Syria became many Iranians' window to the outside world. Where else could an Iranian too poor or too pious to travel to Europe go for a break, once the great pilgrimage cities of Kerbala and Najaf, both in Iraq, were closed off? Sayida Zeinab, near Damascus, became a popular substitute: the Islamic Republic rebuilt the shrine there, dedicated to the grand-daughter of Mohammed and sister of Ali. Only a few days before the end of the war, in July 1988, the summer crop of Iranian tourists was already on hand, preparing to spend the next few weeks or months on the relatively cool Damascus plateau. Renting flats to them was a steady source of supplementary income for the Palestinians in their nearby camp.

Prisoners of war

The treatment afforded to prisoners of war on both sides was one more example of the belligerents' different views of the world. Being a prisoner-of-war is never a pleasant experience; in the Iran-Iraq war it was a particularly nasty one. Never had the International Committee of the Red Cross (ICRC) made so many public appeals (code-word for denunciations of unacceptable practices) for one conflict and in a comparable period of time as those published between 1984 and 1988. An appeal is by its nature addressed to all the signatories of the Geneva Convention: it is not easy to push them into recognizing their collective responsibility for the application of humanitarian law. The word 'appeal' is deceptively mild. In fact, it is the ultimate arm of the ultra-discreet ICRC, wielded only when persistent discussions with the governments involved achieve no results. The ICRC appeals provide sad footnotes to the story of a sad war. In carefully laundered diplomatic prose, they talk about protecting civilian populations, the use of prohibited chemical weapons and, repeatedly, prisoners of war.

Just as the negotiations to end the war began, more evidence came to light in a report by a UN mission sent to both countries during the odd limbo between the time Iran said that it would accept the cease-fire and the moment the fighting actually stopped a month later. The report, freed from the ICRC's self-imposed straitjacket of silence, corroborated, with far more detail, the careful accusations of the appeals.[22] It presented a harrowing picture of physical ill-treatment of prisoners in Iraq, held one hundred at a time in an underground dungeon with a rudimentary toilet in one corner and, next to it, a few plastic buckets of drinking water. The Iraqi guards were accused of brutality, but Iraq was given comparatively high marks for at least formal co-operation with the ICRC and the UN mission. The ICRC was allowed to visit most of the prisoners throughout the war and the Iraqi authorities did sometimes listen to, and act on, remarks made, even punishing guards accused of brutality once the commanding officers were told about it.

In Iran, the situation was almost a mirror image as reflected in the deforming glass of a carnival side-show. Prisoners, who were far more numerous,[23] lived in much better physical conditions: they slept in bunks rather than on blankets on the ground, lived in decent barracks and were usually given adequate food. They were, officially, 'guests of the Islamic Republic', not POWs. In the early years of the war, the Islamic Republic had refused to recognize most of the usual rules of international affairs and in 1982 its delegates at the UN were denouncing human rights as 'an imperialist decadent Western notion'.

However, as guests, the prisoners were expected to learn the ways of their hosts. The camps' 'cultural committees' were responsible for applying the appropriate psychological pressures; in plain language, brain-washing. The aims, methods and results of such treatment are just as intolerable in international law as the beatings on the other side. In several camps, the visit of the UN experts sparked off violent demonstrations: against Iraq, against all international organizations, including the ICRC, against any Western or non-Islamic influences.

Three years after the end of the war, the ICRC was still trying to persuade both sides to exchange the last of their prisoners-of-war. At the same time, the Islamic Republic was trying to persuade some of its over two million refugees, most from Afghanistan and a few hundred thousand from Iraq, to go home. Iran was consistently given high marks by the the office of the United Nations High Commissioner for Refugees (UNHCR) for their hospitality,[24] which the Iranians modestly say is normal. When the Soviet army entered Afghanistan in December 1979, there were already approximately 500,000 Afghans in Iran – nomads making their normal rounds or migrant workers. Two million more came after 1979 (and began trickling back after the signing of the Soviet withdrawal agreement). Until 1984, Iran bore the cost of the refugees alone; after that, the amount of international aid going to Iran was a tiny fraction of that accorded to Pakistan, where the number was not much larger, slightly over three million. The refugees in Iran were all the more assimilable since almost all of them speak Pushtu, which is simply Farsi with an Afghan accent.

Very few of the Afghan refugees in Iran lived in camps beyond a short transit period imposed mainly for quarantine purposes. The refugees brought with them diseases that had been all but eradicated in Iran: measles, leprosy and cholera. After a few weeks in the camps, most managed their insertion into the economy. For ten years, hardly a house was built without Afghan workers and they provided welcome agricultural labour as Iranians went to the front. Despite persistent rumours, there were no forced enrolments of Afghans into the Iranian army. It was, however, probably not difficult to persuade some that going to fight the 'infidel Iraqis' was a highly meritorious occupation. The ICRC did not find a single Afghan among the prisoners in Iraq.

Iran after two wars

It was difficult to imagine what kind of Iran would emerge from its long and painful war with Iraq. In the latter half of 1988, it became clear that the country had gone through very hard times indeed. To return to Shahram Chubin's maxim: for Iraq, holding out against an enemy three times larger was in itself victory; for Iran not to win was in itself defeat. When, in early July 1988, Iran suddenly announced that it accepted the cease-fire resolution voted by the UN a year earlier this was, according to Professor Chubin's reasoning, a confession of defeat. In the internal debate that seems to have taken place during that year, those who were in favour of abandoning the war in the face of increasing domestic difficulties needed to find some way of doing so while not losing face. The Americans, by shooting down the Iran Air airplane on 3 July, may have given it to them. The enormity of almost 300 civilians being killed by what was probably a mistake in judgement for once tilted international opinion in favour of the Iranians; even at the United Nations a resolution condemning the attack was given almost unanimous support.

As soon as the peace negotiations started, there was a curious reversal of roles between the two countries. Iraq, proud of what it considered a great victory, thought that it could impose its own will and quickly tried to add preconditions and modifications to the UN resolution, which was the negotiating agenda originally agreed. In the meantime, Iran suddenly became the model negotiator; its shrewd Foreign Minister, Dr Ali Akbar Velayati, smoothly agreed to everything the UN Secretary-General proposed, simply asking that the resolution be applied as written, which implied strict adherence to the Algiers agreement. The Iraqis called the agreement null and void but outside experts continued to hold it as an integral part of the corpus of international law.

As the months went by, Iran began to return to normal international life. Diplomatic relations were restored with most Arab countries[25] as well as those European ones with which they had been broken, but not the United States. The 'Den of Spies Bookshop' opened in a corner of the former Embassy grounds specialized in presenting volume after volume made up from documents found when the students went over the wall just behind in 1980.

The attitude towards the outside world was a mixture of eagerness, suspicion and cautious watchfulness: many Iranians felt sincerely misunderstood.[26] Overtures were made to the Gulf states and the Soviet Union at the same time as other officials thundered against all foreigners. Inside Iran, the debate went on between the purists who continued to oppose all contact with the corrupt and corrupting world of the infidels and those who thought at least technical co-operation was desirable if not indispensable. On an economic plane, the debate was keen between those who opposed all foreign borrowing,[27] and those who insisted it was necessary to put the country back on its feet (industrial capacity was running, in late 1989, at about 30 per cent of capacity). The second group were more or less the same people as those who had wanted, for analogous reasons, to stop the war and were mostly people close to Hashemi Rafsanjani. During the first post-war winter they had seemed to be gaining ground, but few observers saw their ascendancy as the prelude to a return to the *status quo ante revolutionem*.

Events were quickly to prove them right, with the unlikely bias of what was to become known as the 'Rushdie Affair'. In the autumn of 1988, Salman Rushdie, a British citizen of Indian Muslim origin, published his fourth novel, *The Satanic Verses*. At the time and in the ensuing months several groups of Muslims living in Britain, and particularly the large Muslim community in Bradford, protested against the work which they considered blasphemous and insulting; letters were written to editors and some ceremonial book-burnings were organized. Neither the author nor the publisher, nor the literary establishment at large took the protests very seriously. In the second half of January 1989, violent demonstrations broke out in India, then in Pakistan. Saudi Arabia had already banned the book, and other Muslim countries followed. On 14 February, the 'judgement' of Ayatollah Khomeini was made public. The old man, still the guide of the revolution despite his eighty-seven years, condemned Salman Rushdie to death for blasphemy (but not apostasy) and called on all Muslims, wherever they or Rushdie might be, to carry out the sentence. Cash rewards were subsequently promised to the assassins (not, it was quickly explained, directly by the Ayatollah but by 'private foundations'). Paradise assured was the principal reward. The British government reacted violently to what it considered an intolerable act by immediately breaking off what little remained of diplomatic relations with Tehran. The other members of the European Community showed their solidarity by recalling their ambassadors, but carefully did not go beyond that measure.

This is not the place for a literary criticism of Rushdie's complex work of fantastic fiction. What seems certain is that only a minute percentage of those who condemned and burnt it, who attacked bookshops and sacked the British Councils (which certainly had not time to stock it in their libraries) had read the 550 pages of difficult English text. If indeed the intention to vex, to mock or even to insult was there (which is possible, considering the caustic sarcasm of Rushdie's previous books),[28] it was blanketed under several layers of difficult English and literary conceits: dreams, irony, hyperbole, the symbolic distortion of names are only four among others. The names of the great figures of early Islam are not the only ones to appear in transformations: the then British Prime Minister is called 'Maggie Torture' – but then her government made no claim to divine authority.

The result of the Ayatollah's condemnation was not only that Rushdie and his wife went into prudent hiding under police protection and that his book became an instant best-seller. Literate people in the Middle East and in the West were both dismayed and heartened to see that such a political and diplomatic storm could be provoked by a work of literature. For weeks after the pronouncement, the newspapers were full of the Rushdie affair and just when it seemed to be calming down, the rebound came with the murder, on 30 March, of the head of the Muslim community in Belgium and Luxembourg and his assistant.[29] Later, some doubts were cast on whether the double murder was really a result of the Imam's mild defence of Rushdie's right to remain alive or simply a settling of scores within the Brussels community. In any event, the murders served notice that the affair was not finished. They effectively added to the confusion among the ordinary Muslims in the immigrant communities and convinced even more Westerners that Islam was indeed the religion of violence and folly.

Irrespective of what one may think of the novel itself, the political capital made out of it was a brilliant stroke by the Ayatollah and his close advisers. The tenth anniversary of the revolution had gone by in early February with relative indifference. The unsatisfactory ending of the war had inevitably led to a loss of prestige, inside and outside the country. Iran had officially abandoned the forced export of its revolution and not much remained to offer even as an example.

Thanks to the Rushdie anathema, suddenly Iran was once again calling the tune of militant Islam.

The European countries were caught in the trap, and the Muslims, including the Arabs, even more so. They were forced to go along with the Ayatollah's condemnation, on pain of being accused of laxness, and in doing so they acknowledged, *de facto*, the Ayatollah's leading role within the *umma*, the very thing many of them feared most. Political leaders and intellectuals were equally embarrassed and most kept silent or tried to skirt round the problem. One of the few who did speak out publicly was King Hassan II of Morocco, whose Muslim credentials are impeccable: he is the only Muslim ruler who can, today, legitimately avail himself of the hereditary title of 'Commander of the Faithful'. Almost all the Muslim countries, plus some with only small Muslim populations, banned *The Satanic Verses*; European publishers and booksellers dithered in the face of threats; committees and individuals who had worked for decades to further understanding between Muslims and non-Muslims were in despair. With time, the Rushdie Affair could well appear as one of the most brilliant of modern political manipulations of public opinion.

As an element of domestic policy, it also seems to have been a detonator for other signs of what, in the absence of a better term, one might call the re-radicalization of Iran. Just before another fruitless round of negotiations began with the Iraqis in Geneva, a veritable purge struck several of those who seemed to be working for an opening not so much towards the ex-enemy, but towards the outside world at large: the Iranian ambassador to the United Nations in New York and the deputy foreign minister in charge of European Affairs were among the victims.

The death of Ayatollah Khomeini, in June 1989, brought an end to the first period of the Islamic Republic. In a quick and surprisingly smooth transition, Ayatollah Ali Khamenei (until then President of the Islamic Republic and often considered a fairly colourless figure) was named *faqih*, or guide of the revolution. The Constitution was amended to give more power to the President and the elections were advanced: as soon as the period of formal mourning was over, Ali Akbar Hashemi Rafsanjani, the former speaker of the Majlis, was elected against only token opposition. Even during the lifetime of Ayatollah Khomeini, Rafsanjani was considered a moderate. This does not mean that at heart he is some sort of Westernized semi-social democrat. He is a cleric, a hojatolislam (the next rank below ayatollah), from a fairly wealthy family of businessmen; but – like most of the Iranian clergy – he has neither studied abroad nor even travelled further than Najaf or Kerbala for any length of time.

The first months after President Rafsanjani took office were spent in expectation. The faithful still chanted 'Morg bar Amrika' at Friday prayers on the campus of Tehran University and a new term appeared in the vocabulary of abuse: 'American Islam' – what Saudi Arabia was accused of practising, as opposed to 'the true Mohammedan Islam' as practised in Iran, a tautology that causes many Muslims to wince. The tentative diplomatic rapprochement with the Soviet Union was made no easier by the unrest on the Azerbaijan border where, in the first days of 1990, violent rioters called for open passage for Azeris on both sides. Unacceptable to the Soviet Union at a time when half a dozen other Republics were asking for special dispensations, the demands may or may not have been blessed in the highest spheres of Iranian diplomatic policy-making. They would have gone against the desire for good relations with this most important neighbour (1,800 kilometres of common border), but, on the other hand, Tehran could hardly speak out officially against attempts to express any extension of the unity of the *umma* out from the Iranian centre. The handling of the Azerbaijan affair provided yet another case of conflict between those who believed that no compromises should be made in the ideals of the Islamic revolution and those who were ready to come to terms with the outside world and with those members of society who are less zealous than themselves.

The post-war period brought a veritable identity crisis in Iran. With the death of Ayatollah Khomeini, a good deal of difficulty was encountered in defining the limits of authority between the civil – or presidential – authority and that of the *faqih*, the jurisconsult or guide as Khomeini's successor continued to be known. Even some Iranian liberals were saying they missed the old man, who alone had the power to curb some of the wilder instincts of his disciples. He himself, before he died, had once again allowed the playing of Persian classical *tar* music – forbidden at the time of the revolution – and authorized a few games, including chess which had been played in Persia for over 2,000 years.

The so-called hard-liners continued to favour the claustrophobic inbreeding of a fanatically Islamic Iran, whose only contacts with the outside world would be those needed to further the establishment of Allah's reign on earth. In the second post-war winter, they still held the majority in the Majlis and at least a blocking power almost everywhere within the government. The result was often paralysis. One of the most difficult tasks facing the government was dealing with the organizations that had both made the revolution and grown out of it. The Revolutionary Guards, the *Pasdaran*, had become almost a state within the state: their empire ran from publishing houses to arms factories and, of course, their own military and security structures. The *komitehs*, the local guardians of morality which had often degenerated into little more than vengeful gangs, were no longer so feared by the population, but were occasionally unleashed for new campaigns of individual terror, directed mostly against women for real and imagined breaches of morality.[30] The *bassij*, the very young or over-age volunteers who had provided much of the Iranian cannon-fodder during the war, were even more difficult to deal with; most came from the poorest sections of society, where support for the regime was strongest but where, let loose with no work and no prospects, they would also be most likely to cause real trouble. Unemployment in the cities was reckoned to exceed 15 per cent by early 1990, and mutterings were heard from the countryside where even simple peasants were tiring of the excesses of political mullahs.

President Rafsanjani, surrounded by rivals but also by political allies including most of what remains of the educated elites, is a patient man and a clever politician. He knew, after his election, that he could count on a period of grace afforded by the population and that it would last, at most, a year. In the first few months, he was busiest trying to neutralize the most conservative elements of the theological-revolutionary establishment, who had coalesced around the figure of Ayatollah Khomeini's son,

Ahmad. Fortunately for Rafsanjani, Ahmad had inherited his father's name but neither his brains nor his charisma and the so-called 'hard-line' did not produce a single figure of undisputed authority.

Saddam Hussein never understood Iran. He understood it no better when, on 15 August 1990, two weeks after the invasion of Kuwait, he suddenly reversed all his previous positions, returning to an acceptance of the Algiers agreement (publicly torn up ten years earlier), giving up all claims to the Shatt al-Arab and accepting all Iran's terms for peace. It was all too obviously a ploy to garner Iranian support against what was rapidly becoming a powerful international coalition. But despite Saddam's new-found Islamic fervour (which apparently did impress some of the more naïve clerics), those who decided policy in Iran remained unmoved. Official Iran – and on this most of the factions did agree – said, in effect, thank you very much for finally giving us our due, but we accept neither your invasion of a neighbouring country nor your bellicose stand in the whole region. On the other hand, Iran remained opposed to the presence of foreign, that is, non-local, troops in the area, and included the Egyptians as well as the Americans. Declaring itself neutral, it said it would nevertheless join the embargo against its recent enemy.

By and large that policy held, minor smuggling notwithstanding. In the tension of the following months, the so-called 'radicals' did several times push for Iran to reverse its position and join Iraq in a 'jihad against the West'. But it was also a sign of the maturation of the Islamic Republic that they were allowed to state their position, though they were not allowed to influence policy. Indeed, placating the radicals is a necessary ingredient of the subtle art of governance in Iran.

In March 1991, once the Americans called a halt to the coalition's march on Baghdad, Iranian policy grew bolder. Its support of the revolt of the Shi'a in southern Iraq was unquestioning – but not unlimited. The subtle Iranian policy-makers did not want a head-on collision with the United States. Whatever one may think of the justification for the war, it is difficult to remain indifferent to the aborted revolt. The Americans actively encouraged the Iraqi people to revolt against the tyrant who governed them; when the appeal was heeded, it was as though the Americans had suddenly seen a genie emerging from the Aladdin's lamp they had so recently rubbed. Iran, hidden behind the code-words of break-up or anarchy, haunted the Americans. They rescinded the orders denying the Iraqi air force the right to retaliate. (Helicopters, which the Iraqis were allowed to operate, are at least as effective for fighting an insurgency as the fixed-wing aircraft that were piously kept grounded.) It will never be known for certain whether or not Iran would have annexed a wide swathe of southern Iraq had the revolt not been so brutally crushed. At the time, the United States and Saudi Arabia were fearful that Iran would do so. The American phobia of Iran has barely abated; Saudi Arabia made its peace with the Islamic Republic in time for the 1991 pilgrimage in June.

In the following year, Saudi Arabia became a main sponsor of Iraqi opposition groups and was particularly active in trying to coordinate the work of the secular (even Communist) opposition with the Islamic movements, including the Shi'a groups based in Tehran. The Iranian government, in the meantime, showed its capacity for subtle diplomacy on two fronts. It continued its opposition to outside powers in the Gulf by firmly opposing the Damascus agreement: signed by the GCC, Egypt and Syria in 1991 (see Chapter 10). Oman, the UAE and Qatar were inclined to think that Iran had a point in that it did indeed have more stake in the Gulf than the two Arab partners. At the same time, Iran continued more vociferous opposition to the continued military presence of the United States.

By early 1992, some pressure was taken off the Gulf by Iran's increasing involvement in Central Asia, in direct competition with Turkey, as the newly independent republics of the Community of Independent States groped towards finding their place in the outside world. But, Iran has the capacity to play on several diplomatic fronts simultaneously and the Persian Gulf remains and will continue to remain a vital part of its overall political horizon.

CHAPTER 4

Kuwait: Dangerous Opulence

The Kuwaitis did not need an Iraqi invasion to be made fully aware of their identity. Kuwait had a special place in the Gulf, where it was – and, perhaps ruefully, still is – often taken as an example of what could happen elsewhere. Kuwait was, and will again be, one of the world's richest countries; in 1989, the World Bank figure for gross GDP per inhabitant was over US$14,000; if there had been any way of computing the sum per Kuwaiti citizen it would have been far higher. The Kuwaitis have a long and well-deserved reputation as tough, clever businessmen – but also as a people who had to some extent succeeded in creating an organized country in their 29 years of existence as a modern state. There was indeed a great deal of money, but there was *also* a sense of responsibility. Kuwaitis undoubtedly lived well, but many of them also worked hard. Some of the hardest workers were women; a surprising number of them had responsible jobs outside their homes.

Among other Arabs, Kuwaitis were more often respected than really liked. They were often perceived as 'arrogant'; the judgement contained more collective than individual truth. Kuwaitis do often show a decidedly un-Middle Eastern sense of efficiency that could be taken for brusqueness; far less time is allotted to tea-drinking and relaxed conversation than in neighbouring countries. People in the Gulf often quote a remark attributed to King Faisal of Saudi Arabia in the 1970s, after some fruitless discussions with his Kuwaiti neighbours: 'In the eyes of the Kuwaitis there are three big powers in the world: the

United States, the Soviet Union and Kuwait.' *Si non é vero, é ben trovato*. This perhaps exaggerated idea of their own importance is tempered by a streak of almost ruthless lucidity – another Kuwaiti hallmark.

Kuwait was, and perhaps will again be, admired and often envied for its incipient democracy, its relative political liberalism, its experiments with a budding form of parliamentary monarchy, and its lively and open press. Suspended in 1986, under the growing pressures of the Iran–Iraq war, freedom of the press had returned and parliament was in the process of restoration in the summer of 1990. True, it was not a Western-style parliamentary government, but for many years it was the closest thing to democracy between Israel and India, although only about 5 per cent of the Kuwaiti population had the right to vote. The arithmetic is quickly done. At the last census, in 1989, 74 per cent of the population was made up of non-Kuwaitis and 26 per cent of Kuwaitis. Half of the population is female, and women did not, and still do not, have the right to vote. Of the remaining 13 per cent, more than half were under the voting age of 21, which leaves about 6 per cent. Subtract all those Kuwaitis whose families had been naturalized since 1923, or for less than three generations, and the remainder was effectively 4 to 5 per cent. Voters, then, were made up of adult male members of the merchant families and of the few remaining bedouin clans; they were not sociologically homogeneous by any means, but, try as one would, it was impossible to find any destitute Kuwaitis.[1] In fact, although without income tax returns there is no way to be sure,[2] it was generally thought that several of the merchants were considerably richer than the Emir and his family. The poor did exist, but they were immigrant workers.

However, the final authority for decision-making lay not with the Kuwaiti Assembly but with the Al-Sabah family and the cabinet, of whom two-thirds were commoners; the key posts of defense and foreign affairs, as well as that of prime minister-cum-crown-prince were reserved for members of the family. The Assembly's role was to discuss, to question, to probe, even to goad – but not to make policy, especially not foreign policy. The Assembly sometimes went beyond its normal limits, and the government usually listened. Over the years, the Assembly was instrumental in assuring that Kuwait remained faithful to the PLO, one of the few countries that not only paid its Arab League assessments, but made regular contributions to institutions like the West Bank universities and Jerusalem's Maqassed Hospital.[3] That unwavering fidelity became another cause of bitterness after the Iraqi invasion, when Palestinians were perceived as being in the vanguard of the invasion, and of the diplomatic support for Saddam Hussein, too.

The Kuwait Fund for Arab Development reveals much about the state: tough in its criteria, stringent in its controls, and then generous in giving enough to be useful. Neither as individuals nor in the aggregate are Kuwaitis a sentimental people. Some of the rich Gulf sheikhs financed projects on the strength of whim or personal affinity; that is not Kuwaiti style. In the first twenty-five years after its founding in 1962, the Development Fund had accorded 323 concessionary loans of KD 1,458 million (US$5.6 bn), gifts of about KD 30 m ($96 bn), plus scholarships and multilateral aid. Despite the name, money from the Fund went to Africa and Asian countries as well as to Arab ones.

The Kuwaitis are an interesting mixture of near-Western sophistication during working hours and very 'Arab' characteristics in most other facets of their lives. The Islamic influence is strong, far more so than in Iraq where twenty years of Ba'athist secular ideology has deep-seated effects not annulled by Saddam's tactical reconversion. The open hospitality of the Gulf was perhaps not quite so easy to perceive in the urban society of Kuwait as elsewhere. Typically, there were more restaurants in Kuwait than in the neighbouring countries, and the more emancipated women frequented them without necessarily having a man in their group. The real sign that a visitor had penetrated the formal reserves was an invitation to the *diwaniyya* or, at weekends, to a tent camp in the desert. No bedouin's tent had ever been decked out with fridges, mobile telephones and televisions like these. They were the Kuwaitis' equivalent of a hunting lodge. Whole families moved out to the desert in the February school holidays; cars made it easy for those who had jobs in the city to commute. The psychological distance was sometimes more difficult to overcome. Fear of mines will probably quash the custom for years to come.

The *diwaniyya* is a pure Kuwaiti institution, somewhere between a literary-political salon and a weekly stag party. In many ways social life was more relaxed than in other Gulf countries, but *diwanniyas* remained closed to Kuwaiti women. Every head of an extended family, every minister, every man of substance had his *diwaniyya.* Literally, the word means the reception room where gatherings take place, the equivalent of a *majlis* elsewhere in the Gulf; it could be a special building or a large room in the house, furnished with the traditional cushions on the floor or armchairs along the walls, punctuated by small tables for coffee, tea and cold juices. A man did not 'belong' to a single *diwaniyya*, but could and would attend several in the course of a week; that is where discussions of ideas and politics really took place. Being accepted as a full-fledged member of the *diwaniyya* system was a rite of passage for young men and for the relatively few immigrants who were integrated into the Kuwaiti society. The *diwaniyyas* seem to have been misunderstood by the Iraqis. Bereft of any tradition of free talk, even in private, they apparently thought that because of the brisk and sometimes brusque discussions and criticism of the government to be heard in many *diwaniyyas*, Kuwait was ripe for revolution. After a month of occupation, the Iraqis had caught on. Kuwaitis recount with particular abhorrence that they systematically pulled down the pictures of the Emir in the *diwaniyyas* and ordered householders to replace them with portraits of Saddam Hussein. Those who refused were shot on the spot. The Emir and his immediate family were not, perhaps, loved (as the Sultan of Oman is genuinely loved), but they were symbols of a largely concensual system that worked much better than most outsiders realized.

For two days after the invasion on 2 August 1990, the Iraqis tried first to pretend that they had been called in by 'patriots who wanted to form a Free Kuwait Government'; and then, that such a government had been formed by those who had 'asked for Iraqi intervention'. Both claims were pure inventions of the Iraqi propaganda machine; not a single Kuwaiti Quisling could be found, not even among those who the winter before led public demonstrations for the restoration of the then still-suspended National Assembly. The Iraqis had tried to contact the leaders of the Kuwaiti opposition, including Ahmed al-Khatib and Jassim al-Qatami, staunch Arab nationalists who had flirted with both Nasserism and Ba'athism. They and all other Kuwaitis of any account rejected their approaches[4] and became vocal members of the Kuwaiti political establishment in exile.

The gesture towards parliamentary democracy within a monarchy was fairly timid, and the restoration of 1990 (which foresaw a partially appointed Council for an interim period) even more so, but it was honest. That half-open door to democratic government was a beacon to those in nearby countries who considered Kuwait a model. It is one more reason why, beyond the plain fear of Iraq, the Iraqi invasion of Kuwait sent tremors throughout the Gulf.

Geography explains some of Kuwait's problems. Its situation as a very small, very rich country wedged in between three large and difficult neighbours was often uncomfortable. Only 40 kilometres of water separate it from the nearest bit of Iran, and Iraq never properly recognized its border or recognized it unambiguously as an independent state. With Saudi Arabia, tensions are usually kept under the surface. Nevertheless, the Kuwaitis often said that their geological luck provided some consolation for their geography.

Kuwait is not, by any stretch of the imagination, naturally beautiful. The landscape is deadly dull, not even affording the beauty of sand desert and dunes, only stark, pebbly steppe with hardly a hill to break the monotony. It is not good guerrilla terrain. The climate is even worse than elsewhere in the Gulf, just as hot and humid in summer and colder and wetter in winter. The dusty steppe provides little for the eye to catch except the edge of the turquoise waters of the Gulf (repeatedly sullied by terrible oil spills in a decade of war) and some good modern architecture. Along with more indifferent but functional buildings, these features had turned apparently unpromising Kuwait into quite a pleasant place to live. Its small area and concentrated population had made it possible to spend the oil revenues on an infrastructure rivalled by few in the world. Almost nothing remained of the old mud-brick Kuwait, except two scraps of city wall and part of the original emiri palace. Desalination plants had compensated for Kuwait's lack of sweet water. Long before the oil boom, the few brackish wells were insufficient and water had to be brought by boat from the Shatt al-Arab. The Kuwaitis grew painfully aware of their vulnerability during the Iran–Iraq war, but could do nothing about it.

Kuwait and Iraq

In the nineteenth century the sheikhs of Kuwait concluded a series of agreements which led to a loose association with the governors of the Ottoman province of Basra, one of the three later fused into the Kingdom of Iraq. The three provinces, or *senjaks*, were not a single administrative unit. Indeed they, or their governors, were often at odds one with another and the *mutasallim* of Basra ruled almost independently of the *pasha* of Baghdad, who was theoretically higher in the complicated Ottoman hierarchy. Both were usually at war with the nearby Persians, a good enough reason for successive governors to search out possible local allies such as the sheikhs of Kuwait. The on-again off-again alliances were sometimes consigned to writing but more often not; none involved formal incorporation into the Ottoman Empire.

Even before the break-up of the empire at the end of World War I, these associations foundered when Kuwait, whose sheikhs seem to have seen the wind turning, entered into a fairly loose protectorate agreement with Britain – not, it should be emphasized, under any constraint. The first documents were signed in 1899. Well before the three Ottoman provinces of Basra, Baghdad and Mosul became the British mandated territory of Iraq,[5] the protectorate agreement was refined and reaffirmed, without mention of any association with the former provinces. The border between Kuwait and the mandated territory, like most borders in the deserts, was only vaguely defined until 1922, when the treaty of Ugayr was signed just down the coast. On that occasion, the chief British negotiator,

Sir Percy Cox, represented both the mandated territory of Iraq and the protectorate of Kuwait; the third party involved was the Nejd, later to become the Kingdom of Saudi Arabia. Sir Percy's pen-strokes amputated about two thirds of what was then considered Kuwaiti territory in favour of the up and coming Al Sauds. Legend has it that Sir Percy's red wax crayon (and not a pen) had melted in the heat, adding to the imprecision of the drawn lines. The border between Kuwait and Iraq seemed less important in those pre-oil times than setting reasonable limits to the ambitions of Ibn Saud, as the future King Abdul Aziz was known to most Westerners. Sir Percy Cox was also responsible for that aberration in international law, the neutral zone.

The history of relations between Kuwait and Iraq can be examined even further back, though not as far as Iraqi legend would have us think. The claim repeatedly used by Iraqi propaganda that there existed 'unity thousands of years ago', for simple geographical reasons was incorrect. Ur, the early capital of Sumer, was at the height of its development around 2,000 B.C. It was also a port, something difficult to remember when one visits the site, now a vast plain near Nassiriya. Sumerian civilization slowly lost its lustre along with its port as, over the next thousand years, the shallow sea slowly silted up. Kuwait did not exist.

One point should be made before we go further. Until well into this century, lines on a map marking formal boundaries meant little or nothing in the Arabian peninsula. What counted were tribal loyalties and connections and, as a corollary, the economic space to which a family or a group of families considered themselves connected. Kuwait's economic ties – where the traders went and with whom they worked – were multiple and shifting. Sometimes they were strongest with Al Hasa, now in Saudi Arabia, sometimes with Basra or, when they were on speaking terms, with Al-Zubair, the nearest town in present-day Iraq. Bahrain also entered into the Kuwaiti orbit, especially when there were rich pickings to be had in trading in goods purloined by pirates further down the Gulf. There was no such thing as codification of nationality, records were mostly oral and passports non-existent. In the Arabian peninsula a man was who he was because of his family and his allegiance. The

Ottomans were more bureaucratic; they fussed over problems like ownership of rights of way or what to do about the *mutasallim* of Basra who sought refuge in Kuwait from successive pashas of Baghdad.[6] By 1838 or 1839, the Ottomans were sending messengers to Kuwait to persuade the sheikhs to become effective counterweights to the expansion of wahhabism under the Al-Saud.

In the second half of the nineteenth century the Kuwaiti Al-Sabah sheikhs, chosen by the other merchant families to represent them, had particularly cordial relations with the Ottomans. Geographic proximity counted less than the fact that Sheikh Jaber I helped the governor regain Basra after he had been forced out by marauding Iraqi tribes.[7] The result was a treaty of mutual recognition: the Kuwaiti sheikh gave the governor an annual gift of 40 bags of rice and 400 *frasilah* of dates; in return he received a 'dress of honour'. In the context of the times, the agreement was less unequal than it seems. In 1871, the Ottoman government awarded Sheikh Abdulla the title of *Qaim-Maqam* (which means the governor of a sub-province) and decreed that Kuwait was henceforth attached to the *senjak* or *vilayat* of Basra rather than that of Al Hasa, further to the south.[8] Abdulla's son, Mubarak the Great, who is often considered the father of the modern Sabah dynasty, saw things differently. He assassinated his half-brothers – Mohammed (ruler between 1892 and 1896) and Jarrah – largely because he thought they were too close to the Ottoman governors. Thus ended the special relationship. Even though Kuwaiti ships flew the Ottoman pennant whenever they thought it useful until 1914, the protectorate agreement with Britain had begun even before it was formalized into the treaty of 1899.

Iraq, under whatever government, has consistently protested against the very existence of Kuwait. In 1961, it tried to block recognition of an independent state and laid claim to all of Kuwaiti territory. The revolutionary stridence deployed then was only reiterating the feebler claims made in 1954 to the British (still the protecting power) by royal Iraq's last prime minister, Nuri Said. In 1961 Abdul Karim Qassim, Iraq's dictator of the moment, thundered out the familiar litany that Kuwait had once been under the control of the Ottoman Empire and that Iraq, as successor state of that empire, was the legitimate proprietor of its territories. In the following months, Iraqi proclamations included: 'The era of sheikhdom is over … We shall extend Iraq's borders to the south of Kuwait',[9] and 'Kuwait is not and has never been an independent state. It has always been considered, historically and legally, a part of the Basra province of Iraq. There can be no question of an international dispute arising between Iraq and Kuwait since the latter is an integral part of the Iraqi Republic …'[10] The same arguments were used in 1990; that time Iraq sent an army to enforce the harsh words.

Britain had kept its promise to defend Kuwait after independence by sending British troops, soon to be replaced by Egyptian troops. Iraq, by refusing to recognize Kuwait and by raising the spectre of British imperialism, succeeded in blocking Kuwait's admission to the United Nations for two years. The Soviet Union used its veto. These events occurred only three years after Iraq had overthrown the monarchy and become a so-called progressive Arab state. The Arab League, very much under the influence of Gamal Abdul Nasser, did admit independent Kuwait. Iraq stormed out until 1963, when Abdul Karim Qassim was overthrown in the first Ba'athi revolution. Ironically, that first Ba'athi government lasted just long enough to renounce Iraq's claim to Kuwait in exchange for a new delimitation of the neutral zone and an interest-free loan of US$80m from Kuwait, to be repaid in 19 instalments over 25 years.

Since then, Iraqi-Kuwaiti relations have lurched from one crisis to another. In particular there was what was euphemistically called 'the problems of 1973'. Iraq had tried for several years to persuade Kuwait to let it station troops on its territory to protect Umm Qasr, then being built up as a military port. Not having much success, it forcibly occupied a border police fort at Al Samitah. The Iraqi foreign minister of the time, Murtada Abd Al-Baqi declared that 'the whole of Kuwait is a disputed area. There is a document saying that Kuwait is Iraqi territory. There is no document which says it is not Iraqi territory.'[11] Iraq went on to say that it was planning to take Bubayan and Warba islands and would agree to give up the rest of Kuwait for their sake.

That dispute dragged on until 1977 when the Iraqi troops quietly withdraw from Al Samitah. By then, Iraq had signed the Algiers agreement on the Shatt al-Arab with Iran. Saddam Hussein had negotited the agreement and it looked as though Iraq now wanted to use its growing oil revenues to improve living standards for its own citizens rather than flex its muscles in foreign adventures.

The next crisis (encapsulating numerous sub-crises) came with the Iran–Iraq war, which quickly became known as the Gulf war – now the first Gulf war. Kuwait's major concern was to stay out, though it could not avoid peripheral involvement. It first became involved in the Iran–Iraq war as the principal trans-shipment point for Iraq in the early years. The merchants were delighted. After Iran tried to impose a blockade on military material headed for Iraq going up the Gulf, the sea-borne trade dwindled considerably, except for the monthly shipments of Soviet-made weapons and military supplies. To the end of the war, the Iranians inexplicably turned a blind eye.

Direct Iraqi attempts to embroil Kuwait came less than a year after the beginning of the war. In August 1981, three small bomb blasts went off almost simultaneously in Kuwait, one of them at the central electricity control station. At the time, Iran was loudly proclaiming its aim of exporting the Islamic revolution and seemed the obvious instigator. However, the Kuwaiti police quickly realized that all was not as it appeared, but by then several of the attackers had crossed the border towards Basra. Iraq refused to extradite them.

That was Kuwait's first taste of terrorism. In December 1983 bombs went off at the US and French embassies and at the airport; a Kuwait Airways plane was hijacked to Tehran in 1984; an attempt to assassinate the Emir in May 1985 failed, but only just. Then came the murderous explosions in the crowded cafés in the summer of 1986; a car bomb and various other explosions at the time of the Islamic summit in January 1987; and the second Kuwait Airways hijacking in April 1988. The perpetrators, when they were caught, were mostly connected with pro-Iranian Lebanese factions. Beginning in 1985, the liberation of these prisoners became a 'normal' demand of hijackers and hostage-takers all over the Middle East. All such demands were refused. When the Iraqis invaded in August 1990, one of their first acts was to open the prison doors, and let the convicted prisoners free, whether they were terrorists or common criminals.

During those years, Iraq never stopped applying pressure. In 1984, when it was really feeling the pinch of the war, it tried once again to dust off old documents that might support its claim to swampy Bubayan island, whose main virtue is to provide an excellent vantage point at the head of the Gulf, commanding the approaches both to Umm Qasr[12] and Basra. The Kuwaitis hastily finished their causeway to the island and made sure a few soldiers were on permanent alert there. Iraq proposed a 'final border settlement' in exchange for Bubayan, and even requested a temporary military lease on the island. Warba, the second island that became one of the 'Iraqi objectives' after the invasion, was barely talked about during the war. Bubayan is basically a large mud-flat, but firm enough for a French construction company to have built a causeway to it in the early 1980s and for Kuwait then to add some basic military installations. Warba is nothing but a smaller mud-flat.

Kuwait obviously rejected the Iraqi request; Iran had warned that any such deal would be considered a hostile action and also rejected all Iraqi attempts to embroil them in the conflict. To ensure that the money kept flowing from Kuwait (and, of course Saudi Arabia) Iraq decided that asking for protection money was the best technique. Pay up or you'll see, was the approach, and it worked. The official Kuwaiti subsidies, in the form of interest-free government-to-government loans, came to around US$15 billion;[13] there were other loans and gifts, some from individuals, which will never be totted up. Besides, Kuwait sold oil on Iraq's account at a time when the Iraqi production facilities were damaged and the export pipelines had not been expanded.

For Iraq, the attitude towards Kuwait was part of a larger strategy to internationalize the war. The effort to involve others in what was presented as a chapter in the historic Arab-Persian struggle helps explain some acts that would otherwise be incomprehensible. The effort almost succeeded. As the war grew closer and dragged on there was increasing sympathy for Iraq. By 1987, when one asked Kuwaitis whether they considered themselves directly implicated in the war on Iraq's side, most answered yes.[14]

Several times during those years, the Kuwaiti government asked Iraq to agree to a final border delimitation. The answer was invariably: not now, after the war. When, in 1987 and again in early 1988, Iraqi officials were asked why they kept refusing such a good friend, one explanation was: 'We don't want to negotiate from a position of weakness.'[15] In September 1989, just a year after the cease-fire with Iran, the Emir, Sheikh Jaber, made one of his rare forays abroad to Baghdad. A major point of discussion was the border question. According to eye-witnesses, the Iraqis were surprisingly unpleasant toward the Emir. They kept him waiting for hours, a breach of both protocol and of Arab politeness.[16] They high-handedly dismissed all ideas of any border settlement without unacceptable conditions that would, among other things, have made relations very difficult with Iran, where Kuwait was trying hard to mend fences. Iraq began to insinuate that the Kuwaiti loans – interest free, and for which Kuwait was not pressing repayment – be annulled. At the time, although Kuwait never said so officially, it was commonly thought that those loans would, with the passage of time, just fade away.

The oddest part of this difficult relationship is that the Kuwaitis themselves were often divided on the attitude to adopt toward the large neighbour to the north. Well before independence, and in particular in the late 1930s, when the Iraqi monarchy was beginning to assert itself, the merchants had argued that Kuwait would do well to attach itself to the Hashemite kingdom. The ruling family stood against the idea. Their gratitude for having escaped the revolutionary and Ba'athist maelströms partly explains the merchants' abiding loyalty to the monarchical system.

The invasion

Greed was certainly one important element of the Iraqi invasion of Kuwait, though less important than the overweening, unreasoning desire for power. From the first day, the Iraqi invaders looted, burned, pillaged, ransacked, and stole. They also raped, tortured, maimed and killed Kuwaiti citizens and foreigners who had the misfortune to be caught in the country. A cynic might argue that much of that behaviour is normal for an invading army. But in the case of the Iraqis there was a streak of wanton destruction that went beyond the 'normal' behaviour of an invader: it looked as though deliberate destruction was used to wreak vengeance on the Kuwaitis, their possessions, their city and all they had built. One can understand poor Iraqi soldiers, coming from a country that should be rich but where finding a light bulb can be a major problem, going beserk in Kuwaiti supermarkets. One can understand their rampaging through the gold souk, or even stealing computers from the school-rooms. But the Iraqis went far beyond that: they seem to have made a deliberate effort to wipe away all traces that could stand as evidence of Kuwaiti enterprise, of civilization and culture (even the kitsch, like the 'Entertainment City'), of what made Kuwait not just a spot on a map but a country with a character of its own. A year after the war the United Nations' special rapporteur on Kuwait presented a terrible and sobering report on Iraqi practices during the occupation, corroborating individual eye-witness accounts and Amnesty International's.[17]

Kuwaitis are probably the most austere of the Gulf Arabs. Kuwait has long had a law prohibiting alcohol, certainly ignored by some individuals; during the Iran–Iraq war it was extended even to foreign embassies. The Iraqi propaganda made a point of 'the Emir's throwing away of the people's money in casinos'; many people in other Arab countries and in the West believed it. The propagandists got their target wrong since the casino-addicts (who do exist, but not nearly in the great numbers imagined by the popular press) are rarely from the Kuwaiti princely family. Even abroad, few Kuwaitis conformed to the ostentatious, hard-drinking, high-living caricature. The Kuwaitis have a puritanical streak and the *diwaniyya*, with its impassioned talk, is more typical than wild partying. Many Kuwaitis were genuinely shocked by the sudden influx of alcohol into Kuwait: not only beer (of which the Iraqis are particularly fond) but whisky was being sold openly.[18] After seven months of occupation, alcohol had become a common solace.

Kuwait and its money

Before 2 August 1990, Kuwait was known to the outside world almost entirely for its money. Ever since the first big 'oil shocks' of the 1970s, it had enjoyed one of the highest incomes per inhabitant of any country on earth, alternating at the top of the list with its Gulf neighbours, Qatar and the United Arab Emirates. There was enormous disparity in wealth between Kuwaitis and most immigrant workers (only some Palestinians had made fortunes), but economists usually agree that there was a better distribution of the wealth among the citizens than in most other oil-producing countries. In a nation that was practically a city-state almost all Kuwaiti families had benefitted from a nest-egg provided by generous compensation for expropriations. All the amenities of a modern society were provided in plenty and often with luxury: schools, hospitals, water works, electricity plants, a university. Water, once brought from the Shatt al-Arab by boat, was now provided by desalination of sea water.[19] At the end of the Iran–Iraq war, discussions on reviving an old project for an aquaduct collapsed with the impossibility of getting a final agreement on the border.

Kuwait had had time to go further than most of its neighbours and by 1990 was already in the second generation of development. A model school for handicapped children from all over the Peninsula had been operating for over ten years, and the Kuwait Institute for Advanced Scientific Research (KISR) was almost unique in the developing world. The unstinting support given to KISR revealed a turn of mind, a willingness to admit questioning as the basis of real learning, of human progress, that is not very common in the Muslim Middle East.

A double system of public investments made tiny Kuwait a major partner in the world of international finance. Its reserves, estimated at US$95 bn in July 1990, are held in two funds: the State General Reserve and the Kuwait Reserve Fund for Future Generations. The General Reserve Fund has made many direct investments (not to be confused with development aid) in countries like Egypt, Morocco and Tunisia;[20] the Fund for Future Generations has more holdings outside the Arab world. Iraq obviously hoped to get its hands on this enormous amount of money.[21] Its efforts were frustrated by the immediate freezing of Iraqi and Kuwaiti assets in most Western countries. These assets were not seized, but, in juridicial terms, placed under sequester.[22] The Kuwaiti assets were frozen in most countries including the United States, Britain and Switzerland from the day of the invasion, even before the requests of the Kuwaiti government had been received. Predictably, Iraq protested against the sequester for its own holdings and, after announcing the annexation on 8 August, those of Kuwait.

The cash-flow problem was short-lived for the Kuwaiti government. By the third week in August, it began to function in exile, in Taif. By that time, too, the United States, Britain, Switzerland, Saudi Arabia and several other countries had authorized known bona fide representatives of the government to start signing cheques on its own account. Individual Kuwaiti citizens did not always fare so well. Their cash was worthless, their credit cards blocked. The Kuwaiti embassies became, among other things, social-welfare centres. Some countries, especially those of the GCC, allowed as a gesture the one-off exchange of a small fixed sum of Kuwaiti dinars for Kuwaiti citizens and residents. In Europe, the rules varied. Switzerland, where a good number of wealthy Kuwaitis had bank accounts, first blocked them, then allowed identifiable individuals to make cash withdrawals for their current needs. 'Identifiable' meant either that the client was personally known to the banker, or that he could prove his identity, in person. Telex or telephone withdrawals were systematically turned down, but one banker who was closely involved in the operation now says that in fact he heard of no concerted Iraqi attempts to get at Kuwaiti accounts.

Inside Kuwait, the economic system quickly broke down. Big and small shops and warehouses were systematically looted. At the huge food storehouses in Shuweiq port what was not carted away immediately was burnt. Banks were closed. On 7 August, one day *before* the announcement of the annexation, Iraq officially devalued the Kuwaiti dinar to the same rate as the Iraqi dinar; the two currencies, went the announcement, could be used interchangeably. It was a strange step to take, and one that could be explained only by a desire for revenge rather than by sensible economic rationale. In 1979, the Iraqi dinar and the Kuwaiti dinar had indeed been almost on a par in their exchange value against the US dollar and in purchasing power. By the end of the Iran–Iraq war in 1988, the Kuwaiti dinar was the strongest currency in the Middle East (official exchange rate 1 KD = US$3.65). The Iraqi dinar was still artificially quoted at 1 ID to US$3.50 (rate at which visitors were forced to change at least some of their money). On the open market, a Kuwaiti dinar brought 10, sometimes 12 Iraqi ones. One of Iraq's first targets in Kuwait was, not surprisingly, the Central Bank. Iraq found considerably less gold than it had presumably hoped for and foreign currency amounting to only about US$4 m. However, approximately 365 million Kuwaiti dinars, in cash, was taken to Baghdad – and then the KD was devalued.

This leads to the question of why relatively little gold and currency was found in the vaults. Had large quantities been sent abroad and, if so, why? There were indeed some transfers during the tense month of July, but more intriguing is that quite a large amount is said to have been transferred earlier. At the beginning of 1990, the Central Bank of Kuwait held over 2.5 million ounces of gold. In March, the international markets were put in a spin by an unexpected sale of gold; part of it was known to be Russian but the other big seller was never publicly announced, which is unusual in the tight-knit world of gold dealing. Most specialists say the selling was being handled by the National Commercial Bank (NCB) of Jeddah. Even for the biggest gold-dealers in the Middle East, selling about 2.4 million ounces in a matter of days is unusual. Specialists at first thought the gold came from SAMA, the Saudi Arabian Monetary Agency (which acts as the Central Bank), but with hindsight the Central Bank of Kuwait seems a much more likely source. At the time, the few people who noticed it were gold specialists, not political analysts, and they could make no sense out of the whole business. In perspective, one cannot help wondering whether, even then, the Kuwaiti Central Bank governors were worried. If this account of what happened to the Kuwaiti gold is true, and it probably is, it effectively ends speculations that there may have been a secret vault in the cellar of the Central Bank. According to that story – denied by

Kuwaitis in a position to know, but relayed by many other people in the Middle East – the underground vault was built in such a way that any unauthorized tampering set off an explosion designed to catapult it straight into the sea. Such is the stuff modern legends are made of. The Kuwait foreshore is very shallow and even amateur divers could easily retrieve that fabulous treasure. What was probably left in the Central Bank at the time of the invasion was approximately 125,000 ounces of gold, worth some US$50 m; presumably, much less than the Iraqis had expected. Gold is not voluminous: 125,000 ounces, or four tonnes, of gold would have been easy to place on one flat-bed truck for carting away to Baghdad. At the end of the war, one of the first steps towards normalization was the return of the gold, with bar after bar being weighed under United Nations supervision.

Occupation

Kuwait radio and television continued to broadcast independently until mid-morning of 3 August when they became relay stations for the Iraqi media broadcasting from Baghdad. Within days, a programme of singers and dancers in Kuwaiti costume was featured, singing the praises of Saddam, and reciting odes to the 'joy of Kuwait at being reunited with the fatherland'. For perceptive Kuwaitis, this was one more small sign that the invasion and occupation had been carefully prepared; the best-oiled ministry of information could not have had the poems and music written and dancers and singers costumed and drilled in such a short time.

At first, life in occupied Kuwait was fearful, unpleasant because of its confinement, but not yet unbearable for the Kuwaitis. The water and electricity plants continued to function until they were destroyed by the departing Iraqis. Foreigners were leaving, if they could or, in the case of Westerners, being rounded up or going into hiding. Arab foreigners were not necessarily treated better. Egyptians seemed to be the target of particularly unpleasant treatment, partly, though perhaps not entirely, because of the Egyptian government's stand against the Iraqi invasion. Once again, the Iraqis seem to have been settling scores, working out old resentments.

Kuwait is not a good place for a resistance movement to take hold. Most of it is a city, with roads, public buildings and houses planted on what was only recently empty desert. No romantic dunes, no trees, not even scrub serve as cover. Kuwaitis are not fighters, barely even hunters. In Saudi Arabia, the UAE or Oman, there is hardly a man who doesn't know how to handle a rifle, even if he is not a trained soldier. A Kuwaiti's recreation is more likely to be deep-sea fishing. After the invasion, the reaction at first was to stay home. Kuwaitis stopped going to work, to their offices and shops; with the exception of the cooperative societies, most activity ground to a halt. Only a few expatriates kept essential services going.

The invasion was marked by almost unimaginable looting. At first much of it was from public buildings or from shops; except for the Emir's palace, and that of the Crown Prince, dwellings were mostly left alone. The Kuwaiti supermarkets and shopping malls must indeed have looked like glittery visions of heaven to the Iraqi soldiers; they were gutted and emptied. Cars, those powerful symbols of modern well-being, were prime targets. Some drivers were forced out of their cars at gunpoint; dealers' showrooms were even better hunting grounds. Dozens of new cars were driven off by happy soldiers, and dozens more were simply crushed under the treads of tanks. Toyotas, Mercedes and Chevrolets were popular; Oldsmobiles not, because the Iraqis were worried about getting spare parts. Black Mercedes were often spared; they were too closely identified as the cars of high officials. At the time of the liberation, Yussuf al-Ghanim, one of the biggest car dealers in Kuwait, had already filed suit against the Iraqi government in American courts: he asked for £195 million in damages for his sales office and show-room.

The resistance worked in keeping life, however grim, possible for those who stayed. The early protest marches by Kuwaiti women stopped after at least four women were shot dead during one demonstration. As public services broke down, deliberately neglected or sabotaged by the Iraqis, the social solidarity committees assured the distribution of food, the clearing of refuse and the protection of foreigners. Engineers managed to keep a system of communications going by using small portable dish satellites; the Iraqis were never able to tap into them and the resistance movement was in daily touch with the exiled government and the coalition forces. This was particularly useful just before the military action began, and during the seven weeks of war.[23]

At first, Kuwait still believed that Iraq really would withdraw in a very short time, as it had promised. Kuwaitis were soon disillusioned as they saw Iraqis being bused into Kuwait. The first were poor families from Basra, then they came from further afield. Soldiers went to houses and flats, establishing which were occupied (many rented by foreigners were now empty) and guided the newcomers. A decree went out that all Arab foreign residents of Kuwait (which presumably included the newly-arrived Iraqis) were now the owners of their flats.

The major beneficiaries of the munificence were, of course, the Palestinians: officially they numbered about 350,000, actually at least, 400,000. Many had lived there most of their lives; some were of the second generation, and most were hard-working, settled and well off, with good jobs. A few were millionaires. There were more opportunities to make money, to organize their own businesses, than in most Arab countries, and many Palestinians were sending considerable amounts of money to Jordan, to Gaza and the West Bank. Kuwait officially levied a 5 per cent tax on all their incomes, the so-called 'Palestine tax', which went directly to the PLO. That tax was over and above all private contributions and the more or less voluntary assessments for the PLO central fund and that of the Palestinian factions. Palestinians in Kuwait (as elsewhere in the Gulf) were almost all solidly affiliated with Fatah.

Fatah and the PLO itself were founded in Kuwait, which took a certain proprietorial pride in both and in Yasser Arafat; he had done well, first in the Kuwait public works department then as a contracting engineer before he became a full-time politician. The Kuwaiti newspapers were largely staffed by Palestinians, and became the best press in the Arab world after the demise of Beirut.

However, those same Kuwaiti Palestinians inevitably felt some resentment. Many worked hard for the government, as technicians, middle-level executives and specialists. Paradoxically, the better they did, the more resentment built up as they realized that the head of the department, the plant manager, the bank president, those with the titles, would always be Kuwaitis. Even if the Kuwaiti in question had less experience or competence he would be paid more, get more perks – and hold the ultimate power. And like all foreigners, the Palestinians were excluded from the privileges that came with the simple fact of being Kuwaiti: better educational opportunities for the children; better insurance coverage; the prospect of owning, rather than renting, property; even the possibility of playing the Kuwaiti stock market – a privilege which brought enormous riches (and some calamities) to Kuwaitis in the successive booms.

Fewer than 10 per cent of the Palestinians had been given Kuwaiti citizenship and, in the two years before the invasion, there had been signs that the notion of Kuwait as a Palestinian paradise might require revision. Palestinian families who sent their young people abroad to study, as many did (often with UN or Palestinian scholarships, rarely Kuwaiti ones), knew that it might be impossible for them to return. Right of birth did not confer right of residence. Some Palestinian journalists, and others in what were considered sensitive jobs, were dismissed and expelled. Those expelled were not only Palestinians, but since the majority were, they considered it a blow aimed directly against them.

Under the circumstances it was understandable that the Palestinian population was not really unhappy about the invasion. One Kuwaiti Palestinian said simply: 'We used to work for Kuwaiti masters; now we have Iraqi masters who promise to treat us better. Fine. Why not?' Some Palestinians became active collaborators. Apparently the Fatah office in Kuwait was better able to provide the Iraqi army with lists of names and addresses of Iraqi dissidents in Kuwait than even the Iraqi embassy. Some young Palestinians donned Iraqi uniforms, added a checked *keffiya*, and started working with the police, the army or the special forces. Kuwaitis now suspect that when the Iraqis boasted of Kuwaitis who joined their ranks, they were referring to those young men who speak Kuwaiti Arabic.

Immediately after the invasion, most Palestinians continued going to their jobs, where they still existed, and where they did not, they sometimes found replacement work. But, at the end of August and in early September, came the problem of money. Many government employees realized they were not going to be paid at all; others in the private sector may have hoped for a salary, but then realized that 300 Iraqi dinars were not the same thing as 300 Kuwaiti dinars. Their savings had been wiped out. They began to remember the bright side of their life in Kuwait; Salmiyya shopping centre, in the area most populated by Palestinians, had been raided a little later than the other emporia, but even there the opulence was gone. Many Palestinians, inside and outside the country, began to realize their attachment to a place that had, in fact, been their home. Others were torn between personal feelings and political loyalties. The political education of Palestinians in Kuwait began practically in the cradle. Three-year-olds strutted around in camouflage suits toting toy pistols and singing nursery songs in praise of Arafat. The Palestinian leadership, and especially Arafat, disappointed many foreign supporters with their pro-Saddam statements from the beginning of the crisis. For many Kuwaiti Palestinians the disappointment came later; at first they were ready to follow their leader and the signals that came out of the influential Palestinian embassy in Kuwait.

As the Iraqi occupation turned to annexation, one might have expected the occupiers to grow more lenient, to return to the plateau of terror on which the Iraqi people had been living for over a decade. Instead the Iraqi forces grew harsher and their repression increasingly erratic. By mid-September, when the Iraqis announced the appointment of Ali al-Majid as Governor of Kuwait (the '19th Governorate' in Iraqi terminology), those who knew their recent Iraqi history began to expect the worst. Al-Majid, cousin and faithful follower of Saddam, had been governor of Kurdistan during the bloodiest days of the repression there. He was the man who, in 1986, tore families apart, imprisoning the men while wives and children were sent to live in 'new villages' on the desolate plain north-east of Kirkuk; he was the man in charge, at the end of the Iran–Iraq war, of poison gas attacks on villages near the Turkish frontier and the evacuation of a thirty-kilometre 'security zone' around the borders of Iraq.

The ferocity of Iraqi destruction often appeared senseless. Why dig up roads, knock down lamp-posts and traffic signals or destroy school science laboratories if you are going to annex a country? The schoolbooks for the new academic year had been distributed; they were burnt. At the Kuwait Institute for Scientific Research the laboratory equipment, the computers and the furnishings were either stolen or destroyed. They can be replaced. What cannot be replaced are the protocols of research in process, the results, often in embryonic form, of work done or planned. Years and years of thought and intellectual endeavour have been irrevocably destroyed. The library itself is only partially replaceable.

Kuwait University was not spared either. With an ironic twist that can hardly have been completely unconscious, the Iraqi invaders quickly turned the building which housed the Faculties of Law and Arts into a detention and interrogation centre for Kuwaitis caught defying the occupation. Those minor offenders, who were accused of writing anti-Iraqi graffiti or passing out handbills, were kept there, tortured, and made to confess. For 'more serious offenses' the punishment was shooting on the spot or being taken to Baghdad.

Of the 70,000 teachers in Kuwait during the school year 1989–90, 50,000 were Egyptian. After the invasion, those who were not on holiday saw the writing on the wall. If they were caught fleeing across the desert the Iraqi soldiers seemed to take special care to humiliate them: besides receiving the standard punishment for robbery, they were often kept waiting in the blazing heat and then, after one or two people in each car were shot, the rest were let go – but only after the soldiers confiscated their water supplies. No one has been able to estimate how many Egyptians died in those August weeks in the desert.

Other expatriates – those who were not considered hostages – were free to go, but sometimes hesitated. The Indian government was one of the first to comply with Iraq's ultimatum to close embassies by 24 August.[24] At the end of August there were still an estimated 100,000 Indians in Kuwait. At first many thought that they might as well stay; they thought the occupation would be short and saw no point in going home with no job; for many, their savings in Kuwaiti banks were wiped out. Then, as the Kuwaiti economy dwindled to nothing, with their employers out of the country or trying to leave and, in any case, not able pay them, they saw that staying was pointless – even if no particular exactions were visited on them. It was the Indian community itself that with great efficiency organized travel for its nationals in convoys at set intervals, trying to time them so that transport home to India would be available once they reached Jordan. By the end of the year, the community had dwindled to less than 6,000.

The round-ups of Kuwaitis and 'hostile' foreigners began immediately after the invasion. The Emir himself left his palace with the Prime Minister exactly six minutes before the first Iraqi soldiers arrived in the very early hours of 2 August. Some Westerners had difficulty understanding why the Emir, the crown prince, other members of the Al-Sabah family and the government left, or as they put it 'ran away'. After the liberation a few Kuwaiti voices joined in. Such criticism (in which the example is often given of King Haakon V of Norway during World War II as compared with some of the Balkan royalty) must be considered in the context of Gulf societies and of the Iraqi dictatorship. For Kuwait, it was of the utmost importance that the Emir was safe and that he continue to function as both symbol and cement of the society and the state. The Emir realized that perfectly; as soon as a dozen ministers had managed to cross the border to Saudi Arabia, the first cabinet meeting was held, at about 11 am on 2 August, at the Saudi police post at Khafji. As the days passed, it became evident that not a single credible Quisling could be found to head a puppet government in Kuwait.

The continued existence of the legitimate Kuwaiti government, in exile but in no way 'provisional', also made it very much easier for the international community to take decisions. Without a legitimate government, it would have been difficult to ensure the application of the UN resolution No. 662, refuting the annexation. Without a legitimate government to back them up, it would have also been far more difficult for the Kuwaiti diplomatic missions and the Kuwaiti quasi-governmental and state-related organizations to carry on.[25] Kuwaiti newspapers quickly began publishing, almost as though nothing had happened: *Al-Qabas* in London, *Al-Siyassa* in Jeddah, and *Al-Anba* in Cairo. By December, Kuwait Airways was defiantly running full-page advertisements in publications like *The Economist*: 'London to Cairo, the Gulf and Onward. *And any day now to Kuwait.*'

Middle Eastern diplomats unanimously agree that had Sheikh Jaber and Sheikh Sa'ad, the Crown Prince, been captured they would almost certainly have never been seen alive again. They would either have been killed immediately or else taken to Baghdad, put through an Iraqi-style show trial, and executed afterwards. In any case, the decapitation of the Kuwaiti government and society would have led to the same results. Saddam Hussein and his Iraqi advisers may have made several other bad misjudgements about Kuwait (such as counting on Quislings and a popular uprising), but they were right about the importance, both real and symbolic, of the Emir and his immediate associates.

Westerners were shocked that so many men left without families. In the first days of August, no one expected that the occupation would last more than a week or two, or at most a month. The idea lingered that however abominably the Iraqi soldiers had behaved in the first few hours, they would still respect the old Arab code of war of not harming women, children and old people. On balance, the risks of the very real dangers of fleeing across the desert in the heat of summer seemed greater than those of staying. If necessary, the men thought they could send for their families who in the meantime would be able to keep their homes occupied and so prevent looting. The bedouin, who could come and go more easily than others, organized a trekking service. At the Saudi rendez-vous points they were told exactly who should be fetched and guided. By mid-August the tribes had established an accepted rate for these services: 500 Saudi riyals for one person and 2,000 for a family. Some offered their escort service for free.

Alas, the traditional Arab code of honour was not observed by the Iraqis. Very early on there were accounts of extreme violence towards children, women and old people, of rapes and wanton cruelty. These continued with every reliable witness who escaped. Critically-ill patients were turned out of hospitals. The

Bahraini Embassy frantically tried to cope with more than 70 desperately ill countrymen who had come to Kuwait for specialized treatment. The ambassador attempted to organize direct transport home for them; the Iraqis insisted that they be taken by the long land route through Baghdad and Jordan – an impossible journey for many for them. The psychiatric hospital, one of the most advanced in the Arab world, was ransacked, and patients expelled into the street. As for the jail, it was one of the first targets of the invading Iraqis. So far as we have been able to piece together the story, ordinary criminals were simply freed, while political prisoners, including 15 hijackers of a Kuwaiti plane imprisoned since 1983 and presumably linked with *Al-Dawa al-Islamiyya*, were taken to Iraq.[26] No one knows what happened to them there.

The most harrowing stories came from the hospitals. Most patients, even those who were very ill, were simply turned out of their beds into the streets. In the ensuing weeks, oxygen supplies, dialysis, incubators and life-support machines were switched off, smashed or loaded on to lorries going north. The Iraqis carted away the ultrasounds and computers from Al-Sabah Hospital, the dental equipment from Adan Hospital, the books and periodical collections from the medical faculty libraries.[27] The explanation was: 'Kuwait is now a small town in Iraq and should not have more facilities than Baghdad or Basra. It's just redistribution; we're not stealing.' This 'redistribution' was obviously planned, with lists prepared in advance.

The first stories of rape were played down by Kuwaitis fleeing the country. It was considered normal that an invading army stole and raped. Sadly, there was even less outcry than there would otherwise have been because the first documented cases almost all involved Filipino and other Asian household workers. It was not until the second wave of Kuwaitis fled the country, in mid-September, that serious accounts of the rape of Kuwaiti women began to be heard. Rape is a traumatic experience anywhere. In a traditional Muslim society, it is literally worse than death. The Iraqi soldiers, some from regular army units, others from the 'Popular Army', usually under the control of Ba'ath party militia commanders, stormed into houses to demand food, to loot valuables and to hunt for particular individuals, often government officials who were reportedly still in the country. Occasionally, the pretext would be to look for young men suspected of having committed 'crimes of resistance'.[28] Once inside the houses, particularly if no men were in evidence, the soldiers would rape young women. One 19-year old victim struck back. The day after she was raped in her own house she found petrol and a small quantity of explosives, put them in her car, proceeded to one of the Iraqi army command posts and, driving past the guards at full speed, blew herself up at the gate. Very much an amateur operation, it did the Iraqis little harm.[29]

With the liberation the dilemma to leave or not to leave turned into a polemic between these who left and those who stayed. With the long memories of the Arab world, the question will be debated for years and could become a source of deep bitterness. It is generally admitted that the Emir and the Crown Prince – but not necessarily the whole government – did well to leave; what is less generally admired was the manner of their return. Many people felt deep unease in seeing the French, the British and the American ambassadors return to their embassies, not knowing what they would find there, while shots were still ringing only a few miles away – while the dignitaries of the regime waited for days, and in the case of the Emir, weeks, to return. Sheikh Jaber was never an open, demonstrative man, but the aloofness of his return from exile in Saudi Arabia did nothing to bring him closer to his people. The stern announcements that followed included the imposition of martial law, strict censorship of the press and no elections for another two years and were perhaps necessary measures to cope with very real possibilities of grave disorder. However, the manner of their imposition showed little sensitivity to the feelings of Kuwaitis of all political persuasions who had abandoned their differences and united in their support for the liberation. It showed even less sensitivity to the rest of the world.

One could argue – and many Kuwaitis did – that the opinion of the rest of the world made no difference, that Kuwait was free to do whatever it wanted to do. Kuwait was indeed free again, but it owed that freedom largely to the efforts of the United States, Britain, France, Egypt and Syria and, of course, its neighbours in the GCC and all the other countries that took part in the coalition. That the resistance to the Iraqi aggression was right from the point of view of international law is unquestionable. However, to go beyond the resolutions and debate once it became clear that Saddam Hussein would not listen to reason, required action and, especially in the United States and in Europe, public opinion began to feel a proprietorial interest in the Kuwaitis they had defended. It may, indeed, have been unreasonable and unworkable for the Emir to return to Kuwait and to announce the hasty introduction of multi-party democracy and the organization of free elections. But even the most sympathetic observers as well as many Kuwaitis felt that caution was carried too far. Indeed, they felt cheated of their freedom and their victory. Vengeance seemed to come more easily to the returning rulers than confidence in their own people.

A year after the liberation of Kuwait, the combined effort of hundreds of contractors had erased or hidden most of the physical signs of the occupation. The seven hundred burning oil wells had been extinguished (the legendary American Red Adair found himself being beaten on his own ground by the ingenuity of Romanian and Hungarian teams working for half the price); by the end of 1992 Kuwait was expected to be back to pumping and exporting its OPEC quotas of oil. Most buildings had been returned to their pristine inelegance; roads were back to their normal state of clogged excellence, though a little less clogged than before because the population of 1.8 million before the invasion had been reduced by about half. Most Kuwaitis had returned; a few, discouraged, had decided to wait for pleasanter times, clipping coupons in Switzerland or France. The big difference was in the foreign population of Kuwait. Palestinians were no longer being lynched or brutally thrown out with no warning as had happened in the first days after the liberation, but they were still being expelled. Every Tuesday and Saturday some 50 to 60 of them were escorted to the Iraqi border; the ICRC had negotiated with the Kuwaiti government a procedure that gave them a few days to wind up their affairs after the expulsion order was served. It would not be long before only a handful were left of the once thriving community. For the unfortunate stateless Arabs of uncertain lineage who had drifted to Kuwait's booming job market over the decades, the situation was even worse. Most of those the Western media began to call 'bidoun' ('without', in Arabic) were originally from southern Iraq; many were to be found in the ranks of the Kuwaiti police and army. Easy scapegoats after liberation, there was real danger that they would be very badly treated by the Iraqis too. Those who could choose preferred detainment camps to being sent across the border.

One of the *leitmotifs* of the restoration was that Kuwaitis would be expected to get along with far fewer foreigners and to do their own work. The idea was excellent, but the reality very different. Even the idea of bringing in Egyptians and Syrians from Arab countries with surplus labour – an element of the aborted Damascus agreement setting out cooperation between Arab nations, rich and poor – was held suspect. Docile Asian workers were preferred. They came cheaper and would never, it was thought, ask for too many rights. This lack of confidence in fellow Arabs also manifested itself in the preference for long-term security arrangements with the United States rather than the arrangements outlined in the original Damascus agreement. Following the agreement, in March 1991, 35,000 Egyptian and 10,000 Syrian troops would be stationed in northern Saudi Arabia and Kuwait; but, by May, on Kuwaiti insistance this was revised to an 'Arab Force' of 10,000 Saudis, 10,000 other GCC troops, 3,000 Egyptians and 3,000 Syrians. By the time the 'final draft' of the agreement was approved in July, the text stated only that any GCC state had the 'right to employ Egyptian and Syrian troops'.

All of this was observed with some acrimony by the outside world. Then the attention shifted, and the Kuwaitis were left alone with their bitterness. The invasion had not lasted long, and the immense Kuwaiti financial reserves – including a part of the famous Fund for Future Generations – had been used to erase the physical scars with almost incredible alacrity. But the psychological scars were deep, indeed surprisingly deep for only seven months of occupation. Perhaps the pain is greatest in the first part of any ordeal; time dulls even very sharp pain. The government's attempts to pour financial balm on the psychological wounds were not received with whole-hearted enthusiasm; most Kuwaitis did not need to have all their debts cancelled, nor to be given free electricity. Indeed, thinking Kuwaitis rather bitterly thought that such measures were almost insulting lollipops being handed out by a government not as sure of itself as it once had been.

Once the elections promised for the end of 1992 are held and oil exports return to normal, Kuwaitis may feel that the time has come to draw a curtain over the bad times of 1990 and 1991. Some changes will have to come – they were indeed promised during the government's exile. For example, it seems inevitable that the method of categorizing Kuwaiti citizens (into those who could or could not vote, or have other privileges) be revised, and probably disappear.[30] Reinstating the former prerogatives of the Assembly and probably developing them, is another change that was promised. The question of women's political rights will be thornier. Not only are the Islamic groups bitterly opposed, but for the Saudis, who remain sceptical about the various Kuwaiti experiments in liberalization, such a move would be completely unacceptable. And this is not the time in history for Kuwait to defy Saudi Arabia.

In fact, many of the demands even of the Kuwaiti opposition require nothing more than a scrupulous application of Kuwait's constitution, an important point that has sometimes been forgotten and sometimes deliberately obscured. Most Kuwaitis strongly hope that the apparent hardening of the positions of the Emir, the Crown Prince and a few other members of the ruling family will not rob them of what they consider, rightly or wrongly, their victory.

CHAPTER 5

Saudi Arabia: The Quest for the Absolute

When a Swissair flight touches down at King Abdul Aziz airport in Riyadh, the pilot extinguishes the tail lights. This is not a blackout precaution left over from the time of the Iran–Iraq war. Turning off the tail lights is simply conforming to the rule that says no sign or symbol of any religion other than Islam can be displayed in the Kingdom of Saudi Arabia. Together with Air France, Swissair was the first foreign company to be granted landing rights in Riyadh in 1984. Until then, foreign aircraft could land in Jeddah on the Red Sea or in Dahran on the Gulf, but the Wahhabi heart of the Kingdom was forbidden territory. During the negotiations, the Saudi Government asked Swissair to remove or to hide the cross on its tail assembly. The company replied that, with the best will in the world, it was technically impossible to repaint the planes each time one was to go to Riyadh just as it was impossible to reserve special aircraft for that route. Finally a compromise was found. Swissair would keep the tail lights off, and thus its cross would not be visible during its stay in Riyadh, where its flights arrive after dark and take off before first light. From the point of view of Riyadh, such a demand is perfectly normal, just as the request made to the Swiss government to mask the cross on the plaque of its embassy and not to fly the flag except on very special occasions is normal. Symbols, visual and verbal, are important.

In October 1986, the king announced that he should no longer be addressed as 'His Majesty, King Fahd'. The correct form henceforth would be 'Custodian of the two holy shrines,

King Fahd'. The change of title (which is fortunately less awkward in Arabic than in English) is due neither to chance nor to a whim. Saudi royal affairs leave little room for whims. It was a precise response to the worries of the moment in Saudi Arabia – not very different from those that have preoccupied the Kingdom from the time of its foundation. The new title was introduced, as though by premonition, only a few months before the dramatic events of the 1987 pilgrimage season. On 31 July, the last Friday of the *hajj*, a bloody demonstration provoked by Iranian pilgrims left more than 400 people[1] dead in Mecca. These demonstrations marked a turning-point in the life of the Kingdom. Inevitably they were compared to the attempted seizure of the great mosque of Mecca in 1979 by a group of fanatics. Despite certain parallels, the causes of the two events were as dissimilar as their consequences. Both, however, were telling revelations of the situation in and around the Kingdom at the time: that is why we shall consider them both in some detail.

The founding of the Kingdom

The Kingdom of Saudi Arabia is the giant of the Gulf and the peninsula by almost any standard. The figures are staggering: over 2 million square kilometres of territory, ten times that of Oman, more than four-fifths of the total of all the Gulf Co-operation Council countries combined, just a whisker less than that of Algeria and almost twice that of Egypt, which has six times the Saudi population. In the heady days of 1982, the Kingdom's gross national product was $153 billion. In 1985, when the post-boom period was already well under way, the state budget could still count on revenues of 200 billion Saudi riyals, of which 149 billion were supposed to come from oil. For 1988, the budget was calculated on revenues of only 105 billion riyals, but as the oil price has dropped once again, the accounts will have suffered even more. But it is still difficult to feel sorry for the Saudis.

The only figure where superlatives are not in order is that of population. Officially there are somewhere between 8 and 11 million inhabitants in that vast space, of whom probably 5 to 6 million are Saudi citizens. The last census dates from 1974 and was not very convincing even then. The Yemeni tribes at the extreme south-east fringe of the Kingdom provide only one small example of the difficulties of a census. They are fairly numerous and they knew very well that it was in their interests to get themselves counted as Saudis: more subsidies go to Saudis than to Yemenis. Still, natives of a border province whose status is not finally determined, they probably feel themselves to be at least as much Yemeni as attached to the house of Saud, if, indeed, they have any real loyalties beyond the tribe.

Here we come back to the heart of the problem. The huge expanse called Saudi Arabia is far less homogeneous than one might think when looking out from the airconditioned glass and concrete of Riyadh or Jeddah towards the oil wells and pipelines. The Kingdom is not a modern nation-state and makes no real pretence at being one. It is a kingdom held together only by the allegiance that the tribes and certain individuals grant to the king and his family. When one king succeeds another, his accession to power is not marked by a ceremony of enthronement or coronation, but by the *bay'ah* or triple nose kiss. There is no grand ceremonial at all, just a series of visits, hardly even on an organized basis, to the new king's *majlis*,[2] his audience. Family members, the heads of the tribes, all the important men of the Kingdom and even many of those who are not so important but want to show their loyalty, come and manifest their allegiance to the new king by the *bay'ah* – and that is all.

The other foundation of the Kingdom, even more basic because it underlies all other claims to legitimacy, is Islam. It is hardly a unique trait among the countries of the Islamic world to declare Islam the state religion. What is more uncommon is for Islam to be the whole *raison d'être*, the underlying and overwhelming basis for the very existence of the state.

When the Egyptian diplomat Tahsin Bashir said 'Outside Egypt, there is no nation in the Middle East; the others are only tribes with a flag', he was probably thinking of Saudi Arabia in particular. In fact, the Saudis would probably agree, acquiescing with some pride rather than regarding the remark as a slight. Saudi Arabia is the only country in the world, with the exception of Liechtenstein, to bear the name of its ruling family or tribe.[3]

Its green flag, the colour of Islam, carries only the profession of faith written in a superb hand: 'La ilaha illa 'allah wa Muhammadan rasulu.' 'There is no god but God and Mohammed is his prophet.' Fortunately calligraphy is still an honoured branch of learning in Arab schools. Otherwise one would feel sorry for Saudi school-children who want to draw their flag: scribbles in place of the holy letters would be considered a sacrilege.

The history of Saudi Arabia is that of an alliance between two dynasties which began in the year 1745. The Al Saud, whose chief was at the time the Emir of Diriyya, not far from Riyadh, linked their destiny to that of the great reformer Muhammad ibn Abd al-Wahhab whose descendants are now known collectively as the Al Sheikh. For over two centuries, the Al Saud have, with varying fortunes, taken care of temporal affairs, the political, economic and military questions of their domain – whatever physical extension it may have had at any given moment – in association with the descendants of the founder of Wahhabism who were specially charged with religious, moral and spiritual questions. This remarkable partnership ensures that the Al Saud derive their legitimacy from this strict form of puritan Islam and, in turn, serve as its secular arm. It has not always been easy to ensure the functioning of this extraordinary symbiosis, no more so in times of opulence than in those of wretched poverty.

The faithful do not call themselves Wahhabis. To do so, they say, smacks of veneration of the founder and as such would contradict his own principles. They prefer to call themselves *muwahiddun*, those who believe in the unity of God.[4]

Muhammad ibn Abd al-Wahhab was born about 1703 and died in 1792. He had no idea of creating a new sect with his reform; indeed the Wahhabis today say they are simply good practitioners of the Hanafite school of Sunni Islam. He simply declared that his sole aim was to purify Sunni Islam: what he saw around him seemed defiled by a return to pagan practices. Rigorous and puritanical, stripped to the bone to extirpate outside influences, Wahhabi practice forbids all veneration of human beings, alive or dead. Kings, like their subjects, are laid to rest directly in the earth, wrapped only in a shroud, and their grave is lost in the desert.

The prohibition of idol-worship[5] was taken so literally that for a long time even after the founding of the modern Kingdom all portraits were forbidden, including, or perhaps particularly, those of the king. A compromise was reached, and today portraits of the King and the Crown Prince are displayed in all official (and many non-official) premises. The introduction of television caused an enormous uproar which was finally resolved by explaining to the conservative *ulama*, the doctors of the law and guardians of the faith, that this new invention could also be used to propagate the Holy Koran and its teaching – as it abundantly is in the Kingdom. The same argument had been used a generation earlier to justify the introduction of a national radio, well after 'The Voice of the Arabs' had begun spreading the ideas, considered dangerously revolutionary, of President Gamal Abdul Nasser to the furthest corner of the desert.

Two centuries before and without benefit of transistor radios, Muhammad ibn Abd al-Wahhab's revolutionary ideas had spread over the whole peninsula with devastating speed. The reforming preacher and his warrior sheikh had captured the Nejd (the desert heart of the peninsula) and a grandson of the first sheikh, Saud bin Abdul Aziz, proclaimed himself master of Mecca and the whole of the Hijaz before crossing the peninsula to advance on Kerbala and the great Shi'a holy cities of Iraq.[6] In 1802, the Wahhabis sacked Kerbala completely; for them its gold domes and silver-encrusted shrines were intolerable expressions of idolatry. Not long after, the old emir, Abdul Aziz – father of Saud – was assassinated in the mosque of Diriyya by a native of Kerbala who was avenging the massacres that accompanied the destruction of the shrines. After the Iranian revolution, as tension grew between Shi'a and Wahhabis, some Iranian authors revived the historical references to these events of almost 200 years earlier.

When the Wahhabis, whom they considered dangerous upstarts from the desert first conquered the holy cities in the Turkish-held Hijaz, the Ottomans were most displeased. Muhammad Ali, who by then had managed to make himself the master of Egypt, was sent to reconquer the Hijaz; for good measure, he pursued the Wahhabis all the way back to their strongholds in the heart of the Nejd. There, in 1818, his overwhelmingly superior modern artillery pounded the fort of

Diriyya into surrender. Sheikh Abdullah al-Saud was taken prisoner and sent to Istanbul where he was beheaded. The ruins of Diriyya still stand, only a few kilometres from modern Riyadh, and have become an ironic sort of monument to the dynastic history of the Al Saud. There can, of course, be no real monument because any direct reference to the family glory would immediately be construed as idolatry. In a final twist of fate, the curator of Diriyya is an Egyptian archaeologist.

After the fall of Diriyya, the family and local history degenerated into long decades of internecine fighting which only ended when a serious rival for supremacy over the Nejd emerged. In 1892, the Emir of Hail, Muhammad ibn Rashid, captured Riyadh and the heads of the Al Saud family were forced to flee to Kuwait. The story would probably have ended there had there not appeared in the next generation a remarkable man who managed to ensure that the family would not disappear from the scene. Faisal Abdul Aziz Abd ar-Rahman, whom foreigners later persisted in calling Ibn Saud. He was not yet twenty when he started his life's work of reconquering his kingdom.

The rest of the story has been told often enough: the near-miraculous reconquest of Riyadh with only 15 warriors one Ramadan night in 1902 was followed by one victory after another. When the Rashid were finally eliminated from the scene in 1906, Abdul Aziz began to negotiate with the British. The masters and protectors of most of the Gulf were looking for allies against the Ottomans, still the titular masters of the Red Sea coast of the peninsula and thus potentially dangerous for the route to India.

Meanwhile, Abdul Aziz was working hard to ensure the support of the tribes, sending them preachers to exhort them to follow the path of the true faith, to encourage them to settle and to enroll as volunteers for his army – or all three at once. The alliance with the Al Sheikh was reaffirmed as one of the cornerstones of his policy. He established military-religious settlements whose inhabitants took the name *ikhwan*, or brothers. To promise bedouin tribesmen water, green pastures and flowering shrubs and above all a real mosque is to offer them a vision of Paradise. If, in addition, they can be given the opportunity to fight in a holy war, as Abdul Aziz presented the conquest of lands less pious than his own, with the hope of plundered booty, then Paradise is all but attained.

Abdul Aziz also embarked on a carefully planned campaign of dynastic marriages in which his virility proved an undisputed asset. He fathered forty-five legitimate sons and an indeterminate number of daughters by twenty-two wives chosen from all the great tribes. This policy assured the future king of indispensable alliances and provided loyal incumbents for most of the sensitive posts of the Kingdom. Today the Al Saud family boasts approximately 4,000 male members.

In 1916, Sherif Hussein, the Hashemite ruler of the Hijaz, rose up against his Ottoman protectors. The principal architect of the revolt, which quickly spread to other Arab vassals of the Turks, was the British special envoy, Colonel T.E. Lawrence, Lawrence of Arabia as he liked to be known. The Sherif's independent reign did not last long despite the help he had given to the victors of the European war, which had engulfed him. He had had hopes of assuming the title of Caliph, head of all the Muslims, after the defeat and overthrow of the last Ottoman sultan, but he was to be granted neither the time nor the opportunity to achieve that ambition. Ibn Saud and his desert warriors swept over the holy cities and the port of Jeddah in 1925. Hussein, broken in spirit, had only one small consolation: his sons were given thrones in the new kingdoms carved out of the ruins of the Ottoman empire, Faisal in Iraq (it was supposed to be Syria, but the arrangements between the mandating powers, France and Britain, were unable to accommodate that) and Abdullah in Transjordan, where his grandson, another Hussein, reigns today.

Mastery of the holy cities

With the conquest of the Hijaz, the future Saudi realm was almost complete; only the extreme southwest remained to be conquered. Even then all would not go smoothly. The insurrection, later called the Revolt of the Ikhwan, was a direct consequence of the difficulties linked to the absorption of the Hijaz. It is worth examining, because in many ways it was a prefiguration of the occupation of the great mosque in Mecca in 1979. The revolt of the Ikhwan was the most important crisis during the consolidation of the Al Saud territories, the 1979 occupation of the great mosque, the most dangerous during the Kingdom's literal golden age.

After the conquest of the Red Sea coast, the Ikhwan were hard put to reconcile their ideas of absolute Islam with what they saw of life in the Hijaz, in and around the holy cities for whose liberation they had fought their holy war. The Nejd was almost a closed universe, turned inwards upon itself. In contrast, the Hijaz, criss-crossed by caravan routes from ancient times, was a meeting place for merchants and pilgrims from all over the Muslim world; it looked towards the outside world and was open to ideas and customs that had nothing to do with the austerity of the desert. It was easy for the Nejdi Ikhwan to follow the most radical of their leaders, those of the *ulama* who preached that all contact with non-Muslims is in itself evil, that those who came in contact with non-Muslims are contaminated: such an anathema would encompass almost all the inhabitants of the Hijaz. The Hijazis simply did not understand what the Ikhwan were talking about.

One of the first demands of the Ikhwan after the conquest of the holy cities was that the tradition of the *mahmal* be abolished. For centuries, Egyptian pilgrims had jealously held to their privilege of bringing with them at the *hajj* season a new gala cover for the *kaaba* – the cubic structure at the centre of the great mosque in Mecca (and therefore at the very centre of the Muslim world) which protects the black stone that Abraham himself is said to have placed there. The cover of finest wool – its name is the *kiswa* – was carried to the *kaaba* in a joyous Egyptian procession complete with bands, songs and festive shouting. To the Ikhwan, all music was sinful frivolity and the slightest bit of traditional folklore added to religious devotion, a sign of pagan survival. The *mahmal* seemed to them a sacrilege. And still the new master of the holy places, their prince, refused to issue an edict abolishing the custom. The Ikhwan decided to take matters into their own hands. During the pilgrimage of June 1926 they fell on the Egyptian procession, killing a dozen pilgrims and wounding many more.

For the Ikhwan, the continuation of the *mahmal* was one more example of the concessions that their own princes, the Al Saud, were willing to make towards people they themselves regarded as 'infidels'. The definition was very broad; those Iraqis (like all the inhabitants of southern Iraq, Shi'a) who dared to bring their flocks to graze on the sacred Wahhabi lands and the Sunni Hijazi merchants whose shops in Jeddah were open to all comers were no better than the 'Ingliz' with whom Ibn Saud was negotiating to construct the first satanic telegraph line across the desert. Once it was built, the Ikhwan cut the wires several times. The revolt, of which the attack on the *mahmal* in Mecca was only the beginning, was inevitable; so was the fierce repression which followed.

Today, for the Al Saud, the mastery of the holy cities is both a right and a duty, the symbol and justification of the perpetuation of the dynasty. The enormous wealth of Saudi Arabia is certainly an instrument of power, but it is never presented as a legitimation. I am not a theologian and still less a theologian of Islam, and I dare not go into the subtleties used to explain the rights of guardianship of the holy places. Still, even for a lay observer, an examination of some of the signs and symbols that accompany these rights can help to explain the functioning of the Kingdom.

The mastery of the holy cities has given Wahhabism and its *ulama* considerable prestige within the whole structure of Sunni Islam where there is no real hierarchical organization, neither pope nor ayatollah. If a single ecclesiastical authority in Sunni Islam had to be designated, it would probably be vested in the sheikhs of Al Azhar, the great theological university of Cairo. But even then, there would be no real foundation for that primacy other than tradition, which is, admittedly, an important source of Islamic authority. In theory, the Saudi *ulama* have no particular status outside the Kingdom. In practice, in recent years the faithful of many other countries have increasingly looked towards Mecca for guidance and the *fatwa*, rulings on points of canon law, of the Mecca *ulama* are increasingly solicited on subjects as diverse as whether *jihad* or holy war should be undertaken or whether listening to rock music is a permitted form of leisure activity. Radio announcements by the

Grand Mufti of Mecca have replaced the local sighting of the new moon in dating the official beginning of various Muslim feasts for some Muslim communities, particularly in the peninsula. The Islamic University of Medina is almost as venerated as that of Al Azhar[7] and it is no accident that the Islamic Conference Organization established its secretariat in Jeddah. The organization, which includes about forty countries where Muslims form a majority of the population, is largely supported by the Saudis (the other major donor countries are the UAE, Kuwait and Libya). Saudi Arabia also plays a preponderant 'spiritual' role in the organization, together with Pakistan and Morocco – both of them countries where Islam is the underlying legitimating power. Other important Islamic organizations are also based in Saudi Arabia, from where they carry out their missionary activities: the Muslim World League in Mecca, the International Organization of Islamic Science in Riyadh and the World Federation of Arabo-Muslim schools in Jeddah, among others.[8]

Religion, or rather reference to Islam, is omnipresent in every detour of 'ordinary life' – except that the very idea of trying to make a distinction between the two would no doubt be refuted by the Saudis (and not only the Saudis) as a Western distortion. In Islamic thought there is no frontier between secular worldly activities and religion. In much of the Muslim world trying to make such separations leads to incomprehension. In Saudi Arabia, the symbiosis has become dogma and the examples are legion.

When a foreigner innocently asks why the Kingdom has no constitution, the Saudi interlocutor will explain that he has not understood the position. The Kingdom does have a constitution – the Koran – and needs no other. When documents are prepared for distribution abroad, the Saudis, as a concession to foreign ignorance much contested by the purists, first write the day and the month according to the lunar calendar that dates all events from the Hegira, the flight of Mohammed to Medina (in the year 622 according to Western reckoning), and then add 'corresponding to' and the date of the Gregorian calendar.

Contact with non-Muslims

For the strictest of the *ulama*, the ideal would probably be to apply to the letter the Koranic verses that can be interpreted as forbidding Muslims all contact with Christians and Jews.[9] As for the others, those who are not even 'people of the Book', the question does not arise; they are without any position in human society, practically non-people. This attitude is not unique to Saudi Arabia but can be found all over the Islamic world. It is particularly prevalent, however, in the heart of the Arabian peninsula, perhaps because ordinary people, until very recently, had so little occasion for contact with non-Muslims.[10]

The whole question of contact with non-Muslims goes beyond a rhetorical or polemical discussion. If Saudi Arabia really wants to be faithful to its idea of absolute Islam and at the same time enter the modern age of technology and comfort, the question becomes a dilemma and, inevitably, a choice must be made. Up to a certain point, there is the option of dealing with foreign Muslims; that is the preferred solution while waiting to have enough Saudis trained to do the work. In schools, particularly for girls, it is becoming possible to replace some of the Egyptian teachers; teaching is one of the very few acceptable professions for women. Elsewhere, whether in specialised technical or scientific fields or the humblest of occupations, dealing only with Muslims, even inside the borders of the Kingdom, is not a feasible policy, and probably will not be for a long time to come. One manifestation of the dilemma is what is often described as Saudi xenophobia. The phenomenon exists but, consciously or not, its roots probably lie in the defence mechanism prescribed in the Koranic verses rather than in any innate meanness. The very real xenophobia expresses itself far more often in official or public acts and utterances than in direct relations, more in rules than in person-to-person contacts. This is almost the direct opposite of the common manifestations of xenophobia in the West, where rules and regulations are usually fairer than the acts of individuals.

Thoughtful Saudis often worry about the constant ambivalence between the temptation of isolation, the refusal to know, to understand or even to have any contact with those who are different, and the possible benefits of such contacts. An imposing number of articles, lectures, and books have been devoted to this problem, sometimes disguised under the generic title of 'The Arabs and Western Civilization'.[11]

The successive rules applied to foreign diplomatic representatives in the Kingdom are another example. Until 1984, all embassies were in Jeddah, along with the Ministry of Foreign Affairs. They were, in a sense, in quarantine; by keeping a numerous but unavoidable group of foreigners far from the heart of the Kingdom, there was, so to speak, less risk of contamination. The law is the same in Jeddah as in Riyadh, but sometimes it can be applied a little more subtly. When the diplomatic missions were given the order to move to Riyadh, various interpretations were essayed. The obvious reason was that the government had reached a stage of sophistication that made it necessary to concentrate all the ministries, including that of Foreign Affairs, in one place. During the reign of Abdul Aziz, there was hardly any fixed capital at all; the government departments, such as they were, just tagged along with the court, which followed the king in his travels all over the country. But speculation on other theories flourished. One had it that the government wanted to reduce the importance of Jeddah, still slightly suspected of too much liberty, two generations after the revolt of the Ikhwan. Another, a logical progression from the first, was that by moving a large part of the foreign population of Jeddah, the part that was most likely to show some independence, to Riyadh, it would be easier to keep an eye on them, especially since all the embassies were instructed to keep to a reserved quarter, a huge foreign compound called the diplomatic area on the outskirts of the city. Under the pretext of ensuring their security, it was possible to establish a *cordon sanitaire* around all these foreigners, which was impossible in Jeddah where chanceries and residences were scattered all around the city. Now only consulates remain in Jeddah, with smaller staffs and less influence, but usually with enough room to house their diplomats down for a weekend from Riyadh to breathe the slightly headier air of the coast.

There is something very powerful about the spirit of place in Riyadh. From the moment one touches down in the new airport

– even to someone who is not a particular fan of airports it is an architectural marvel – the ghosts of those austere founders of the Kingdom make themselves felt. A European woman, even when she is dressed with a great deal of what is called 'modesty' in these parts, i.e. a long skirt, long sleeves, the most unrevealing of necklines, will still be made to feel half-naked without at least a scarf on her head. Jeddah, as long as one is reasonable, is very different. Jeddah was for a long time a kind of safety valve in the very strict rules of conduct of the Kingdom, and the grandees knew it. They were supposed to be resident in Riyadh, the nominal capital, but almost all had a second house in Jeddah – and of course a third in Taif, the summer capital in the hills, above the burning heat of the desert, plus others in Geneva, on the French Riviera, in the Caribbean, or on the Costa del Sol.

The distance to be kept from those who are different, the non-Muslims, which can become a veritable fear of contamination, is also the underlying reason for the prohibition of all non-Muslim religious practices within the Kingdom. This rule is applied just as strictly to Christians – that is, to people of the Book – as to devotees of any other religion. In principle, even the embassies are expected to respect the ruling, despite their formal extra-territorial status. In fact, it very much depends on the convictions of the individual ambassador just how much he will help his fellow countrymen in getting round the rules. In recent years, the French embassy has stopped organizing a Christmas mass: French citizens join those of other nationalities for a discreet celebration in another Western embassy where a friend, who happens to be a priest, is invited at the appropriate time of year. Those who suffer most from the prohibition of religious services are probably certain Asian workers, in particular the pious Filipinos, too numerous and too humble to be invited to embassy parties.

A few companies arranged for priests to come as part of their personnel, under another occupational label, and help arrange 'recreation evenings'. The practice was illegal, but was usually known to the authorities and tolerated; with the tightening of the rules after 1979 – as a consequence of both the Islamic revolution in Iran and the seizure of the mosque in Mecca – it became increasingly difficult. In May 1982, the two Roman

Catholic priests of Jeddah and the single Protestant pastor were exposed and expelled. In December 1983, an Italian priest who lived in Riyadh was arrested in Hafr al-Batn, 700 kilometres to the north, where he went once a month to say mass for the American, Filipino and Korean Catholics building the huge military city. On the insistence of the American and Italian embassies, he was released and left the country. He was replaced by an American priest, carried on the roll of a private company as an anonymous employee. As a precaution against a repetition of what happened to his predecessor, he did not go to Hafr al-Batn, but in August 1984 he was nevertheless arrested as he was saying mass for a group of Filipinos in a private house in Riyadh. For two weeks he was questioned about his activities: who came to mass; who were the other priests and pastors working in the Kingdom; how had he been able to enter the country; who was his sponsor? In the end, his personal belongings and all the religious articles were confiscated and twenty-five days after his arrest he was expelled. Since then, any meetings, even in private houses, that look the slightest bit suspicious are carefully controlled and sometimes forbidden.

This attitude can be understood only in the Saudi perspective according to which the Kingdom not only happens to be a country where two holy cities are located, but, by virtue of that fact, the whole country is sanctified. A simpler formula puts it this way: the whole of the Kingdom of Saudi Arabia should be considered as one huge mosque. That is how Sheikh Abou Bakr Djabir, president of the section for the propagation of Islam at the Islamic University of Medina, put it in a letter he wrote to the Paris daily paper, *Le Monde*. The letter read, in part:[12]

> The kingdom of Saudi Arabia is, it is true, the only one of all the Muslim countries where it is forbidden to have houses of worship for the 'people of the Book' (Christians and Jews) ...
> This is not a sign of profound intolerance on the part of the Saudi royal authorities; on the contrary, this injunction is the result of an Islamic concept which holds the whole of the Kingdom of Saudi Arabia (a minute part of the Islamic world) to be considered within Islam as a mosque, where two religions cannot co-exist.
> Just as it is inconceivable to build a mosque inside a church, so it

> is unacceptable to build a church in a country that is, in itself, considered as a mosque ...

This explanation, which is not universally endorsed by Muslims, also embraces the ultimate justification of the power of the Saudi sovereigns as guardians of the holy shrines. In order to ensure their safety, the whole country is declared a mosque, that is, sanctified land, and the sovereigns who reign over the land and its holy treasures are imbued with a sanctified mission. It is not difficult to see how such a syllogism can annoy even the slightly rebellious inside and outside the country.[13]

The attacks on Mecca

The two great attacks on Mecca, which were really attacks on the Saudi monarchy, did come one from within and one from without, in 1979 and 1987. Both set off shock waves that went beyond the borders of the Kingdom to the very edges of the Islamic world. Comparisons were inevitably drawn between them. They had one point in common, which was neither trivial nor fortuitous: both took place within the precincts of the holy shrine of Mecca, the holiest place of all Islam. For both also the ultimate target was the legitimacy of the Al Saud as guardians of the holy places. Both left hundreds of victims dead. But despite these symmetries, the two attacks seem fundamentally different, and these differences, which lie in both the underlying bases and the consequences, are more important than the similarities.

The 1979 attack shook the Kingdom to its very foundations. It probably prodded the Saudi rulers into a serious reconsideration of their situation and that of the country well before the end of the boom, and provided the impetus for some much-needed reforms. The 1987 massacre seems paradoxically to have reinforced the Saudi position at the head of the *umma*, the community of the faithful, and in consequence, the position of the Al Saud as a family.

The 1979 attack has been documented with a great deal of detail in several easily available books.[14] Here just enough of an outline of the events is given to make it easier to understand what follows. It all began at dawn on the morning of 20

November 1979, the first day of the year 1400 according to the Islamic calendar, which many simple believers took as the beginning of a new century. Because of that, the day took on more symbolic significance than an ordinary New Year's Day, which comes three weeks after the solemnities of the *hajj*, the pilgrimage.

In 1979, the year of the Iranian revolution, the Saudis had been particularly worried about the enormous crowds thronging to the *hajj*. Until about 1950, only a few tens of thousands of pilgrims came each year, but from then on, the number of *hajjis* began to grow steadily, to one million a year, and then two. The increase can be attributed largely to the growth in the number of Muslims in the world and to the ease of travel, and perhaps to increased prosperity. The pilgrimage has always been one of the five pillars of Islam, together with the profession of faith, the prescribed prayers, the Ramadan fast and the giving of alms. The centrality of the pilgrimage to the practice of the faith is another reason why the guardianship of the holy places is so important – and also explains the shock that came in the wake of the massacre of the 1987 *hajj*.

Ancient chronicles tell of months and even years of travel before a fervent pilgrim would finally arrive in Mecca. Now, all the pilgrimage requires is a week or two of the believer's life plus a travel reservation and a little cash, which is sometimes provided by governments or charitable foundations. Some pilgrims still make the long journey overland; those from West Africa may take years to arrive in Mecca, stopping on the way to regroup and to earn enough money to continue, but they are an ever-decreasing minority. Most other pilgrims are still fresh when they discover the arrangements made to ensure order and as much comfort as possible: the largest of all the many huge modern Saudi building projects were destined for the *hajj*. The special airport in Jeddah is reputedly the world's largest; health and sanitation provisions have been made for two to three million visitors, including some from countries with endemic cholera, leprosy and the like; each year gigantic tent cities spring up complete with clinics and showers, drinking water fountains and sanitary toilets, grocery shops and, of course, mosques. Lots of money has been spent, but there are also enormous efforts of organization and, each year, a few more security measures.

The year 1979 was probably the zenith of the oil boom and even more so of the euphoria that went with it. At the same time, the brand-new Iranian revolution was striking sparks in the popular imagination of many Muslim peoples. The two phenomena were superimposed one on the other, but were very difficult to conjugate, particularly as the boom was pushed ever further by Western fears that made the prices of oil rise ever higher. The Gulf monarchies were frankly worried, and Western strategic experts vied with one another to see who could come up with the most frightening scenario of regional, or global, cataclysm. The Iranian revolution was commonly thought to be a forerunner of the fall of the Saudi monarchy. The attack on Mecca in November seemed to many of these analysts a demonstration that all their predictions were about to come true. For Muslims everywhere the shock was so great that reactions were for a time completely unpredictable. I was in the eastern Sudan at the time, and I remember with frightening clarity the consternation that could be read on people's faces as the news spread through Kassala. One of the pillars of their world had collapsed. For others, closer to the events, the result was sheer panic. One notable difference from what had happened in 1926, when the Ikhwan turned on the Egyptian pilgrims, was the speed with which the shocking news was carried far beyond the streets and courtyards of Mecca despite the quickly-imposed black-out. The effect was amplified by the uncontrolled rumours that spread even faster than the meagre information diffused by the state-controlled radios.[15]

Three weeks after the end of the *hajj* the biggest crowds had left Mecca, but the great mosque was far from empty at 5:20 am, as the imam, Sheikh Muhammad ibn Subayyil, prepared for dawn prayers. He had just pronounced the first holy words when he was pushed aside and the opening shot went off, killing one of the mosque attendants. The loudspeakers began to squeal and then the early-morning worshippers could hardly believe their ears when they heard a voice proclaim that the speaker was the long-awaited *mahdi* whose place of refuge was in the great mosque, in accordance with holy writ. The first shot was fired by a young man called Juhaiman ibn Muhammad al-Otaibi and the self-declared *mahdi* was named Muhammad ibn Abdullah al-Qahtani.

This was the beginning of a waking nightmare which lasted fifteen long days and nights and rocked the whole Muslim world. The assailants had prepared for a siege. They knew the geography of the great mosque well and had laid in stocks of food and arms in the cellars. The mosque is built on porous rock that is pierced with hundreds of metres of corridors leading to 300 small cells, or hermitages, where individuals can retire to pray, to meditate and to study the sacred texts.

The *mahdi* is an important figure in Muslim popular belief – a messianic figure who is supposed to appear at the end of time, when he will announce to the corrupted world that the kingdom of God is nigh. He alone will be able to triumph over the army of evil, and thus hasten the end of the world, the prelude to the resurrection of the dead. Belief in the *mahdi* is a central theme of Shi'ism, particularly for the 'twelvers', the form of Shi'ism practised in Iran. He is the twelfth imam in the direct succession from Muhammad and Ali; the twelvers believe that the twelfth imam did not die, but disappeared in a cavern in Samarra, in central Iraq, and they are awaiting his reappearance.[16] Sunni Islam, for whom the concept is more peripheral, has nevertheless seen many proclaimed *mahdis*. The best known was Muhammad Ahmed ibn Abdulla, who set up a madhist state in the Sudan – the Mahdiya – in 1881, which continued even after his death in 1886 until it was finally overrun by the British and Egyptian armies in 1892.[17]

When Muhammad ibn Abdullah al-Qahtani proclaimed himself the *mahdi* he was acting in conformity with yet another tradition: he was in fact only the spokesman for the real leader of the attack, Juhaiman ibn Muhammad al-Otaibi. Insofar as one can separate fact from *ex post facto* legend, Juhaiman was a fanatic born in about 1948 in one of the great north Arabian tribes. From childhood on, he seems to have been fascinated by the memory of the Ikhwan. He joined the Saudi Royal Guard, but found the atmosphere uncongenial because it was not pious enough; then, for a short time, he was a student of the famous blind sheikh Abdul Aziz al-Baz at the Islamic University in Medina. Juhaiman was later to turn against his master, denouncing him as lax and a lackey of the established powers, though Sheikh Abdul Aziz al-Baz is considered by many others as the very epitome of the guardian of orthodox traditions, preaching, among other doctrines, the geocentricity of the universe. Juhaiman seems to have thought himself invested with the mantle of the rebellious Ikhwan, of all those who reject the Al Saud, who denounce what they see around them as disorder and licence, accusing all others of having forgotten Islamic purity as wealth began to pollute the original values of the Kingdom.

Juhaiman began to preach his doctrine in the small towns of the Nejd, and then to write, or to inspire others to write, violent diatribes against what he called the mortal corruption of the Kingdom. The first pamphlet was printed by the Talia press in Kuwait, the production centre for the local Islamic fundamentalist groups. Tiny cells of followers sprang up all over the Kingdom and Juhaiman and his disciples really seem to have believed that their fellow-citizens were only waiting for a sign to join the revolt. Who better to begin with than the faithful present in the great mosque on the first day of a new century, and then the inhabitants of the holy city?

Blinded by their own faith, Juhaiman and his followers seem to have completely misunderstood the real situation in the Kingdom, where the majority of citizens were far too comfortably ensconced in their new well-being to be potential revolutionaries. The oil wealth was certainly not distributed by the rulers with any mathematical equality, but enough had filtered down into society for the great majority of Saudis to have had at least a taste of the cake. What Juhaiman and his followers forgot, is that in the Arabian peninsula few people ask for an absolutely egalitarian distribution of wealth. Many foreign observers have made the same mistake, but they are more easily pardoned for it. Some degree of hierarchy is regarded as normal, on the prime condition that wealth be accompanied by generosity. Overriding greed and avarice, on the other hand, are unforgivable.

In the November dawn, the zealots were surprised that their cry of revolt was not immediately taken up by all those present. Most of the worshippers managed to flee from the mosque and sounded the alarm. But the authorities could not be sure that all had been able to get away, an uncertainty that made the operations that much more difficult.[18] Before the day was out, King Khaled called together the most respected of the *ulama* to ask for a *fatwa*, a ruling, allowing the use of armed force inside the holy shrine. Most of the leading princes hurried to Mecca, but Crown Prince Fahd, who was attending an Arab summit in Tunis, deliberately did not rush back, in order to show a calm face to the other Arab leaders.

All telecommunications were quickly cut between Mecca and the outside world on the orders of Prince Nayef, the Minister of the Interior. In the absence of real information, rumours ran riot: the rebels were in control of the city, the king's palace in Riyadh had been bombed. Prince Sultan, the Minister of Defence, took over the formal command of operations with efficient support from Prince Turki al Faisal, the head of foreign intelligence.

Over the next two weeks the regular army, the national guard (which foreigners often call the white army) and the bedouin militia specially charged with the protection of the royal family,[19] plus various police forces, fought to take back the mosque, gallery after gallery, one courtyard after another. On 1 December Saudi television once again showed prayers being performed in the great mosque. But the last of the rebels only emerged from the underground passageways five days later, after the French anti-terrorist intervention group, the GIGN,[20] for whom the *ulama* had issued a special ruling allowing non-Muslims to enter the sanctuary, had drilled holes into the walls of the underground galleries and filled them with gas. 170 people surrendered: Muhammad ibn Abdullah al-Qahtani, who had proclaimed himself the *mahdi* a fortnight before, was not among those who came out of the underground warren and his body was never clearly, or at least not publicly, identified as among the 61 dead rebels and the 25 bodies belonging to worshippers who had probably been taken hostage.

On 9 January 1980, 63 rebels were beheaded in eight cities scattered around the Kingdom. The purpose was to bring the example as close as possible to the maximum number of citizens. Among those executed 41 were Saudis, 10 Egyptians, 6 South

Yemenis, 3 Kuwaitis, 1 Iraqi, 1 Sudanese and 1 North Yemeni. Almost all the foreigners were long-term residents in the Kingdom. The inevitable rumours of foreign inspiration or intervention seem to have had no basis in fact. After long interrogations of the prisoners, the Saudi authorities were convinced that there had been no foreign involvement; they would have much preferred that there had been. The arms found were of mixed provenance and were all of the sort that can easily be bought in any bedouin *suq*.

Despite the unresponsiveness of the local population, the occupation of the great mosque inevitably raised worries that the troubles could spread throughout the country. It was, indeed, surprising that the incident awakened so little echo elsewhere in the Kingdom. The population of Mecca is rather special; its residents feel themselves imbued with a holy mission by the very presence of the great sanctuaries and they, in turn, assure the city special treatment. Trouble was feared particularly in the Shi'a communities on the Gulf coast and demonstrations did break out there; however, they were probably less a direct consequence of what was happening in Mecca than of a coincidence of the calendar.

The great Shi'a feast of Ashura falls on the tenth day of the first month of the Muslim year, in other words, nine days after the beginning of the occupation of the great mosque. The Shi'a of Al Hasa, the eastern province of the Kingdom, form a community of at least 250,000,[21] and they were particularly sensitive to what was happening in Iran. In that year of the revolution, they were preparing to transgress the long-standing interdiction of the traditional Ashura celebrations. Many Shi'a were employed by Aramco[22] which had, in the course of decades, practically became a state within the state. They were not only workers, but engineers, managers and skilled technical personnel, smarting all the more under the political yoke. They knew that their province was the principal source of wealth for the Kingdom and this made it even harder to accept the profoundly unjust rule of the Al Jiluwi governors and their innumerable vexations and discriminations. The Wahhabi Al Jiluwi seemed to have a hereditary grip on the governorship of Al Hasa province, taking it as a mission to oppress the Shi'a and their beliefs.

The Ashura processions went ahead despite official disapproval, and there was trouble and violence on both sides. In Qatif, at least 17 people were shot by the police. But these demonstrations never escalated into an insurrection and the Saudi authorities quickly realized where the real danger lay and, what is more to the point, did something about it. The dynasty of the Jiluwi governors was broken. The last of them had been particularly brutal; according to those who knew him, referring openly to the Shi'a as 'dogs' was only one of his failings.[23] He was replaced by Prince Muhammad al Faisal, a sign that the house of Saud was finally ready to listen to the population of Al Hasa. The construction of the enormous industrial city of Jubail which had been decided on in 1977 was accelerated, the eastern cities became the objects of particular care, and even the Riyadh-Dammam railway was rehabilitated. In 1987, at the time of the second great crisis in Mecca, the *hajj* massacre, worried official eyes turned again to Al Hasa – but nothing happened there. There have been almost no demonstrations at all among the Saudi Shi'a since they wanted to celebrate the first anniversary of the return of Ayatollah Khomeini to Tehran in 1980. Does this signify a real improvement in the local situation? disillusion with the revolution across the Gulf? tighter security? It is impossible to disentangle the strands to find out which has been most responsible. No doubt they have all played a part.

After 1979, the *hajj* became an increasing source of worry for the Saudi authorities. In 1982 and 1983, two and a half million pilgrims came; in 1984, three million. The Iranian delegation grew from 50,000 in 1979 to 155,000 in 1987. Each year the Iranians brought portraits of Ayatollah Khomeini and pamphlets attacking the Saudi government and the legitimacy of the Al Saud family as guardians of the holy shrines. These touched a sore point, because the Al Saud have not forgotten that they acquired that honour by force of arms and that they must prove their fitness to keep it.

Within the Kingdom, enforcement of Islamic codes of conduct has become even more stringent. The *mutawwah*, the religious police, have been reinforced with young puritans whose ideas seem even stricter than those of their elders, as though the zealots of the stripe of Juhaiman had found a new haven. Too short a sleeve can bring a severe reprimand. There were also some difficulties about football, which is a favourite form of recreation in the Kingdom. Finally, despite some hesitation, those male thighs were permitted to be shown on the pitch, in front, of course, of an all-male public. Within the royal family itself, a few black, and even gray, sheep were made to feel the royal displeasure. Saudi students, especially those in the United States, are watched far more carefully by the embassies' social services just to be sure they do not go astray; those who do are not given many warnings before they are whisked back home. In the summer of 1987, an order went out to all Saudis, including the princes and grandees of the Kingdom, to leave the Côte d'Azur, the Costa del Sol and the Caribbean beaches and return forthwith. Ostensibly the order reflected security concerns following the Mecca troubles, but some observers think it may have been the other way round: the troubles had provided an opportunity to crack down on some high jinks that had become embarrassingly visible.

It has become practically impossible for Saudi women to study abroad and even a foreign woman is subject to travel restrictions. I had to have a special permit to board a plane alone from Riyadh to Dahran in transit for Bahrain. The rules on work for women have been tightened. Women are not allowed to work in any position or place where they could come into contact with men. A fundamental restructuring process is under way: the buzzword is 'saudization', as, in other places, there is bahrainization, omanization, etc. According to the fourth development plan 1985–90, 176,000 women should be working outside the home by 1990, as against 136,000 in 1985. There were relatively few women among the 2.6 million foreigners officially reported to be working in the Kingdom in 1985, so very little replacement can be counted on. Saudi women who work outside the home are practically confined to teaching and the health services, except for a few offices where the labour pool is large enough to make complete segregation possible.

Every *hajj* season since 1979 has brought trouble. Some years it was minor, in others, and especially in 1986, it became serious. According to the *ulama*, it is impossible to bar any Muslim from going to perform his religious obligation of pilgrimage unless he is a convicted criminal – and even then there is a divergence of views. The Saudi Government has nevertheless tried to control the waves of pilgrims. Each request for a visa goes into a central computer and those who are noted as having participated in demonstrations (demonstrating pilgrims were deported as early as 1980) usually draw refusals in subsequent years. In 1984, Lebanese Shi'a complained bitterly about the slowness with which their visas were being granted; two weeks before the beginning of the pilgrimage the consulate in Beirut was burnt down. This was also the year when a plane carrying Libyan pilgrims was found to contain twenty cases of arms and ammunition; plane and passengers were turned back. In 1986 explosives were found in the luggage of Iranian pilgrims. Saudi television made a film which was not shown until a year later, after the tragic events of the 1987 *hajj*.

Even though the Mecca riots of 31 July 1987 shook the Saudi establishment far less than the 1979 occupation of the great mosque, they still provoked a grave shock in the Muslim world. A dense crowd was milling around the outside perimeter of the great mosque on the morning of the last Friday of the *hajj* when a few dozen Iranian pilgrims carrying banners proclaiming 'God is with us' and inscribed with the name of Imam Khomeini began a noisy demonstration, waving portraits of Ayatollah Khomeini and Ayatollah Montazeri, his designated successor. All of this, of course, in the bastion of Wahhabi orthodoxy, where pictures are still suspect and the slightest hint of idolatry is anathema. According to scenes shown on Saudi television, scuffles broke out when the Iranian pilgrims began to shout slogans and burn effigies of the American President Reagan, and to insult other pilgrims, attacking them and ordinary citizens of Mecca with long staves; then they began burning cars. Still according to the televised reports, this was when the Mecca police went into action and tried to separate the demonstrators from other pilgrims by the use of batons and tear gas grenades. In the ensuing stampede, hundreds of people fell and many were trampled on; witnesses later said they heard shots. Officially there were 402 dead, of whom 275 were Iranians, and at least 600 were wounded.

Paradoxically, it can be argued that the riots of July 1987

strengthened the position of the Saudi monarchy as legitimate guardians of the holy places. As the news spread, messages of support came to King Fahd not only from friends, but even from many who were not quite that, such as the president of Algeria. The immediate reaction of the head of the Libyan Jamahariyya, Colonel Qaddafi, was to support the Iranian demand for the internationalization of the holy cities; then he remembered that he was both Arab and Sunni and changed his mind.

It was almost certainly the shock of the Mecca attack that nudged not only Libya but also South Yemen[24] into joining the other Arab states in their harsh condemnation of Iran at the Amman Arab summit in November. The Islamic seal of approval was added at the Islamic Conference Organization ministerial meeting the following March – after the Iranian delegation had walked out.

In contrast to 1979, there was no doubt that the 1987 troubles had been directed from outside the Kingdom and, no less important, from outside Sunni Islam. As a consequence, although far more people were killed than in 1979, it was also much easier to react to the outrage, immediately and in the following weeks and months. The Iranian charge that the events proved that the Al Saud were not fit to assume the guardianship of the holy places was much more serious than any immediate physical danger. Whatever support might come from governments, such an accusation could easily spread among the common people, perniciously digging into the collective conscience within the Kingdom and outside. It could, but it did not. Apparently the attack was so monstrous, and enough journalists and other witnesses were present to talk about it and to describe what really happened, that the temptation to follow the Iranian line of thinking was overwhelmed by indignation. There was no rioting in front of embassies, not in Egypt, where the risk was probably the greatest, nor in Tunisia[25] nor India, Pakistan or Indonesia, nor anywhere else.

Saudi Arabia's reaction was a spectacular turn-about in its attitude towards the Gulf war. Until then, despite all the help given to Iraq, the Kingdom, like the other Gulf states, had remained officially neutral. After the events in Mecca, some members of the government and the ruling family were in favour of declaring war on Iran and openly entering the fray. They were dissuaded by cooler heads, and it is possible that the arguments for moderation put forward by Oman and the UAE in the consultations among the GCC members played a part. In September, discussions were heated among the GCC foreign ministers; by the time the rulers met at the end of the year, passions had cooled down.

Since 1980, *hajj* visas have been distributed to national delegations, with the Saudis explaining that some limitations were necessary to cope with the organizational problems. The Iranians countered that they did not believe that this was the true reason, and that, if it were, it would be a good argument against the Al Saud claims to guardianship of the holy places. The question of pilgrim contingents was high on the agenda of the foreign ministers' meeting of the Islamic Conference Organization (ICO) in March 1988, the first high-level gathering of Muslim leaders after the *hajj* of the previous year. The Saudis asked for, and received, approval for a system of quotas, allowing each country one pilgrim per thousand Muslim inhabitants.[26] If the total number of Muslims in the world is estimated at 900 million, there should be 900,000 pilgrims; in 1987, over 2 million went. Iran, which had sent between 100,000 and 150,000 each year since 1983, was allocated a quota of 45,000, plus 5,000 more as a sign of good will. That did not stop Ayatollah Khomeini from declaring a few days after the meeting that Iran would send as many pilgrims as it wanted. In June, however, there was another about-face: Iran would send no pilgrims at all. Its idea of boycotting the *hajj* opened up interesting theological perspectives on what to do about the pilgrimage obligation. In fact, there had been a tentative pronouncement by Ayatollah Khomeini in January 1988, expounding that, in times of crisis, the obligation could be superseded.

Dealing with the modern world

Like the other oil-producing states, Saudi Arabia has felt the effects of lowered oil income, and some of the problems of structural adjustment proved difficult to resolve. Nevertheless, gloomy predictions that the Kingdom would go bankrupt bear more resemblance to science-fiction scenarios than to realities on the ground. Like almost everywhere in the Gulf, the big projects are mostly completed, the basic infrastructure is in place; a slowdown was inevitable. The smart businessmen have adjusted: instead of coming up with proposals for other huge projects, they are learning to sell maintenance contracts. Luckily, Wahhabism has no objections to architectural beauty. Besides the highways and round-abouts, there was time and will enough to build some of the world's best modern buildings. Two examples among many are the new sea-front in Jeddah, which almost makes it possible to forgive the quasi-disappearance of the old houses with their wooden verandahs, and Japanese architect Kenzo Tange's complex for the King Faisal Foundation in Riyadh.

New universities have provided scope for more breath-taking constructions. There are seven universities in all in the Kingdom and their combined budget in 1988 was 4.8 billion riyals, down half a billion from the year before but still a hefty sum. Despite the money, the universities pose some problems, the first of which is that of the quality, not of the buildings, but of the products they turn out, i.e. the graduates. The foreign faculty members are not alone in their misgivings. Dr Ghazi A. Algosaibi, who taught at the University of Riyadh before he became a minister, worries about it openly.[27]

A particular aspect of the problem is the lack of both competition and stimulation. With the mushrooming of the universities, it has become difficult for even the best Saudi students to escape mediocrity unless they are very rich and, despite the legend, not all Saudi families are. There are fewer grants for foreign study and even those who can pay have difficulties entering and staying in first-class American and European institutions where the work is more demanding than in their own universities.[28] The phenomenon has not been completely studied, but during the transitional period, when King Faisal was systematically sending his best young people to study abroad, embassy cultural services were often able to persuade admissions offices of top-flight universities to bend the rules a little and many of the beneficiaries lived up to the trust placed in them. The system does not work like that any more. It has become practically impossible for girls to go abroad; even the American women-only universities do not provide sufficient guarantees of separation of the sexes.

Even more than in other fields, Islam becomes the central preoccupation when it comes to education. The West has had its quarrels in the past between science and religion. Copernicus, Galileo and Columbus all got into trouble with the Church in their time. In Saudi Arabia, the dilemma of reconciling scientific thought with religious certitude remains acute, but one can hardly speak of a debate. Absolute Islam requires absolute submission, *is* absolute submission.[29] Given that fact, it is almost impossible to stimulate philosophical or scientific speculation or to teach students to ask fundamental questions. Applied science poses no major problems, but when it comes to questioning basic premises the situation changes. It is not only in the field of political speculation that the problem comes up; any technologically advanced society that does not want only to apply techniques will eventually be faced with the problem of scepticism. Doubt is a necessary ingredient in scientific advance and doubt is fundamentally incompatible with the pure tradition of submission. There is room for *aggiornamenti* and many people in the Kingdom disagree with the fundamentalist Sheikh al-Baz and his preaching of a geocentric universe: indeed, the *ulama* have approved the legality not only of the radio and television but of blood transfusions, contraception and organ transplants. Such adaptations to the modern world denote a real broadening of the spirit, but it remains difficult to imagine a Saudi equivalent of the Kuwaiti Institute for Scientific Research (KISR) where much speculative fundamental research goes on.

It may indeed be the factor of submission that makes curiosity such a rare trait among the natives of the Arabian peninsula,[30] with rare individual exceptions. In general, they know far more than they seek to know. This holds for the most ordinary situations (consider the behaviour of most Arab tourists), as much as for the basic questions of speculative philosophy. A philosopher who feels it necessary to prove the existence of God is unimaginable: God exists and that is that. Such certainty inevitably colours many other attitudes, including those of the young people studying abroad.

One of the mysteries of Saudi Arabia is its incredible capacity for reabsorbing those of its sons who leave temporarily or, to turn the axiom around, the immense adaptability of the students who return after years abroad. All the foreign observers (and here I include many non-Saudi Arabs) who think that they will become elements of disaffection, unwilling to accept the strict rules of the society to which they are returning, have been proved wrong. The students melt back into the Saudi landscape as easily as they change from jeans into a *thobe*. The transformation could be only surface conformity, but usually it is not. Examples abound, but one anecdote can help to explain the prevailing attitude. A young Riyadh lawyer with a degree from one of the best American universities turns down all invitations three evenings a week; on those three days the elder members of the family have decreed that all their male descendants and collaterals are to be present for a family council. A friendly dinner party is not a good enough excuse for absence. Almost no Saudis live abroad permanently and nowhere is the tiny handful of self-exiled political opponents numerous enough to merit being called a community.

Saudi malcontents do exist, more than there are members of organized opposition movements. Those who live within the country are neither vocal nor virulent in their opposition. The country has known political prisoners, in particular the officers who were judged guilty of having participated in a Nasserite conspiracy in the air force in 1969. In Saudi Arabia, where the Shari'a, the Islamic legal code, is applied in its integrity, capital punishment exists for murderers and several other categories of convicted criminals (convicted according to the terms of Shari'a even if the procedure is different from the ideas of Western criminal law). Hands and even feet may be amputated for theft and an adulterous woman can be stoned.[31] But Saudi Arabia does not execute purely political prisoners: Juhaiman al-Otaibi and his companions were beheaded for their part in the killing of at least 100 people and not for their opinions. As regards the Nasserite officers arrested in 1969, the most fantastic rumours flew around the Arab world, including one that they had been thrown out of aeroplanes over the Rub al-Khali.[32] All this speculation was proved wrong when the officers reappeared about a decade after their arrest. Similarly, all those who were arrested as agitators during the al-Hasa riots in 1979 had been released by 1981 at the latest.

A few dissidents are active abroad, in the United States and in Europe. They put out pamphlets and even a magazine, '*Saout at-Talia*' ('Voice of the Vanguard'), published by the 'Liberation Front of the Arabian Peninsula'. The Saudis do not worry about it or them. More than one ex-revolutionary has come back and become an ordinary citizen again, despite the noisy proclamations of those who call themselves the 'Organization of the Islamic Revolution' and the heirs of Juhaiman al-Otaibi. In 1984, one of them said that the 20,000 Saudi students then in the United States were 'horrified by the backwardness and the subjugation in which their country was kept.'[33] This statement seems to be one more example of the amalgam that has too easily been made between the situation that obtained in Iran before the fall of the Shah and that of Saudi Arabia. It is particularly surprising since it seems to have been made by an insider.

There are certainly patent contradictions both within Saudi society and in the Saudi state, but they do not have at all the same significance that they would have in a Western country. To take one example, it was Saudi influence, and that of Prince Muhammad al Faisal in particular, that set in motion the international network of Islamic banking based on a strict interpretation of the Koranic injunction against taking interest[34] and which works on the principle of direct sharing of profits and losses. The system has attracted much attention, praise and criticism, and Islamic banks are now found everywhere from Bangladesh to Morocco. Yet the first Islamic bank opened in the Kingdom only in the spring of 1988. The Al Rajhi brothers officially transformed their huge and profitable chain of exchange houses, which at the end of 1987 included 230 offices and had over 4 billion riyals in deposits, into a bank that would operate according to the Islamic system.[35] Most Saudi banks work exactly like any other bank in the rest of the world.

Payment of interest has become a sensitive subject since the beginning of the recession. Cash flow crises plagued many businesses after 1984; it was not too difficult to suspend payment to employees or to contract creditors (especially if they were foreigners, whose passports were sometimes confiscated to make sure they did not leave the Kingdom). Sometimes it was possible not to pay suppliers, again especially foreigners. Some complained but could not do much about obtaining redress: the courts are overworked and arbitration is a long and expensive process. It was only when the payment crises began to affect the banks directly that they were taken seriously. This led to a series of conflicts which were mainly concerned with differing concepts of commercial practice. A bank running into cash problems would ask its debtors to pay up, including back interest. The debtors would refuse, arguing that taking interest is contrary to Islamic law. The courts, which naturally apply Islamic law, have often found in favour of those who refuse to pay interest; they try to walk a legal tightrope by also applying another principle that says that contracts, once entered into, should be honoured according to the good faith of the contractants. Such problems inevitably loom far larger for foreign companies than for the Saudis themselves. Like Arab traders in general, Saudi businessmen do not worry over much about the prompt payment of debt. In the absence of traditional conditioning to the principle of interest, the idea of money having value intrinsically linked to finite time is still a foreign notion. A Saudi lawyer also explains that such incomprehension could be linked to the fact that there are no regular times for paying taxes.[36]

If this is so, it could soon change. The Kingdom of Saudi Arabia is not on the verge of bankruptcy, but it is in the process of reorganizing its economic and financial systems to face the outside world. There has been a sharp turn-about since the years when the major problem was trying to spend all the money that was available or, in the jargon of the time, a question of absorption. The public reserves are still there; an independent expert estimated them at more than $100 billion in 1988, of which at least $40 billion were in US Treasury notes: $20 billion less than in 1986. The International Institute for Strategic Studies is less optimistic and gives only $40 billion dollars in all for 1988.[37] While continuing to dig into reserves, the Kingdom is trying to establish a financial system closer to what is considered normal in ordinary advanced free-market economies. It is not always an easy job.

The fate of a proposal which would have made foreigners pay income tax is instructive. The whole business, from the publication of a decree announcing that henceforth foreigners would be subject to direct income taxes to the announcement saying 'King Fahd has ordered the abolition of the proposal',[38] lasted two days, from 3 to 5 January 1988. The idea was not without precedent; before 1975 income taxes had been levied in Saudi Arabia.[39] The decree of January 1988 announced a flat 30 per cent tax for all salaries over 60,000 riyals, which is near the minimum wage for anyone with the slightest skills. The first protests came not from the future tax-payers, whose voices would probably not have counted for a great deal on their own, but from their Saudi employers who quickly realized what the consequences would be if there were to be a mass outflow of skilled labour. The employees showed their displeasure with a veritable epidemic of resignation letters. Foreigners still make up about 60 per cent of the Kingdom's workforce.

Even though it backed down on this occasion, the government is going ahead with other income-generating plans. Import tariffs on most products, with the exception of foodstuffs, were raised to 12 per cent, and 20 per cent for building materials. The problem is that these figures are higher than the GCC general limit of 7 per cent. The tariffs are not only supposed to bring in money; they are also frankly protectionist measures to favour new industries. Saudi Arabia is not a member of the GATT, the General Agreement on Tariffs and Trade, but has put in complaints about what it calls discriminatory measures on the part of the European Community towards the products of its new petro-chemical factories and its surplus of excellent wheat. The wheat, the most surprising of all Saudi export products, is grown with the help of subsidies that range from free water to guaranteed purchase prices five to six times the world price. Despite the fact that agriculture has been integrated into the security system of the Kingdom, even there the austerity policy is beginning to pinch, only slightly less than elsewhere.[40] The 1985 defence budget was 64.09 billion riyals ($17.3 billion); in

1987, it was 60.8 billion riyals and in 1988, 50.8 billion riyals.[41]

State budgets and accounts, collecting taxes and tariffs, cutting subsidies, choosing between the rubrics where it is possible to slice a few expenses and those where more spending is indispensable, all this will seem drearily normal to Western readers. Yet, not one of these notions would have been even thinkable in 1980 in Saudi Arabia. All have been examined since then. Saudi Arabia, the fabulously extravagant Kingdom, is becoming very ordinary, at least fiscally speaking.

The follies of the Kingdom during the *anni mirabili* have been abundantly reported. A corollary of these sometimes wild flights of fancy (on the part of those who conceived them, but also of those who talked about them later) was that an idea took root in the collective conscience of many people in the West: sooner or later, the Kingdom was going to sustain shocks like those that brought down the monarchy in Iran. Or, as a variation on the same theme, a revolution in Saudi Arabia would be averted only by a Western intervention: this time the Americans were not going to be caught napping nor let their friends down as they had been accused of doing in Iran.

Relations with the United States

The relations between the United States and the Gulf states will be discussed later, in Chapter 10. But Saudi Arabia is different. The Saudi-American relationship is not only political, although the staunch anti-communism which they share no doubt cements the friendship. A Lebanese scholar who has little love for the Saudis in general has an interesting theory on the strange bond between two peoples who are so different. He maintains that 'The Americans relive here in the desert the adventure of the conquest of the great American west ...'[42] And he remarks that, while 'the Saudis feel at ease with these Europeans unencumbered by a cultural heritage', the reason for the non-genocide of the native tribes probably owes more to the spirit of the age than to any change of heart. If the oil rush had happened in the nineteenth rather than the twentieth century, the tribes might well have been subject to the same treatment as that of the American Indians who happened to be in the way of the expanding railways – a harsh judgement, indeed.

Most Arabs are fascinated by America, even those who resoundingly vilify it: imperialists, anti-Arabs, biased Zionists – the expletives are familiar, but however loud the screams, they almost always hide a love-hate relationship at the core. Few Arabs have collectively arrived at the stage of near-symbiosis achieved by the Saudis, however. A major part of the oil fields are still run by Aramco,[43] whose extraordinary more or less autonomous position continues, with or without nationalization. For decades it has paid the Kingdom for this favoured position not only in the form of royalties but by being its faithful advocate before the Congress and the President of the United States.

In addition to the ordinary and open economic, commercial and financial relations, a parallel network of technico-military arrangements has been spun; its activities range from contracts for training the National Guard to the building (by the American Army Corps of Engineers) of the enormous military cities (as they are officially known) in Hafr al-Batn and Tobuk. Selling arms to the Kingdom was for many years almost an American monopoly, despite the noisy wrangles in Congress each time a new contract for advanced systems was in the offing. Preventing such sales had become a priority objective for the American-Israeli Public Affairs Committee (AIPAC), the efficient co-ordinator of the pro-Israel lobbies. It is not entirely clear why AIPAC was particularly virulent about Saudi Arabia, far more so than about Jordan. Perhaps Saudi Arabia seemed more vulnerable to pressures since it depended more directly and exclusively on American arms, perhaps also the quantities involved were so big that their symbolic value became that much greater. Jordan, like Kuwait, had refused to be intimidated by such pressure and turned to the Soviet Union for arms that the United States did not want to sell. The Americans did not like such moves, but did not worry unduly about them. They could, they thought, always count on their faithful friends in Saudi Arabia. The enormous investments already made, in which almost every element depended on compatibility with the next bit of the American puzzle in order to be used to its best advantage, were reassuring. When, in addition, they considered the passionate Saudi aversion to communism, the Americans felt reassured.

The first breach in this cozy relationship came in 1986. When the Saudis announced they were buying British Tornado fighter-interceptors rather than American F-16s, it was considered a simple irregularity in the electro-encephalograph of the relationship, and the infidelity was only with that surest of allies, Margaret Thatcher's Britain. The real blow came in March 1988, with the news that the Kingdom had bought Chinese C(SS)-2 missiles. The American analysts were even more perturbed when they heard that the negotiations with the People's Republic had been carried out practically under their noses by Prince Bandar ibn Sultan, the Saudi ambassador in Washington, and had begun as early as 1986. The United States, once again under the pressure of the pro-Israel lobby, had refused to sell Lance rockets to the Saudis. At the time, the proposed sale had set off a furious row because the Lances, with a range of up to 2,000 kilometres, would have been within easy range of Israel and, moreover, were capable of carrying nuclear warheads.

The Chinese missile affair was deliberately provoked, as it soon became clear. The first announcement was made from the office of the Israeli Prime Minister and was not, as sometimes happens, subsequently denied. Jordan has long had rockets capable of hitting Israeli cities and Saudi Arabia has no nuclear warheads and neither the possibility nor the intention of acquiring any in the foreseeable future. On 26 April 1988, Saudi Arabia announced its signature of the nuclear non-proliferation treaty. Despite the occasional hysterical announcement, no Arab country is close to having a nuclear capacity that could be used to equip missile warheads. To bring in Pakistan, because of the Islamic connection, as a possible source of such weaponry (there have even been rumours about sales to Libya) seems a large leap towards political fiction. Pakistan has been trying to show itself a responsible member of the concert of nations and, just to make sure, American friendship is important enough to it to keep it from temptation.

For the United States, even if the Chinese missiles were, as the Saudis said, acquired with Iran in mind, this in no way affected the basic shock at the idea that the Saudis should show such remarkable determination to disengage themselves from the American network and that their partners in infidelity should be the Chinese.[44] In contrast to Oman, which had entertained excellent relations with the People's Republic even during its violently anti-Soviet years, Saudi Arabia has been far more dogmatic in its opposition to communism. All communism remained anathema, for the simple reason of its traditional opposition to religion. China had, in fact, begun making a few moves towards Islamic sensitivities in recent years, for example, by sending a small delegation to participate in the *hajj*.

Yet neither the purchase of the Chinese missiles nor the prudent steps toward a rapprochement with the Soviet Union (see Chapter 10) can be construed as a reversal of the Kingdom's basic policy. They were, however, a signal to the Americans: even friendship cannot be taken entirely for granted. In fact, there are too many interpenetrations and, with the exception of the policy towards Israel, convergences for a serious quarrel to become likely. Quite aside from the long-term links, the Saudi alliance served the Reagan Government's interests well. It assured a second source of aid for the Afghan resistance and, most discreetly, helped the Reagan Administration get financial help to the Nicaraguan Contras at a time when Congress was adamant in refusing its authorization. The support of the Afghan resistance movements is easily understandable in the light of Islamic solidarity, but that reason can hardly be invoked for Nicaragua: only pure, old-fashioned anti-communism could be trotted out as the motivation.

No American politician would forget Riyadh on a Middle East tour. Even sophisticated Americans may not be very sure exactly where to place Abu Dhabi or Basrah on the map, but Saudi Arabia is a central piece in the Americans' global puzzle. It will certainly remain there, at least so long as Iran is not completely reintegrated into a system of Western friendship, and even after that.

No peacock throne

Since 1979, with disconcerting regularity Saudi Arabia has been compared with pre-revolutionary Iran. In 1980, Central Intelligence Agency analysts were predicting an explosion within five years (the fashionable word was 'implosion', as though the Kingdom were a television screen). More or less confidential reports were as adamant as published articles in their warnings. Most of the authors based their arguments on four premises about Iran that they applied to Saudi Arabia. These were: the Shah of Iran had also had enormous oil revenues at his disposal; he, too, wanted to modernize his country; he was an autocrat who, like the Saudi rulers, ruled without any real democratic power-sharing; he was too close to the West and showed it too openly. When 1985 came and went with no revolution, the prophets of doom reluctantly admitted they had been wrong. With the Gulf crisis of 1990 the old arguments were trotted out once more, but with a new twist.

The crisis had opened the Kingdom's doors as nothing before had ever done. An impressive number of foreigners came: hundreds of thousands of Western and other Arab troops (including women soldiers) and hundreds of journalists, most of them completely unprepared for what they would see and try to interpret for the folks back home. Invited into the Kingdom by the government – which had taken care to seek approval of the religious authorities even in the haste of emergency – all those foreigners figured prominently in the propaganda efforts of Iraq and its allies. The Saudis were accused of letting the infidels 'profanate' the Holy Places; that, of course, was nonsense. The Western troops were stationed nowhere near the Holy Cities; the French, at Yanbo, were the closest, over 200 kilometres from Medina, much further from Mecca. However, the Saudis did face the difficult task of extricating themselves from their own previous rhetoric which had stated that all the Kingdom was a mosque. In the face of the propaganda assault, they held an international meeting of Islamic leaders in Mecca in early September that gave its blessing to the influx of foreigners. After all, Saddam had held his own Islamic meeting a few months earlier in Baghdad, where the tame *ulama* had dutifully bestowed upon him the title of 'Hero of Islam'. Some of those present on that occasion repented and showed up in Mecca.

Apart from declamation, one important aspect of the

reasoning went as follows: if the Kingdom were to maintain an army big enough to contain a threat like that of Saddam, it would require a disproportionate part of even that very rich (but underpopulated) country's human resources. Better to ask friends for help in cases of temporary need. In other words, let those who can help defend the Kingdom come, infidels or not, but be sure that they leave when the crisis is over. This was explained to me by Dr Abdullah Nasseef of the World Muslim League, an Islamic scholar who took the trouble to come from Mecca to Jeddah to meet me – an unusual step in itself.

One surprising effect of the crisis was a timid opening-up of the society. Saudi Arabia was very close to a war situation even before the first Iraqi Scuds landed on Riyadh, and war usually leads to tighter controls. In this case, from the first week of the crisis in August, there was a surge of freedom, especially in the press. The Saudi newspapers suddenly became interesting. Timid efforts were made to interest the citizens in their own welfare; that was the main virtue of the quickly-established, but largely untrained home guard. Even women were encouraged to sign up for carefully circumscribed nursing services – rather like European women in the First World War. All this activity led to talk about reforms, perhaps too much talk.

The war came and went quickly, but the crisis ended with little satisfaction in Saudi Arabia. The Kuwaitis went home; so did the ground troops, although a more discreet contingent of foreign specialists stayed. The press pack turned its attention elsewhere. But the taste of freedom lingered. As 1991 went on, a discreet movement to push the King and the senior princes into finally allowing the establishment of a consultative council picked up momentum; but, so did state opposition to any dangerous innovations. The long-promised wholly-appointed *Majlis al-Shura* finally came into existence. By no stretch of the imagination is it a parliament in any Western sense of the word, but it is a tiny first step on the way to wider participation of the increasingly well-educated Saudi population in the working of its own country.

Is the establishment of the *Majlis* enough to guarantee that the dire predictions of incipient revolt will once again come to nought? Such predictions were mostly made through Western eyes, or through Western eyes wearing Levantine spectacles. As a conclusion to this chapter, it is worthwhile trying to look at Saudi Arabia with spectacles better adapted to the Gulf and the Arabian peninsula (sun-glasses would probably be best). First of all, the sparse population of the Kingdom can be considered both as a liability and an advantage: a liability because of the problems this creates in organizing defense and in simply running a modern state, and an advantage because even with lowered oil income the Saudis remain among the most privileged peoples on earth. What is more, the citizens are, on the whole, well aware of that fact. In Saudi Arabia, as elsewhere in the Peninsula, the idea of a revolt of foreign workers is almost unimaginable.

Many members of the large royal family were in a position to take advantage of the boom years to build their personal fortunes; so were many other Saudis. The very real privileges of the Al Sauds are spread over something like 4,000 princes (counting only the male members of the family). Through a network of family and client relationships they, in turn, bring benefits to far wider circles – including that of the religious leaders. The Pahlavi family and their intimates numbered only about 40 individuals in a native population almost ten times that of Saudi Arabia. Saudis are not all millionaires, but there is nothing in Riyadh, Jeddah or Dahran even remotely equivalent to the slums of south Tehran before 1979.

The Saudi King does not rule alone. As a minimum, he must have the consent of the politically active members of his family. The first of Abdul Aziz's sons to succeed to the kingship, Saud, ignored that simple fact to his peril: his brothers and uncles deposed him as incompetent and unworthy to rule. The new *Majlis al-Shura* will not spread the power of decision much further, but it will widen the perception of participation.

There is one final difference between the situation in pre-revolutionary Iran and that of Saudi Arabia that is probably the most important of all. The Shah based his policies on a forced march to the modern world. The pace could be adjusted, but few spheres were completely ignored – with the exception of the religious establishment, which remained almost entirely shut out of the system. Failure to count that factor was probably what cost the Shah his throne. The Al Saud are also trying to modernize their Kingdom, but they never forget that Islam remains the first pillar of their reign. Leaving aside for the moment the differences between the Shi'a and Sunni relationship to the established power, and at the risk of over-simplification, it can be said that the Al Saud rule and reign with the consent of the *ulama*, using Islam both as a factor of legitimation and a direct support, while the Shah ruled in opposition to the religious establishment.

The result is that so far, with the important exception of the 1979 occupation of Mecca, there have been no real threats to the Saudi throne. Perhaps, too, because it is not really a throne. In his *majlis*, the king receives his visitors sitting in an armchair, no fancier and no less fancy than all the others around the enormous hall. Actually, what he prefers, particularly during the hunting season, is to receive his visitors in the desert, in a tent – a very big tent, but a tent nevertheless. A Persopolis extravaganza would be unthinkable in Saudi Arabia.

CHAPTER 6

Qatar: The Quintessence of the Gulf

Qatar is the quintessential Gulf country, a veritable distillation of what the Gulf is, of its problems and qualities, its joys and its sorrows. It is a very small place: an arid limestone peninsula the size of Wales or of the state of New Jersey, sticking out from the eastern flank of the Saudi shore like a hitchhiker's thumb pointing due north. Its whole population is little more than 360,000, of whom far fewer than half are native Qataris.[1]

Qatar is also arguably the richest country on earth; its citizens almost certainly are.[2] In 1987, Qatar was producing an average of 293,000 barrels of oil per day; that was also the year it went back to sticking to OPEC rules, after a serious dressing-down from its partners for overstepping its quota. Like its neighbours, Qatar felt the oil price collapse of 1986; its gross domestic product dropped more than 20 per cent after a 10 per cent decline in 1985 and annual slides of an average of 5 per cent each year since 1982. However, in Qatar, it was all felt differently from the situation in the neighbouring states. Extreme caution was and remains a fundamental character trait of the Emir, Sheikh Khalifa bin Hamad Ath-Thani. Even during the wildest years of the Gulf boom, he was constantly putting a brake on extravagance for himself and his country. When the financial downturns eventually turned to shocks, the effects were diluted by the fact that Qatar is in fact just one large village, with all the advantages (and some of the problems) that can bring. Nobody really wanted to cause serious harm to his cousin or his neighbour. Things were arranged in such a way that there were no resounding crashes like those that shook Dubai, Abu Dhabi or the Saudi cities. There were no lawsuits, no public declarations of bankruptcy, no bitterness, no need for quick revisions of laws that had been made obsolete by the enormous amounts of money sometimes erratically floating about. Doha makes no pretence at being a financial centre.

In Qatar, the big merchant families are not only connected among themselves but also, without exception, related to the Ath-Thani clan – either directly, through marriage, or at the very least in business dealings and personal friendships. There are some 1,700 male Ath-Thanis, and 3,500 members of the family. In other words, one Qatari in fifteen is an Ath-Thani; in Gulf terms, that inevitably makes for a close political and economic network. People may dislike a cousin, but would not want to let him sink completely. Besides, cousins who are well taken care of have less chance of becoming trouble-makers.

Even in the black days of 1986 Qatar saw nothing more dramatic than some blocked payments and a few shut-downs which could almost be taken as the pruning away of dead wood. In such a small society even tiny problems can loom large, but for Qatar there was always a saving factor, a tiny light shining on the horizon. Every Qatari knew about the enormous reserves of natural gas waiting just off the north shore of the peninsula. The first development contract for the gas was signed with a flourish in May 1987. That does not necessarily mean that the next boom is just around the corner, but hope, far from eternal for the bedouin of Qatar before the 1960s, has sprung up again. The exploitation of a gasfield is a far more costly proposition than that of oil, and gas is subject to greater marketing problems in times of glut. Nevertheless, Qatar's North Field, covering about 6,000 square kilometres, contains recoverable reserves estimated at 4,440 billion cubic metres. This makes it the largest reservoir of non-associated (not mixed with oil) gas in the world and means that Qatar owns approximately 4.3 per cent of the world's total gas reserves, and 12 per cent of OPEC's.[3] Thanks to the North Field, tiny Qatar knows that it is potentially the world's second largest gas exporter after the Soviet Union.

International businessmen know it too. At a time when the samsonite brigade have practically disappeared from view elsewhere in the Gulf, they are flocking back to Doha. They will probably not have an easier job than the first time around.

During the years of folly, the Emir of Qatar was known throughout the Gulf as a hyper-conservative, a Mr No; there were even occasional hints of stinginess – a damning accusation. In Arab society, and particularly in the Gulf, generosity is a cardinal virtue and niggardliness one of the deadliest of sins.

Looking back on that period, the Qataris are both proud of and grateful to their prince for his sagacity. When every sheikh around was building a new airport, bigger and more luxurious than his neighbour's, the ruler of Qatar said 'no' to all comers. As a result, Doha airport has remained much in the image of the country: efficient, convenient because very close to town, unpretentious and uncluttered. There is no comparison with Abu Dhabi's miniature version of Paris-Charles De Gaulle, decorated like an Abassid palace, or the luxury supermarket of Dubai, where omnipresent billboards advertise it as the 'best duty-free in the world'. But Doha – with no duty-free shop at all – does have a four-kilometre-long runway, which makes it one of the most efficient landing places in the whole region.

On the sea shore, the same reasoning applied. The construction companies were for years beating a path to the Emir's door, trying to persuade him to order a new general-purpose port, something on the lines of Dubai's Jebel Ali. However, Qatar has little maritime tradition; before oil, some Qataris were pearlers or fishermen but most, and they do not deny it, were simply desert bedouins. The Emir thought that simply adding three new jetties to the existing four, a bit of cementing and a machine or two were really all that was needed. He was quite right, because the result is nicely proportionate to the real port traffic in Doha. In the space saved, some rather pretty bay-side promenades have been established, and the only people who are really disappointed are the contractors who missed out on fat commissions.

Government House, or the *diwan amiri*, remains remarkably modest, even faintly musty. Its walls and columns could do with a touch of paint here and there and the curtains are slightly faded. The whole palace is like a rambling, much-used and well-loved family house with more charm than architectural distinction. All the doors, including those of the several ministers whose offices are in the *diwan*, are open. It is a sad commentary on changing times that in the course of the 1980s it has become impossible, at least for a foreigner, to stop by and see whether the bedouin guards at the gate are still busy with their game of *tawla* or backgammon.

Security has not killed the custom of the open *majlis*. Twice a week, very early on a Sunday or a Tuesday morning, any Qatari can come to the *diwan*, talk directly to the Emir, present a request or a complaint. He will be listened to and will obtain an answer. If necessary, his business will be sent on to the appropriate government department. The Emir does not sit on a throne, but on a blue-upholstered armchair exactly like those of all his subjects and guests. The *majlis* usually lasts about half an hour, while one man after another approaches the Emir, sits in the chair on his left and has his say. A secretary is there to take notes. At the end of the session, the director of the Emir's personal office holds his own *majlis* in the antechamber – with more coffee and tea – to follow up the details.

All this is obviously as far from a Western constitutional democracy as Qatar's appointed Consultative Council is from a European parliament. Nevertheless, in this very small society, it is a system that ensures a sense of participation and a supplementary link between those who govern and those who are governed. The Consultative Council exactly corresponds to its name: it is not there to make laws, but to serve the prince as extra eyes and ears. The members of the Consultative Council are no more given to obsequiousness than are the ordinary bedouin at the morning *majlis*. 'Ya, Khalifa,' they begin as they address the Emir by his given name – no fancy titles here; the Qatari comes before his prince as a free man, not as a fawning subject.

Qatar is the only country in the Gulf to share officially with Saudi Arabia the Wahhabi form of Islam. But Qatar has managed to temper the very strict application of the rigorous Wahhabi faith with something approaching good humour. The rules governing the purchase and consumption of alcohol are, as so often, a good barometer. Alcoholic drinks are strictly prohibited on all official occasions and are never served in public. Even the famous room 501 of the Gulf Hotel, which used to be a semi-public saloon bar, has been closed down and redecorated. But non-Muslim residents may obtain a permit to buy a limited amount of liquor (woe betide them if they are caught selling it on the black market). A permit may also be had by Qataris who, because of their socio-economic or professional situation, are likely to have to entertain foreigners. That rule is also a telling commentary on the reputation of foreigners, who are considered incapable of going without drink for the duration of a visit.

Culture as identity

There are surprising facets to this extraordinary little country. Its Wahhabi rulers would be horrified by anything smacking of licence, but they are not opposed to all the pleasures of life. Most of the arts are encouraged under the benevolent patronage of the prince and his advisers. The theatre is almost a Qatari speciality. Qatari theatre can be lively and witty, taking the risk of an occasional mild whiff of social criticism and even partially breaking the taboo against any contact between men and women. It can breathe fresh air into what is often a fairly stifling social order. In a completely different register, there is something in the Qatari theatre reminiscent of the black South African troupes or the El-Hakawati theatre in East Jerusalem: theatre becomes a way of expressing things that otherwise remain unsaid.

In Doha, one can find women on the stage and in the audience (but almost none, except foreigners, in the streets). Some performances are billed as ‘women's evenings’; in practice, this means that a man, a brother, husband or father is allowed to accompany the female spectators, but no men are allowed into the theatre on their own. Several Qatari playwrights have had the luck to be provided with extraordinary working conditions that would be the envy of most of their Western colleagues: a regular salary, often paid as a cushy sinecure at Qatar television, the certainty of a theatre production and high hopes for a good press. The last is by no means guaranteed. The local critics are inordinately proud of their independence and local pride does not necessarily blind their aesthetic judgement.

The general climate of favouring all forms of culture and communications extends to publications, radio and television. Radio Qatar is listened to all over the Gulf and both its Arabic and English information services have earned an excellent reputation. French broadcasts were begun in 1987. News broadcasts from Qatar go well beyond the court circulars that sometimes pass for information in these parts: an enumeration of audiences, a careful report on which minister was seen off at the airport by whom, and completed by a list of the congratulatory cables sent by and to the local ruler.

The Qatari journalists can be surprising. Press conferences in the Gulf, at GCC meetings for example, rarely go beyond prepared statements and polite noises, except for the less polite ones sometimes made by visitors from outside the area. The Qataris stand out among the Gulf journalists by their readiness to ask pertinent, sometimes even mildly provocative, questions, cutting through the pervading fog of obsequious conformity without ever being impolite. Three daily papers in Arabic (plus one in English) are published in Doha. They have none of the international ambitions of the Kuwaiti papers, but go well beyond the simple local rag or government information bulletin. They must have government permission to publish, but are privately owned. Their publishers are hardly likely to make money, but simply keeping them alive in a population of 350,000, where, among Qataris, 90 per cent of the population was illiterate not so long ago seems some sort of miracle.

The Qatar National Museum is another source of astonishment. It is probably the most interesting of its kind in the Gulf, a small triumph of design, housed in a fastidiously restored complex of old houses (old meaning the first half of the twentieth century) that once belonged to the family of the sheikhs. The museum has become a centre of local life, not perhaps very difficult in a city where public attractions are rare. Still, few museums in the world can have a larger number of visitors in relation to the population and with no help from the tourist trade; there are no tourists in Qatar. The Qataris have kept coming for fifteen years.

The museum contains no masterpieces nor even important

archaeological remains such as can be found in Bahrain or Riyadh. The most important exhibits are reconstructions of places and situations in the daily life of Qatar only a generation ago. Whole families come in the afternoon to gape at a fully-equipped bedouin tent; nothing is missing, not even the stuffed falcon at the door. They sniff at the exhibits of all the perfumes of Araby, pure musk or ambergris, sandalwood or benjoin, and listen to a tape that accompanies a stone mortar and blackened coffee pots displayed on a glowing open hearth. Fewer visitors linger in the petroleum section, which is too close to daily life to provide even a whiff of dreams. The oil market is as much a part of normal conversation in Qatar as is the weather in England.

It seems more than pure chance that the Gulf Folklore Centre, a reference and training centre for specialists from all the Arab countries of the Gulf including Iraq, is in Doha. It was, however, pure chance that made its expansion possible. Just as the Centre was looking for more space, the house next door become available. The Libyan embassy was shut down after its diplomats were strongly suspected of having been directly involved in the planning of a rocket attack to be launched against the Emir and his guests at the GCC summit in November 1983.

The list of Qatari cultural endeavours could go on: subsidizing the publication of historical texts on Gulf topics and organizing conferences on history and archaeology are two other examples. But why this cultural and intellectual activity in a tiny Gulf state that hardly seemed destined to become a mini-Parnassus?

Consciously or not, each of the Gulf states has found a particular niche, some specific trait that differentiates it from the others. Originally, it may have been simply an idea, a cliché or even a stereotyped prejudice; but continuous reinforcement can turn a stereotype into a positive factor of identification. A good example is the 'pragmatism' of Dubai, a firmly held belief outside the emirate and actively encouraged within it, or the 'freedom' of Bahrain, or the fact that Kuwait is so progressive. The cultural interests of Qatar are in the same vein, deliberately fostered to provide a positive image in opposition to all the negative or hollow stereotypes. From the 1970s on, the princpal architect of this policy was the Minister of Information and Culture, Issa Ghanim al-Kawari, who is also the Emir's special adviser and office director. A man of charm, sensitivity and character, Issa Kawari becomes innocence personified when asked why Qatar has gone the way of culture: 'It just happened,' he answers when pressed. Yet this flowering of the arts in such an unlikely environment could not have happened without deliberate encouragement from the government, that is, from the Emir and from his chief adviser on such matters. So the question has come full circle.

A second individual worked for a long time in the shadow of the first. Dr El-Tayeb Salih, a Sudanese poet and novelist who once worked for the BBC's Arabic service, was for years the Director-General of the Ministry of Information. After a spell in Paris at UNESCO headquarters he returned to live in Qatar as UNESCO representative for the Gulf. Between them, these two men worked out and constantly supported a cultural policy that is not only astonishingly rich but so discreet that it has gone almost unnoticed. It is, in fact, a good example of what could be the motto of Qatar: do whatever you want and think is right – but don't make waves.

The French connection

Even on the political level Qatar shows flashes of originality. Saudi Arabia has long had its special relationship with the United States; Oman and Bahrain remain unabashedly anglophile. Meanwhile, Qatar is quietly proud of its French connection. It all began in 1975, when the Emir went to Paris, his first state visit to a European country and the first official visit to France of any of the Gulf rulers. The French had the excellent idea of taking the visit seriously and ever since the friendship has flourished.

Statistically, the French presence remains small: in all there are no more than 500 French residents compared with almost ten times as many British. At first, the francophilia probably fed on the old resentments against the British. Qatar, which became part of the system of imperial protectorates very late, only in 1916, was always considered by the British to be a mere dependency of Bahrain. The British liked the urbane atmosphere of Bahrain and looked down with disdain on the poor fishermen across the way. The Qataris, understandably, rather resented this, and the old resentment was also one of the reasons that led them to reject the 'Federation of Nine' when the British left the Gulf in 1971 (see Chapter 10).[4]

Since the Emir's visit, the French connection has taken multiple forms from arms purchases to a rush to learn French. Like all the Gulf countries, Qatar spends considerable millions each year on arms; just how many is, as always, difficult to say, because arms procurement is rarely included in the published budgets.[5] A large part of these arms are French; Qatar is rumoured to have more Exocets in its armoury than any other Gulf country, including Iraq. Exocets aside, the Qatari penchant for French weaponry makes the work of military harmonization within the GCC even more complicated. It was a hard enough job with the mixed Anglo-American equipment of most of the Gulf countries, spiced by a few Soviet purchases in Kuwait. And that was before the Saudi Chinese missiles entered the scene.

Qatar has retained more of the traditional forms of government than any of its neighbours, with the exception of the individual emirates of the UAE, which are, by the nature of the Federation, in an entirely different situation. The adaptation to the modern world has been executed with the lightest possible hand. The Emir really is the tribal chief who is personally involved in the workings of government, going into quite extraordinary detail. During his holidays abroad, Qatar practically stops functioning. To take only one example, any government cheque for more than half a million riyals must be countersigned by the Emir himself. For lesser sums, almost every payment voucher must go through the Ministry of Finance, where bills can pile up for months. In a very small country, where an inordinate number of business dealings are somehow linked into the public system, such bottlenecks can have disastrous results, precipitating local crises that should never have happened. In 1984 and again in 1986, the country narrowly escaped bankruptcy, simply because too many people forgot too many signatures.

Members of the princely Ath-Thani family hold more than

half the ministerial posts. This does not mean that they always agree with the Emir or with those of his sons who hold the key ministries. The Crown Prince, Sheikh Hamad bin Khalifa, has managed a veritable *tour de force* in making himself acceptable to the most traditional members of the tribes at the same time as he has made for himself a reputation of being open to the modern world. He is a Sandhurst graduate, having gone through the full course with no favours for an 'Arab prince's diploma', and is proud of it.

The Emir's second son, Abdul Aziz, is better known abroad. He holds the Ministry of Petroleum and Finance. The conjunction is not fortuitous, and he is, by those who know the family well, considered the brightest of all the sons. Yet his father still likes to keep him, literally, under his paternal eye. After several years in which, it was said, he began to kick up his heels a little too skittishly, the Emir ordered him to move his personal office back into the *diwan amiri*, close to his own. After a year he returned to his own modern ministry building, just down the Corniche.

The Emir also appoints the thirty members of the Consultative Council. Their prerogatives are strictly limited to what concerns the life of the society around them; international relations, oil and finance are outside their scope.

State accounts and budgets do not, in any case, mean quite the same thing as in the West. The budget – and this remark is true of all the Gulf states – is more a general statement of intentions than a project for the exact distribution of revenues. It is also often used as an *ex post facto* justification. In Qatar, one of the most telling signs of the precarious financial situation in 1986 was the nervous non-publication of the budget, which was delayed month after month. Finally, the year went by with no budget at all. In February 1987, the solemn promise that the budget would indeed appear for 1987 was enough to nudge business into a slightly more buoyant mood.

Fundamentalist stirrings

Even the strictly circumscribed Qatari society saw some Islamic fundamentalist agitation in the first year after the Iranian revolution. It would, however, have been difficult to point an accusing finger at anything resembling a public flouting of Islam or laxness. There is certainly individual transgression of the strict Wahhabi precepts, but it is almost always discreet. The Islamists therefore decided to attack the monarchy as such. But even at the height of their influence, they never aroused a wide response among the population; they never went beyond talk and were never suppressed with any degree of violence. After 1983, whatever influence they did have began to wane.

When the university was established in Qatar, the planners decided on some very mild measures pointing towards the beginning of equal treatment for male and female students. Mixed lectures are the norm in Kuwait, Bahrain and Oman, even though social and residential facilities are separate. At Al Ain, the UAE university, segregation of the sexes is extremely strict, and in the Saudi universities female students attend lectures by male professors via closed-circuit television. In Qatar, no one ever dreamed of co-education, but even the small concessions made went too far. A few weeks before the students were scheduled to move into the new university buildings, a pleasing architectural concept based on interconnecting honeycomb structures, the members of the Consultative Council were invited for a preview. During the visit, some old sheikhs discovered that the male and female students were going to be using the same science laboratories – at different times, naturally. It was too much for them to swallow, and their veto was final. During the time required to build and equip duplicate laboratories, temporary buildings were thrown up in a corner of the site. As one might expect, it was not the male students who were relegated to the garden sheds.

The war had little effect on Qatar; nothing, since the money started coming in, has had much effect on Qatar. True, the oil income dropped, but then there was the gas. Qatar's luck is perhaps to be found in its lack of delusions of grandeur. It remains something of a quiet backwater, but that is also a reason for much of its undoubted charm, for those who are willing to look beyond superficial appearances.

CHAPTER 7

Bahrain: Just Enough Oil to Lubricate the Brains

Bahrain in 1979 looked very much as though it would be the tinder box from which a revolutionary spark might set the whole Gulf on fire. Relatively populous and, within the Gulf context, relatively poor, it is the only country in the region with a significant indigenous proletariat that has some experience of collective action. It also has a Shi'a majority that has never, after two centuries, completely accepted being ruled by a Sunni dynasty. No spark caught fire, no revolution began, but Bahrain has had a few difficult moments to live through.

Until 1970, the Shah of Iran considered Bahrain, British protectorate or not, as part of his 'natural empire', based on the Shi'a majority and a few incursions over the centuries. The British managed to persuade Iran to renounce its claim formally on the eve of independence, but an empty desk marked 'Province of Bahrain' was kept standing in the *Majlis* in Tehran. After the Iranian revolution, the old pretensions were not formally renewed, but then such a step would in fact have been superfluous in the eyes of the Islamic Republic. Bahrain seemed to be the perfect proving ground for exporting the revolution. It would indeed, in Iranian eyes, have hardly counted as an export, just the extension of its scope of action to the nearest natural zone of application.

Since 1980 Bahrain has survived at least three coup attempts – all more or less inspired by Tehran. It has never had any particular political ambitions apart from survival. At the end of the Gulf War, it had accomplished this, and remarkably well, by the technique of keeping its head down as far as possible. The next problem will be how to retain its originality within the new political parameters of the Gulf.

Bahrain is different

The Bahrainis like to think of their country as the Singapore or Hong Kong of the Gulf, seasoned with a dash of Monaco. The Singapore analogy rests on the idea of a small island country – 676 square kilometres scattered over 33 islands of which only three are really inhabited – and even more so on the efforts made to turn Bahrain into the regional centre for financial and other services. Hong Kong evokes the idea of a small, dynamic country working beside a slower-moving giant. And Monaco suggests the pleasures of life – always, of course, seen in the perspective of the Gulf.

Bahrain was the first Gulf state to find and export oil and to benefit from the oil age. Its first commercial well came on stream in 1932 and the first laden tanker steamed out in December 1933. Bahrain is also the first of the Gulf states to be forced to contemplate life after oil. Its wells are almost exhausted and ever since the height of the boom, it has had to think hard about how it could best take advantage of its neighbours' oil. It has a few assets to be capitalized upon.

The first of these is its geographic location. What could be more natural than to make an archipelago in the middle of the Gulf into a communications centre? Another is its population. At the 1985 census, there were 417,000 inhabitants, of whom almost three-quarters are Bahrainis. Certainly an advantage in the long run, this relatively large native population complicates short-term adjustments, since it means that Bahrain cannot use the safety valve of sending surplus expatriate labour home in case of reduced demand. With the general slackening of business and the closing down of several off-shore banks,[1] Bahrain notched up another first: it is the first place in the Gulf where young citizens have experienced difficulties in finding a job to their liking.

The third asset was the educational level of its citizens. Even now that schools have sprung up in all the Gulf countries, Bahrain still has a higher percentage of educated people than any of its neighbours and, despite constant budget problems, of relatively good standard. The first public boys' school opened in 1919 and, more surprising, that for girls only ten years later. Even today, much of the real prestige enjoyed by Bahrainis in the Gulf is based on their reputation as educated people, a population of intellectuals. There is a real belief that the intellectual level of the population as a whole is enhanced – as it probably is – by three generations of reading and writing.

It matters little that today by any yardstick of dinars or riyals the Bahrainis are the poor relations of the Gulf: their reputation is secure, and will probably not be tarnished by the shiny new buildings of the universities dotted about the Gulf. Nevertheless, the Bahrainis see it as a bad omen that the Gulf University, in Bahrain itself, has had so many financial difficulties. The decision to establish it was taken before the founding of the Gulf Co-operation Council and the seven founding contributor states include Iraq. Unfortunately the collaborating countries, with the exception of Saudi Arabia and sometimes Kuwait, forget to pay their contributions.

Interestingly enough, even today schooling is not obligatory, so as to avoid arousing the hostility of the most conservative villagers. Some fathers reportedly still do not like the idea of their daughters going out and getting strange ideas put into their heads. Such families are few and diminishing, however; only a handful of young Bahrainis of either sex have not had at least a few years of primary schooling.

The fourth of Bahrain's assets, which is actually a function of the others, is the presence of an atmosphere of freedom, of liberty, which is difficult to pin down since it has as much to do with psychology as with facts. Talk to almost anyone elsewhere in the Gulf about Bahrain, and there will come a glimmer in the eye, sometimes a sigh and a remark on the lines of 'Ah, Bahrain – you are free there …'

In the Gulf context, liberty implies a whole range of attitudes and facts, without necessarily meaning at all the same thing as in the West. First of all, it means that alcohol is more or less freely available. People who have never lived in a country that practises prohibition find it hard to understand the place that alcohol can come to occupy in the imaginations of those who are deprived of it and who are by no means either drunkards or alcoholics. Drink becomes a fetish, an obsession; innumerable conversations seem to turn on nothing else. Non-Muslims are the first to be affected by the syndrome, but so are many Muslims; alcohol may be forbidden by the Koran but that does not mean that no Muslims partake of it, or, if they are deprived of it, would like to partake. Wherever prohibition is in force, a black market springs up, however severe the regulations; Saudi Arabia is no exception. Foreigners have more difficulty getting access to the black markets and they balk more at the exorbitant prices. They also sometimes risk higher penalties if they get caught. One way out is home manufacture of various beverages ranging from the just-drinkable (embassy wines in Kuwait are usually in that category) to the frankly horrible and sometimes dangerous products of bath-tub stills.

Not really used to drink, the citizens of Gulf countries who do get hold of hard liquor sometimes experience violent and uncontrollable reactions. A little scotch goes a long way on the road and being arrested for drunken driving is no joke. On the other hand, since alcohol does not exist officially, it is difficult to organize any accident prevention campaigns to warn against drinking and driving. There is little physical alcoholism in the Gulf, but there are many people with psychological reactions heightened by compounded feelings of guilt. Some of those who have gone through such a phase then swing to a militant Islamic practice close to that of the fundamentalists.

Little of all this holds in Bahrain. Alcoholic drink can be found in the international hotels, in some of the smarter restaurants and in clubs. Anyone who wants to drink is free to do so, without any questions being asked about religion or nationality. This is one of the pillars of Bahrain's reputation for liberty.

Another is the relative freedom of movement for women. Many women work outside the home, in offices, shops, hotels and there are no restrictions on working in jobs that involve normal contact with the world of men. Bahraini women often work out of necessity. Life is expensive in the islands and a single salary, particularly in government service, is very often not enough to make ends meet. Many more young and youngish families want to live on their own rather than in the extended family house, and Bahrain has offered fewer opportunities than neighbouring states to make a fortune as sponsor or agent for foreign companies.

The relative freedom of women is manifested in dozens of sometimes minute details. They can be seen out shopping in groups of two or three, and sometimes alone, an almost unimaginable sight in Doha or Abu Dhabi. They stop at juice stalls, chat, window shop, with or without an *abaya* (the black cape). Very few of them veil their faces. Bahraini women do not hesitate to enter a restaurant, at least one of the more expensive ones, and can be found on either side of a bank teller's window just as easily as working in the hospital or at the television news desk.

Everywhere in the Gulf, what extra-familial social life does exist revolves around the big hotels. What is special about the Bahraini establishments is the offer of cabaret and dance programmes that hardly differ from shows put on by the same troupes in Paris or London. The pretty Thais and Filipinas who serve in several of the hotel bars provide a touch of raffishness, even though their skirts go all the way down to their ankles and their demeanour is notably prim.

This mildly libertarian reputation, and the hotel infrastructure that is a legacy of the big boom, mean that Bahrain has become a regional tourist centre. Weekend visits – particularly of Saudi guests – are a welcome and quite substantial source of revenue. Nevertheless, the Bahraini authorities have to steer a careful course between two treacherous reefs. How to keep up the reputation of their islands for liberty without falling into the trap of appearing – and it matters little whether the accusation is true or false – to be a den of iniquity. The situation is tricky, inevitably coloured as it is by relations with the big neighbour, Saudi Arabia.

The freedom of which the Bahrainis are justly proud applies above all to individual, personal behaviour. The notion that the individual can be free to choose how he will behave, what his personal codes of behaviour are to be, that there can be choices beyond the imposed norms of society – all this is unique in the context of the Arabian peninsula – and well beyond. In Bahrain, individual freedom exists almost in direct proportion to the discretion with which it is exercised.

On the other hand, public and civic liberties hardly go further in Bahrain than elsewhere in the Gulf countries, and sometimes not as far. The press, radio and television are all more timid than in Kuwait (even after the 1986 clampdown), Dubai or Sharjah. Censorship is tight and the Ministry of Information does not hesitate long before expelling foreign journalists who are considered to have stepped out of line, whether they work for the local papers or an international agency.

Public liberties once made a brief appearance in the islands. A short experiment with a parliament elected in 1973 ended with its dissolution in 1975. The embryonic political parties were outlawed at the same time. Now no one even whispers the idea of their resurrection – apart from a few representatives of opposition groups in exile, far away.

Bahrain, more than any of the other Gulf countries, has attracted the attention of the international human rights associations. Their protests have expressed concern about the number of political prisoners, which are presumed to be of two kinds. The first category includes those implicated in alleged attempts to overthrow the government. One was planned to take place on the Bahraini national day, 16 December 1981, but was unmasked a few days before. Several dozen people arrested then were joined by several dozen more two years later when an arms cache was discovered in the Islamic Centre on the Buddaiyya Road. A third presumed coup attempt was snuffed out in December 1987; a small group of plotters who were said to have been trained and supported by Tehran were arrested before they could do any harm.

The second category consists of what might be called prisoners of conscience, arrested for their open sympathy with outlawed left-wing political movements – the Popular Front for the Liberation of Oman and the Arab Gulf, the Bahrain Popular Liberation Front and the left-wing parties or trade unions which had begun to flourish before the dissolution of parliament. Why is it that the human rights specialists, including Amnesty International or the authors of the annual report of the American Senate's Foreign Affairs Committee,[2] harp particularly on the situation in Bahrain, giving it a far worse human-rights reputation than its neighbours?

Any attempt to answer this question should take two factors into account. The first is that the islands are so small that it is practically impossible to keep anything hidden. Almost everyone knows almost everything, sometimes even more than the strict facts, and someone will always be ready to talk. Despite the existence of an efficient, British-advised secret police, the islands really do not live in a climate of terror. Moreover, most of the opposition groups have representatives abroad and they hesitate even less about talking; they know that they are unlikely to be assassinated for it. Secondly, and at least as important, Bahrain is in a way a victim of its own reputation. The word freedom has been applied to it so often, sometimes in widely divergent contexts, that the disappointment is all the greater in discovering that pleasant, open, relaxed Bahrain does not function exactly like a Western European parliamentary democracy.

The structure of society

The religious structure of Bahrain, marked by a high proportion of Shi'a, is unique in the Gulf. According to estimates (there is no reliable statistical evidence on this point and, in fact, the authorities would prefer to skip over it altogether) the Shi'a could be as much as 65–70 per cent of the native population. It is an unfortunate coincidence that the politico-social cleavage is approximately along the same lines as the religious one: rich and poor, the powerful and the weak, the government and leading businessmen and the proletariat and the Shi'a are consistently on the side of the less favoured.

When the ancestors of the present rulers, the Al-Khalifa family and their followers, arrived in Bahrain from the mainland in the eighteenth century, they found a fairly prosperous population of Shi'a farmers and artisans who owed their well-being to the reasonably abundant sources of fresh water on the islands. Many of the descendants of these original inhabitants still resent the power exercised by those whom they consider, to this day, as usurpers.

The resentment has been carefully nurtured, albeit with varying degrees of intensity, by successive Persian or Iranian rulers. The Shah finally renounced his claim, but the Islamic Republic has played an odd game of cat and mouse with the islands. In the spring and summer of 1979, several more or less violent demonstrations by the Bahraini Shi'a were sharply repressed and the situation remained fairly quiet until the mooted coup attempt of December 1981 when 81 people were arrested, most, but not all, of them Bahrainis. It was not difficult to assume that the operation had been planned by Hojatolislam Hadi al-Modarris, who had been put in charge of destabilizing the Gulf.[3] He had lived in Bahrain long enough to be considered almost a native; when another coup was aborted in 1987, his name was inevitably linked to it again. The plotters were planning this time to take over as many key points and positions as possible on 26 December, while the Emir was away at the GCC summit in Riyadh.

In 1984 an arms cache was found inside the Islamic Centre on the Buddaiyya road. The ironic twist to the story is that the centre had been presented to the Bahraini Shi'a by King Faisal of Saudi Arabia as a sort of consolation gift after they had lost the 'protection' offered by the Shah.

Manama, the capital, is a Sunni town surrounded by Shi'a villages, some of which became enclaves as the city spread. Further out, a few real villages subsist where the population still live from traditional agriculture – which is becoming more difficult each year as the water table falls. The villages have changed surprisingly little. Twenty minutes away from the tinted glass and polished marble of central Manama take you from one world and one era to another. The villages have all been electrified, but in some this seems to be the only change in two hundred years. The contrast is all the greater because they are often interspersed with new developments, frequently inhabited by foreigners. The whole stretch between Manama and Buddaiyya Bay is a huge chequerboard where two worlds co-exist side by side, without ever touching each other. Bahraini

Sunni friends whom I asked to take me to the villages were very hesitant and absolutely refused to stop in one, much less to get out of the car and walk around.

The Emir, Sheikh Issa bin Salman al-Khalifa, is, like many of his more influential subjects, fully conscious of the dangers that can underlie such a socio-religious situation, and has been trying to right the imbalance. Five cabinet ministers are Shi'a and a relatively high proportion of senior officials. But they are not to be found in so-called sensitive positions: the Ministry of Defence or the internal security departments.

In the hope of breaking down the barriers between the sects, the government pushed through two major housing projects designed to become inter-confessional new towns. One may not care much for the aesthetic qualities of Issa Town or Hamad Town (named after the Emir and the Crown Prince; in both cases the English name is commonly used, even by Arabic speakers). Sunni and Shi'a mosques stand practically side by side, families are intermingled, and yet it is more juxtaposition than melting pot; members of the two communities mix very little.

Although the Shi'a form a majority of the population, they are by no means a monolithic force and their very diversity has been a factor of stability, or, if one prefers, of survival of the *status quo*. Not all Shi'a are poor and powerless. There are rich merchant families among them and professional people, and members of the middle class.[4] They also come from diverse backgrounds: families of Persian origin are probably less numerous than the Biharna, whose ancestors at some fairly distant time came from the Indian subcontinent, or those who have simply been Bahraini for longer than anyone can trace.

The most characteristic institution of Bahraini Shi'ism is the *ma'atam*, the prayer room or recitation hall. The faithful gather in their *ma'atam* to listen to the tragic chants that retrace over and over again the life and death of the great Shi'a martyrs, Ali, Hassan and Hussein. For the conservative families in the villages, the *ma'atam* is the pivot around which their lives revolve: school, meeting place and social centre all at once. A high degree of fidelity attaches each family to a specific *ma'atam* for life and beyond. Marriages are decided within the community of the *ma'atam* and although there may be several within one village, there is almost no transfer between them. The fact that there are so many of them and that they all generate a fierce loyalty makes them as much a factor of fragmentation as of cohesion. There is no single charismatic preacher who attracts the loyalty of all, or even a majority, of Bahraini Shi'a, either in the islands or elsewhere.

Bahrain is the only place in the Gulf where the great Ashura processions are held on the tenth day of the Muslim month of Muharram. Even before the Islamic revolution in Iran, the Ashura commemorations of the death of the Shi'a martyrs often afforded an occasion for more or less violent demonstrations.[5] The processions wind their way through the centre of Manama, around the *suq* and outside it; each confraternity and professional group must have official permission to participate. The leaders know exactly how far they can go in their demonstrations of piety and ideology. In recent years the limit seems to have been reached with large posters, the boldest of which say 'The martyr Hussein is dead, but his ideas live on to menace the throne of the tyrant', with no further details.

It would require a large dose of suspicion indeed to imagine the amiable Sheikh Issa bin Salman al-Khalifa in the role of a tyrant. For the Al Khalifa the situation is clear. They are masters of the archipelago by the grace of God and they consider it one of their most important tasks to ensure that the different groups of their Shi'a subjects fight neither among themselves nor with their Sunni neighbours. In other words, they have been set where they are to keep the peace among all the people of Bahrain.

Is there a danger that the peace could be seriously shattered, as many people feared between 1979 and 1981? Is there a real danger of a breach in the confessional truce wide enough to threaten the stability of the country? As I have written in a number of articles, I think it would require intense external pressures to push the majority of the Bahraini Shi'a population to rebel, and all the indications are that such pressures have seriously diminished since 1981. If, perchance, the coup attempt of 1981 had succeeded, even partially, one can speculate that a good many passive bystanders would have joined in fairly quickly; in that case it is possible that the political landscape in the Gulf could have been modified. Since then, however, tension has fallen off considerably and Tehran, even before the end of the Gulf war, had largely renounced direct export of the revolution. During the early days of the Islamic revolution, the Bahraini Shi'a were great listeners to Tehran radio. It may have convinced a few, but many of them grew increasingly sceptical as they became more familiar with the situation across the water.

The causeway and beyond

In December 1986, when the causeway linking Bahrain to the Saudi mainland was opened, the world changed for the Bahrainis. Only 24 kilometres of shallow water separate the principal island from the mainland, but for many Bahrainis those 24 kilometres were not only a sign of insularity but also of independence. The causeway had been under discussion for more than a decade, which is a very long time in the Gulf. Although Saudi Arabia had promised to finance the whole enterprise, the Bahrainis dragged their feet as long as they could. For a long time they could hardly imagine what possible financial benefits could compensate for what they felt was an inevitable loss of part of their uniqueness, even if their independence was not at stake.

Since its opening to the public, the causeway has had mixed reviews. The most enthusiastic supporters, as is to be expected, are the hotel and restaurant owners; Saudi weekend tourism had taken up much of the slack of post-boom over-capacity. The Bahraini businessmen were less happy. The bridge made it easy for Bahrainis to nip across to Dammam for shopping sprees for everything from food to engine parts, all of which could be brought back duty-free, thanks to the GCC. The bigger Saudi market and Saudi subsidies meant that prices were on average 30 per cent lower than in Bahrain. Now that goods can arrive in Bahrain without the expense of trans-shipment – the fleet of little ships that scuttled across from the Saudi ports is one of the casualties of the causeway – the Bahraini merchants are finding it more difficult to justify their inflated prices; they have in many cases lowered them enough to discourage the trip across the causeway for minor purchases.

Ordinary Bahrainis, while happy to have their immediate horizons considerably broadened, are worried about other aspects linked to the causeway. Although official commentaries and announcements have been very discreet, it seems that the number of aggressive acts and brawls grew sharply after the end of 1986; before that, they were extremely rare. The Bahrainis also worried that there would be Saudi pressures to change their liberal social laws, related to alcohol, public entertainment and the like. In fact, the pressures have not come, or not strongly enough to change anything, but the Bahrainis still feel that they are being kept under surveillance. As long as the tension of the war lasted, they were relatively ready to exchange a modicum of freedom for a guarantee of protection in case of need. Thanks to the causeway, elements of the Saudi army can be in Manama within three hours. This was a comforting thought for the Bahrainis, and they drew even more comfort from the fact that no doubt the Iranians knew it, too.

The increased Bahraini-Saudi co-operation has not only been military. A few days before the opening of the causeway, the Bahrainis announced that they were not renewing their contracts for wheat purchases from Australia and would also not be building the projected new grain silos. Instead Bahrain would buy Saudi wheat at preferential prices, presumably the same subsidized prices as those quoted for the Saudi domestic market. Furthermore, the Saudi wheat would be stored in Dammam and brought across the causeway as needed, two or three days' consumption at a time. The new measures made economic sense and were a clear sign of the good functioning of the GCC agreements. Nevertheless, they were greeted in Bahrain with a certain sense of shock. Even before the first wave of cars with their 'S.A. private' number plates appeared, this was a sign that Bahrain was no longer quite an island. Even now, three years later, the Bahrainis are still getting used to the idea.

Bahrain has not had an easy time since 1980. Even though all the attempts at forcible destabilization were discovered in time, the islands are still looking for a new centre of gravity. The economic changes seriously undermined Bahraini self-confidence which had suffered little or not at all from the war.

For a time, the Bahrainis felt that all their good ideas were doomed to failure through no fault of their own. The international off-shore banks, the infant bourse, even Gulf Air, the pride of the four owner states but based in Bahrain, have all had problems.

And yet, since the winter of 1986–7, things have started, perhaps inexplicably, to look up again and optimism has once more become the mood of the times. In Bahrain, the most striking symbol of this was the dockyard, which finally had its first profitable year in 1986 – no doubt thanks to its privileged position as chief repairer for the rocket-damaged victims of the 'tanker war'. That, of course, will not last, but in Bahrain there is real hope that finally a new basis of equilibrium is being reached. The level is slightly lower than had been hoped for even after a slide from the heady heights of the oil boom; nevertheless, for the Bahrainis, it represents a tolerable plateau.

CHAPTER 8

United Arab Emirates: The Difficult Part is the 'United'

The great oil boom was heaven for adventure-story writers. Year after year, wonderful sleazy books with titles like *Bakshish* or *SAS à Abou Dhabi* or simply *Dubai*[1] rolled off the presses. A disproportionate number of them were set in the United Arab Emirates, shuttling, like the titles, between Abu Dhabi and Dubai. More than anywhere else in the Gulf, these two small city-states had insinuated themselves into the Western imagination almost to the point of caricature. Abu Dhabi was perceived as an oriental El Dorado and Dubai was shorthand for Klondyke in the Gulf. There was a grain of truth in the fantasy, enough to make the atmosphere exhilaratingly heady while it lasted. The great boom is now over, but the whiff of magic has not disappeared completely. On the spot no one likes to think that the adventure is over – and, indeed, perhaps it is not.

Yet it is probably in the Emirates that the post-boom adjustment has been most difficult to live with. This is particularly true for Abu Dhabi. Dubai was able to compensate partially: less of its revenue came directly from oil and it benefited enormously from the trans-shipment and direct trading with Iran in the latter years of the war with Iraq. The growing toll of damaged ships also made its dockyard, like that of Bahrain, suddenly profitable. Even the hotels benefited from the war, as Dubai became the favourite haunt of the journalists and military-naval personnel, especially Americans, who arrived with the fleet that began its operations in the spring of 1987. In 1990–1 the excitement was repeated, with the difference that this time the local population felt itself much more directly involved.

Even before the British withdrew from the Gulf, the new oil prosperity had begun to affect the outlook of people in what was not yet the UAE. That was in 1971, two years before the October war prompted the first sharp rise in crude oil prices and sparked off the great boom. A new and more adaptable Emir, Zayed, aided and abetted by the British protectors of the Emirate, had already replaced his brother Shakhbout as ruler of Abu Dhabi. Shakhbout trusted none of the new-fangled intrusions, not even the banks. He kept his considerable stock of banknotes (oil had been discovered on his lands in 1962) in an old trunk, where they were nibbled by mice.[2]

Many Arabs in the Gulf have vilified Oman's Sultan Qaboos because he deposed his father (see Chapter 9). No one ever blamed Zayed for having replaced his brother in similar circumstances and for analogous reasons; in Oman there was the additional urgency of the Dhofar war. But brotherly love is not the same thing as filial piety. Shakhbout lived out his life in the desert oasis of Al Ain[3], but Abu Dhabi today would be a very different place had the British not pushed for the change. Indeed, it is questionable whether, without Zayed, the UAE would ever have been born.

Abu Dhabi

In the early 1950s, when Wilfred Thesiger travelled from Buraimi to Abu Dhabi, it was an adventure.[4] In 1975, when for the first time I visited the oasis with its nine villages divided between the Emirate of Abu Dhabi and Oman, it was still something of an expedition. Nothing really dangerous, except for the murderous road where, during the day, sheer boredom at breakneck speed was the greatest peril. After dark stray camels made driving so treacherous that most conscientious drivers tried to get back by sunset. The only interesting thing to do along the way was to count the burnt and twisted wrecks along the wayside, presumably left there as a warning: once I reached eighty-seven before I gave up.

Things have changed. The awful road has, incredibly, been transformed into, literally, a parkway. Veritable orgies of hibiscus and oleanders line it on both sides, punctuated here and there by date palms, grown incredibly tall in a few years. The sight of so much greenery seems even to have had a soothing effect on the drivers, aided and abetted, no doubt, by the police. Drivers are far more reasonable and 320 kilometres of mesh fencing keep camels off the roadway.

The Al Ain road is in its way a metaphor for much of the change of the last fifteen years. Behind its thick screen of flowering greenery, the desert has all but disappeared from view. Along the whole road, there remains only one old-fashioned palm grove where dates are half-heartedly cultivated; the irrigation ditches are clogged and the ragged trees stand in odd contrast to the manicured hedges. Once upon a time, before oil money changed values, a palm grove was a rare source of food in this near sterile desert: a precious possession worthy of loving care. Now money can buy almost any sort of imported luxury at the nearest supermarket (the local generic name for even a smallish shop) and homegrown dates have lost their relevance.

The sidewalks of Abu Dhabi, like those of Al Ain, Sheikh Zayed's garden city, are shaded and perfumed by flowering shrubs. That statement may seem banal, but almost anywhere else in the Gulf even the idea of sidewalks is practically unknown. After the triumph of the motor car – normal in the Gulf petro-paradises – the great chic is learning to walk again. In Abu Dhabi, a stroll can be an experience of voluptuous joy, during six months of the year: from April to October a nice cool day is one when the temperature does not rise above 40 degrees Celsius.

It all seems terribly simple and normal. However, the picture changes slightly when one considers that the upkeep of each shrub on the parkway costs 500–700 dirhams a month.[5] Thanks to the oil money, Sheikh Zayed has been able to make the great dream of the desert Arab come true. He has created an earthly approximation of the vision of paradise as described in the Koran. Fountains play and birds sing in a city which has become an enormous garden.[6] What difference does it make that this approximation of the Garden of Allah costs a fortune? There can always be economies elsewhere, or later – if absolutely necessary.

The city, as it has become, of Abu Dhabi is both the capital of the eponymous emirate and of the Federation., i.e., of the whole of the United Arab Emirates. And not by accident. When the Federation was founded in 1971, Dubai was already a larger city (as it still is today) and it was closer to the geographical centre, even before Ras al-Khaimah joined a year later. The reasons why Abu Dhabi became the capital are to be found elsewhere, closer to the ambient mentality. Abu Dhabi was, and still is, by far the richest of the emirates. In 1971, its sheikh was also the prime mover, of all the rulers the most enthusiastic about the idea of a Federation. It was natural therefore that Sheikh Zayed should become president and so, in international terms, the head of state. The terminology should not be misunderstood. No wave of a magic wand has turned the traditional desert sheikh into a president in terms of Western political science. The real meaning of the presidency is closer to that of the *sheikh tamima*, the paramount sheikh, than to that of a Western republican head of state. Considering the symbolic importance of place[7] in Gulf society, the choice of Abu Dhabi for the honour of being the capital was inevitable.

Abu Dhabi is a sort of mini-Manhattan, where a grid of streets is lined with tall buildings that have little of Arabia about them. A well-intentioned traffic engineer had the unfortunate idea a few years ago of replacing the original roundabouts garnished with flowering shrubs by straightforward intersections embellished only by traffic lights. Too many of the high buildings were hastily built during the 1970s boom when speed was more important than aesthetics: the few really good buildings are thrown into high relief by so much sad mediocrity. Most amazing of all, 120 (at the last count) mosques are tucked in between the eighteen- or twenty-storey buildings. A careful look will show that whole floors of the buildings are empty.

Biggest and richest of the seven emirates, Abu Dhabi has had a proportionately difficult time in the search for a new post-oil equilibrium. Even though there is still an enormous amount of money coming in, the effects of the recession were felt like successive waves on the local economy and by ricochet on the political institutions of the whole Federation; it is Abu Dhabi – or its sheikh-president – that sustains the UAE.

By 1985, the post-boom period was well under way and the numerous sheikhs and sheikhas were instructed to take this fact into account when the palace issued orders to moderate personal expenditures. The following summer, London hotels and shops felt the effect of those orders directly. The general rule in Abu Dhabi had been that 25 per cent of the net oil income went directly to the ruling family in the form of grants graduated according to the closeness of kinship with the ruler. In the heady years 1980–82, this collective privy purse stood at over $7 million per day. After 1986, the family's share was reduced to 10 per cent, and in a falling market. Nevertheless, few of the ruling an-Nahayan family members risk dire poverty. Most will be able to compensate for the lost oil revenue through their investments abroad.

In contrast to Kuwaiti practice, Abu Dhabi's investments were not made in the name of the state or the community of citizens, but in the name of the ruling family. However, in Abu Dhabi the family – and especially the Emir – underwrite many expenses that almost anywhere else would fall on the state budget or be the responsibility of charitable institutions. Sheikh Zayed's gifts to his subjects have been legendary and his reputation for generosity inevitably attracted seekers of hand-outs from far beyond the borders of Arabia. Particularly if they were able to stick some sort of Islamic label on their proposition, they rarely went away empty-handed. The most spectacular example of this generosity is the reconstruction of the Ma'arib dam in North Yemen. The whole project, which cost approximately $90 million, was paid for by Sheikh Zayed out of his personal funds. The Ma'arib dam is mentioned in the Koran as one of the wonders of the ancient world, and tradition has it that the Emirati tribes, including the an-Nahayan, are descended from Yemenis who fled eastwards after the dam broke in the eighth century BC. The new dam is not an archaeologist's reconstruction but a piece of modern engineering; inaugurated at the end of 1986, it is designed to irrigate 6–10,000 hectares of arable land.

Not all the projects proposed for Sheikh Zayed's consideration were as ambitious as this one, nor as well thought out or useful.

One reason for the new policy of austerity, so goes the local talk, is to make it easier to pick and choose among the horde of mendicants. Still, the system of personal gifts lives on and the criteria for choice and decision remain the personal prerogative of the Emir or of a member of his immediate circle.

Another channel used to distribute some of the wealth was a complicated system that combined direct subsidies with agencies and sponsorships. Even on a fairly local level, the Emir of Abu Dhabi did not confine his generosity to his direct subjects, but spread gifts around to his neighbours, the rulers of the other emirates who, in turn, were supposed to pass it on to their own citizens. In return, he asked only that his primacy be recognized. Little enough, one might think – but not entirely without problems.

A large part of Sheikh Zayed's power no doubt lies in his fortune. But, that does not have quite the same connotation as it would in the West: in the Arabian peninsula one does not simply buy votes (or allegiance) as if running for office in a Latin American election. The relationship between a rich sheikh[8] at whatever level and his tribesmen is more like that which existed between a Roman patriarch and his clients than that of a mafia godfather and the local populace. Certainly, distributing gifts or subsidies will help ensure loyalty, but there is more to it than that. In a society where generosity is a prime virtue, it becomes normal to distribute gifts on a scale unheard of in Western cultures. It is the host who presents a gift to his guest more often than the other way round – could this be a reminiscence of the treatment accorded to a destitute traveller arriving at a desert camp? – and gifts are often obviously given with even more pleasure than they are received.

Real problems only appear when the traditional structure shows signs of cracking and when some sheikhs give the impression of being interested in acquiring wealth for themselves and forget the principles of equable distribution. Equable does not mean equal and the fact that the system was developed in a general situation of relative poverty influenced its rules. It is difficult to reconcile with great disparities between rich and poor and even more so with the values and aspirations of the educated elites.

Quite apart from his wealth and his generosity, Sheikh Zayed is himself a compelling, charismatic figure. Without his personal commitment to constructing a country out of the nebulous conglomerate of tiny principalities called the Trucial States, it is hard to imagine that any such thing as a United Arab Emirates could have been born. His idealism and enthusiasm had an electrifying effect on the younger subjects of his fellow rulers of Dubai, Ras al-Khaimah and especially Sharjah, who flocked to the capital to build the institutions of central government. Even though they all fled home every weekend, they are the people who turned Abu Dhabi into a capital. Their disappointment, commensurate with their earlier hopes, has been one of the factors leading to the Federation's difficulties today; the financial aspects are by far the simplest of them.

There is no historical centre in Abu Dhabi – almost nothing that can recall the past. If you look hard enough, you can find the ruins of a watch tower near the first bridge that linked the island on which the town is built to the mainland; the old fort has been carefully repainted, repaired, and restored to a pristine glory it probably never knew during its time of active service. But that is all. With not even the kernel of an ancient city such as there was in Dubai or Muscat or Bahrain, there was no reason to think about keeping to scale or respecting ancient monuments. Abu Dhabi is hardly less of a new city than Jubail, the huge Saudi industrial complex further up the coast.

By the end of 1986, it was estimated that 18,000 flats stood empty in a city of about 130,000 inhabitants. Not surprisingly, the result was a veritable epidemic of house-moving, with owners trying to attract tenants just as assiduously as prospective tenants had tried to woo the owners a decade before. Prices dropped dramatically and all sorts of perks were suddenly offered – three months' free rent or special installations. The small Swiss embassy can be taken as an example. In 1986, it moved from a 200 sq metre flat, where the annual rent had already dropped from 95,000 to 50,000 dirhams. The new premises, twice the size, big enough to combine office and residence, cost 85,000 dirhams, including (as the former one did not) central air conditioning.

Beginning in 1985, the word went out in Abu Dhabi that

economy was to be the new fashion, but it has been difficult to react coherently to what was certainly an excellent and necessary turn-about. No more 'give me a dozen of each and I'll decide later which one I really like'. The federal ministries felt the pinch first. By 1987, all of them – apart from defence and internal security – had been given orders to reduce spending by 50 per cent across the board.

The Emirates' major problem is one of population: there are not enough native citizens, and especially not enough qualified native citizens, to assure the functioning of the institutions of a modern state, private or public. All the Gulf states (with the possible exception of Bahrain and Oman) suffer from the same problem, but nowhere is it felt as acutely as in the Emirates, and especially in Abu Dhabi. Even Qatar, where according to the statistics the situation should be not much different, seems to have managed better.

Dubai has no more complexes about this problem than about most others. The city is quite unabashed about being almost as much Indian or Iranian as it is Arab, and simply does not worry much about the fact. Abu Dhabi is different. At the beginning of the oil age and even at the time of the establishment of the Federation the native population was tiny, and mostly bedouin. It has grown thanks to better health care and living conditions and the bedouin have mostly settled in housing estates where the reminders of their past life hardly go beyond a few goats in the garden and an occasional camel peering over a courtyard wall. Despite their almost complete lack of formal schooling, members of the first sedentarized generation managed to take excellent advantage of the provisions made to give them a stake in the new prosperity. Every citizen could become a businessman assured of at least reasonable prosperity without prior experience or much risk. The key was in the system of sponsors, the indispensable local partners for any business or service in the newly booming country.

A typical contract gives the sponsor, who usually carries the nominal title of president, 50 per cent of the profits of an enterprise plus a fixed annual fee for the use of his name and his good offices. In a boom economy, where everything from underwater tunnels to the latest hairdressing salon had to be built from scratch, it would have been impossible for the local citizens to accomplish the task alone. Besides the financial advantages, the sponsorship system, at its best, also provided on-the-job training in management skills. The fruits of this were rarely seen in the first generation, but in the next one sees sons taking an active part in the business and not only using the president's office as the modern *majlis* or reception room.

Native citizens of the Emirates are still few, probably not more than 250,000 in all, in a population estimated in 1987 at 1.2 million, despite a remarkably high fertility rate and a life expectancy that has grown rapidly. For years, there were misgivings, often with reason, about the quality of the work these few citizens in the labour force produced. To be frank, very few had been trained to work hard; moving directly from the desert to a manager's chair had been too easy.

The end of the boom brought the beginning of a change in the local workforce. No young Emirati has difficulties in finding a job, but by an effect almost of osmosis, younger people have begun to acquire a real work ethic, a taste for work properly done coloured by a mix of patriotism and a slight worry about the future – all of them completely new notions. Managers have noticed that they can now hire young Emirati citizens and ask them to work in what would anywhere else seem normal conditions: to arrive at the office approximately at a fixed time and remain there until the end of working hours. Even in the early post-boom years, if an Emirati citizen was ready to accept a job, for example in a bank, which was rare – working for the government was more prestigious and the salary was practically immaterial – it was mainly to have a nice card and an office in which to drink coffee with friends between errands in town.

Members of the ruling families obviously remain privileged, and they still get the cushiest jobs with ease. And yet, even there, things are changing. The odd phenomenon is that, while elder sons often remain spoiled darlings (the term playboy is in current use, prefaced or not by decadent), the second, third or sixth sons can often be found really working, using their expensive educations to good effect. One example is that of young Sheikh Musallim al-Maktoum of the Dubai ruling family: influence would not have been sufficient to get him his job as a fighter pilot and he has conscientiously gone through all the training followed by his fellow-pilots and a bit more.

Many of the young Emiratis who have come back from studying abroad learned to make choices, sometimes difficult ones, while they were away. When they returned, they discovered that there was little available in the way of leisure activity, except for the traditional long conversations or the newer tradition of video films. The surprisingly numerous group who are satisfied with neither often take refuge in their work. Interestingly, many are also relatively more serious about practising their Islamic beliefs than their immediate elders. It would be easy to say that they have been influenced by the fundamentalists who work among Arab students in many foreign universities. This may be a part of the explanation, but it does not go far enough. Some ex-students explain that, while they were living in societies where Islam is not a simple fact of life, they were forced to think through their real relationship with it. Islam runs deep in the Emirates and, although a few may have reacted by questioning their faith, in most cases the reverse is true. And yet, as has generally been the case in the Gulf, relatively few have adopted the 'fundamentalist' idea of rejecting the established order of state and of society.

At the time of the great oil bonanza, Abu Dhabi became an enormously varied human mosaic, whose multiple pieces were arranged in a complex hierarchy. At the top there are the sheikhs, then the other native citizens, Arabs first, those of Persian origin next, followed by the Arab immigrants of whom there are about 300,000 divided into several sub-groups. The Iraqis, many of them anti-Ba'athist professionals, vied for first place with the Palestinians. Between 1975 and 1980, there were so many Palestinians holding influential positions in the government and in everything to do with communications that talk about Abu Dhabi as the first Palestinian state was barely a joke.

In absolute numbers, more Palestinians lived in Kuwait, but in proportion to the native population they were far more numerous and certainly more influential in Abu Dhabi, where the structure of both the government and the local society was less firmly established. Yet, oddly, the Palestinians of Abu

Dhabi were never as active politically as those of Kuwait. That Yasser Arafat was head of a construction company in Kuwait before becoming chairman of the Palestine Liberation Organization is only one example. Geography probably also played a part. Abu Dhabi is 1,000 kilometres further from the banks of the Jordan than Kuwait and the general political climate in the Emirates has certainly been less open, especially before 1986.

After the Iraqis and the Palestinians come the Egyptians, more numerous than either but, despite some individual exceptions, a few rungs down the ladder of prestige. As everywhere in the Gulf, the Egyptians form the backbone of the school system, but – an Abu Dhabi speciality – they also provide most of the judges and mosque preachers.[9] Many of them are frankly fundamentalist in their teaching. They have enormous prestige among their own countrymen but their positions have helped spread their influence over the whole emirate – a tendency which worries many people in Abu Dhabi. Oddly, it is practically non-existent in Dubai. The discrepancies in the views propounded by the very traditional judges in Abu Dhabi and their more liberal colleagues in Dubai were vividly illustrated in the long discussions that preceded the adoption of a new code of company law – and particularly in the judgements applied to bankruptcies. In principle, a single code of law applies to all the Emirates, but in Abu Dhabi judges ruled that debtors did not have to pay arrears when interest was involved, because charging interest is contrary to Islamic teaching, while in Dubai other judges ordered the debtors to pay up, on the grounds that they knew what they were doing when they contracted the debt.

The other Arabs in Abu Dhabi include Algerians working in the oil companies, Sudanese, Tunisians, Jordanians, Lebanese and Yemenis, but none of these play an important social or political role as a group. Nor do the 45,000 or so Europeans, most of whom work in private businesses or in the national oil companies. Very few are directly involved with the government, even as advisers; the typical adviser is an Iraqi royalist.

Going on down the social scale, there are the Asians – in 1987, 400,000 Indians, 225,000 Pakistanis, 25,000 Sri Lankans and 75,000 Bangladeshis, Filipinos and Thais. With local variations, the same picture applies elsewhere in the Gulf. But Abu Dhabi seems to have had particular difficulties in accepting these immigrants, not to mention integrating them. In theory the Pakistanis, the biggest group in Abu Dhabi, should, as fellow Muslims and near neighbours, be easier to assimilate than others. In practice this is not so; they are far less easy to assimilate than, say, the large numbers of Indians in Dubai. Is this one more sign of the extreme vulnerability of the citizens of Abu Dhabi, who feel particularly threatened in their fragile sense of nationhood?

Some foreigners, mostly Iraqis and Yemenis plus a handful of Palestinians, have been given Emirati nationality. The policy has made for a larger percentage of citizens on paper, and has given more inhabitants an active stake in the country. Still, within a very small society where genealogy in its primary meaning of 'the science of family knowledge' remains highly prized, more than one generation will be required for the new citizens to progress beyond the undisputed legal and financial advantages to full acceptance.

From 1982 on, the numbers of foreign workers in the Emirates began to diminish; given the system of limited contracts, it was easy to send them home as work grew scarcer. By 1986, the movement was accelerating steadily, if not always very coherently. The Abu Dhabi National Oil Company suddenly announced that it was scrapping 500 jobs ranging from rig workers to management personnel. The biggest shock was that the whole research department was being scrapped.

The end of that year brought an odd reversal in official UAE policy. The reductions in foreign labour continued, but at the same time there came the announcement that a new ruling was to make it much easier for those who remained to bring their families to the Emirates, including workers whose monthly salary was less than 3,000 dirhams. The official reason was that the measure would stimulate internal consumer demand; this was probably true, although no reliable figures have been published about the result. Strangely, however, this new measure includes a real risk of slums developing, unless the families of low-income immigrant workers are given at least a modicum of the substantial benefits previously reserved for citizens. As the ruling comes to be applied, it could change the whole demographic profile of the Emirates. Still odder, a similar ruling was announced a year later in Saudi Arabia.

Though on a different scale, Abu Dhabi suffers from many of the problems of other purpose-built capitals – Chandigarh, Brasilia or even, until not long ago, Washington DC. It has always been unloved, except by a few devotees, and deserted as often and as quickly as possible by civil servants whose homes and hearts were elsewhere. At first the exodus was weekly: every Thursday at noon streams of cars would go up the coast to Dubai or Sharjah, or at least to Al Ain, leaving the city almost entirely to its foreign residents. Then, as the federal ministries were given the order to cut expenses, more and more of the able young men found work in their home emirates. A visit now to one of the Federal ministries is an excursion into surrealism: one walks through the long corridors without seeing a soul, not even a tea-boy. It becomes something of a miracle to find the person one is supposed to be meeting in the midst of these empty offices. Particularly in the purpose-built ministries of the government quarter, one has the odd feeling that life has drained away almost before it began; the buildings are like so many oversized *dishdashas* whose owners have wizened and shrunk.

Plants and shrubs are said to change the climate, to anchor the shifting sands, fix the dunes and combat erosion. As one looks at Abu Dhabi and its thousands of flowering shrubs one cannot help wondering whether they, the visible signs of Sheikh Zayed's dream, will succeed in overpowering the demons of desolation. The dream of a garden nigh unto Paradise also holds true for the creatures who live there: will the dream be able to survive without the dreamer? More than any other place in the Gulf, Abu Dhabi reminds me of what one man who was busily building these new El Dorados told me on my very first visit in 1975. 'Look around you,' he said, 'and imagine what all of that was like fifteen years ago, because in fifteen years it will be like that again – with disillusions to boot.' 1990 brought trouble to Abu Dhabi, in the form of the Gulf crisis, but not the desolation that was predicted. In fact, although the emirate prepared for the war, it felt relatively few direct effects. Too far from the centre of action, it was just barely a rear base.

Abu Dhabi had another trial during that period. In the international banking world and beyond it became known as the BCCI scandal. BCCI, the Bank of Commerce and Credit International, had been founded by Pakistani bankers in 1970. With the help of Saudi and Abu Dhabi backers its assets had mushroomed from US$200m in 1973 to become, by 1990, the fifth largest privately-owned bank in the world with, supposedly, US$20 bn (million million) in assets. It played on both its canniness and a third-world image to lure over a million small depositors and some very big ones. In October 1988 the BCCI scandal broke, first in America, when the bank was charged with laundering US$14 m of drug money, but it was more than a year later that the news reached the general public. Slowly details emerged about drug money laundered elsewhere in the world (including the account of Manuel Noriega, the Panamanian leader forcibly deposed by the United States in early 1990), repeated trouble with bank regulators and exchange controls in Europe (by then the bank was incorporated in Luxembourg) and in third-world countries. Still the depositors – including many Pakistani and Indian immigrants in the UAE and in Britain – came, unsuspectingly, to this bank that smacked a little bit of home.

By the time the whole story, or most of it, came out, it also emerged that Sheikh Zayed of Abu Dhabi was the principal backer of the bank that, according to one of the liquidators, 'lost, stole, gave away or hid an astounding US$15 bn or more. Some of that money may have been sheer invention.' The Bin Mahfouz family, the main Saudi share-holders, had unloaded their part of the capital just before the scandal broke. Sheikh Zayed was, according to reliable accounts, horrified, less by the sheer dimensions of the swindle than by the moral aspects. His first reaction was anger, anger at those who had hoodwinked him and anger at the very bad name the scandal was giving his emirate. Bankers were briefly jailed, employees expelled. But as it became clearer that the situation went well beyond the local scene, Sheikh Zayed apparently was persuaded that it was his moral duty – the legal situation was not quite as clear – to make good what he could. At the end of 1991, when proceedings for the complete liquidation of BCCI were well advanced, Sheikh

Zayed announced that he was willing to contribute up to US$4 bn to a compensation fund for 1.2 million smaller depositors.

Like the Suq al-Manakh crash in Kuwait, the BCCI scandal was a watershed in Abu Dhabi. For many people, it was just as strongly felt as the Gulf War. Still, the fact that much of the BCCI drama unfolded in the eventful years 1990–1 may have taken out some of the sting. Billions disappeared, but if the worst nightmares of the Gulf had come to pass, if Saddam Hussein had been able to achieve his dream of hegemony, those losses – which were absorbed by the munificent sheikh – would have seemed puny in comparison.

Dubai

Arriving in Dubai, 160 kilometres north from Abu Dhabi, the very air one breathes is different. Not that the temperature is any lower in summer nor the humidity a degree less. There is, however, a slightly raffish feeling, an undercurrent of the excitement of life. Dubai is turned outwards to the sea and to the rest of the world, as open to the driftings of varied humanity as its wind towers – very few, alas, remain after zealous modernization – were open to catch every cooling breeze.

Dubai could be a model of how individuals can influence the collective personality in these Gulf societies, where the tribal structure remains primordial and numbers are still very small. As far as we know, Dubai began its career as a port on its deep inlet, the Creek, in the eighteenth century as a dependency of the Bani Yas of Abu Dhabi. The formal secession came only in the middle of the last century, when Maktoum bin Buti led a band of rebels to settle permanently on the shores of such a promising place.[10]

Those who were eventually to become the Al Maktoum ruling family had a hard time carving out a small place for themselves between the Bani Yas, whose hostility towards their breakaway ex-followers was understandable, and the Qawasim of Sharjah and Ras al-Khaimah, who were bitterly opposed to the British. *Mutatis mutandis*, the relationship was something like that of the Americans with Iran after 1979. The Qawasim, in the eyes of the British, were pirates, a regional menace to be portrayed in the most unfavourable light possible; in place of 'pirates', read 'terrorists' and in both cases there is more than a grain of truth wrapped up in a good deal of purposeful propaganda. Faced with such a situation, the first Maktoum, like his successors, naturally became the friend of the British; he soon consolidated this friendship by encouraging Indian merchants to build their godowns on the Creek and to open shops in the *suq*. Then he extended an invitation to Persians from Lingeh or Khamir or Bastak who wanted to escape the centralizing influences of the interior. History was to be repeated when a second, far more important, wave of Persian migrants arrived in the 1920s; this time the merchants were unhappy with the growing power of the newly constituted Pahlavi empire. Most of these Persian immigrants were merchants or pearlers and most were not Shi'a but Sunni Muslims like the tribesmen on what was then still called the Trucial Coast.[11]

All these immigrant merchants remained in contact with their homelands and they became the nucleus of Dubai's vocation as a regional trading centre. The Persian merchants understood the complex regulations imposed by the centralizing Persian Empire well enough to learn how to circumvent them, and they then generously taught all the subtleties involved to their Indian and Arab colleagues. For over a century the Dubai sheikhs have consistently applied an extremely liberal economic policy. With too small a local population to provide a lucrative trading base, the most profitable business has always been in what is modestly called the re-export trade; only foreigners talk about smuggling. Three-quarters of the Emirates' imports go through Dubai and according to the Chamber of Commerce, 60–65 per cent of them are re-exported; and that figure is probably an understatement.

If a business is legal in Dubai, nobody asks what the trading partner's government thinks about it. In the 1960s India imposed strict restrictions on gold imports and demand far outstripped supply: how could marriageable girls be guaranteed a decent dowry without gold? Fortunately the Dubai merchants found a way of getting round the problem with the help of the dhow fleet in the Arabian Sea. Today the gold trade to India, and some others that the merchants are less willing to talk about, are mere shadows of what they were formerly. If you listen to the Dubai merchants, a sad air of conformity has infested most of their trade; it may all be more legal but a good dash of the adventure has gone. The biggest clients now are Iran and Saudi Arabia. Few traces remain of the time when the Saudi ports could not meet the demand for unloading berths, but rising insurance rates and straightforward fear of attack pushed many shippers into preferring to off-load in Dubai, with road transport from there. Some clever merchants, knowing that sooner or later the war-induced trans-shipment business would slacken, managed to turn themselves into regional magnates. One, the general agent for Sony electronics, sells more of his company's products than any other distributor in the world. His territory includes Afghanistan which turned out to be a veritable gold mine for television receiver sales; as the Soviet soldiers began to pack up and go home, literally thousands of them bought television sets and all of them wanted Sonys. Oddly enough, their departure has done little to slacken the demand in Kabul.

Up to 1975, as a few brave people are willing to acknowledge years after the event, Dubai often served as a transit point for drugs going from South-East Asia or Iran to the West. Iran has cracked down hard on drugs and so has Dubai. More typical these days are the arrests of couriers carrying heroin and morphine-base at Dubai airport. Recent cases all involved Nigerians in transit from Karachi to Lagos. Although they were arrested in Dubai, the emirate itself no longer seems to play an active role in the drug circuits.

Business with Iran flourished throughout the war, and by 1987 Iran had replaced Saudi Arabia as Dubai's first trading partner: that year an estimated one-third of all Iranian imports passed through Dubai. Once off-loaded from the big cargoes, the trip across the Gulf was made in hundreds of traditional wooden *boums*, which are now motorized. Every day they jostle for position on the quays, displaying little hand-written signs with the name of the *nakuda* – the captain – and the port of destination. Shipping agents simply stroll down and choose. In the case of some of the goods bound for Iran, passing through Dubai was a way of escaping an embargo, although the Dubai merchants swear that their port was not an important arms supplier. What it did was to supply the deprived Iranians with consumer goods; the quays were full of boxes containing refrigerators and television sets, cookers and small kitchen gadgets – none of which were considered essential imports into wartime Iran. This fact interested no one in Dubai. What the Dubai merchants wanted to know was what was coming in: besides the legal exports of fruit and vegetables, there were rugs and sometimes caviar, most if not all of which had left Iran without the benefit of official customs stamps.

Whether or not it is justified, the spirit of Dubai remains one of optimism and sparkling imagination. Dubai was not entirely spared the economic downturn after1982, but while the people in Abu Dhabi were cursing their bad luck, in Dubai new ideas crackled like fireworks. Some of them even seemed a little mad, like the idea of building a huge complex pompously named the 'World Trade Centre' while office space stood empty all over the Gulf. Yet the tower, which sticks up like a light-house in the flat Dubai desert, manages to attract tenants even as other buildings are losing theirs. Fairs, exhibitions, special events follow one another in rapid succession, including some surprising ones like the 1986 'Chess Olympics'. With massive support from advertising and publicity agencies, its promoters manage to keep the Centre afloat, month after month.

Other audacious ideas can be found in Dubai. One was for a Japanese car assembly plant. It looked like the plan of a madman in a country almost entirely devoid of native manpower,[12] but its supporters mustered several sane arguments in its favour. They are worth looking at, if only to understand Dubai a little better. First, in an age of automatic factories, why could not the Japanese manufacturer set up a robot-run plant employing a minimum number of workers but with a fairly high energy input close to a source of cheap energy and a relatively important market? The project as calculated included the whole Arabian peninsula plus Iran and Iraq in the potential market area – a total population of almost 100 million. On the other hand, even thinking about such a project indicates that Dubai has progressed beyond the too-many-foreigners complex. It was Dubai that first pushed for a new set of regulations to allow lower-income immigrant workers to bring in their families, and it is Dubai – not the Federation – that has enacted it into law. For a long time, the chief official argument against bringing in workers' families was the chronic housing shortage. In fact, this masked a more important one, the desire to sustain what was euphemistically called equilibrium among the ethnic communities – in other words not letting the natives and/or the Arabs be completely swamped by non-Arab immigrants. Although the new rules were presented simply as a response to the sharp drop in internal consumption which had even hit Dubai by the middle of 1986, they are a major change in local policy, an updated version of the first Maktoum's encouragement to Indians and Persians to come to live by the Creek.

Despite appearances, the Emirati Arabs are not entirely at ease with being a minority in their own country, and not even, if the truth be told, in Dubai. Wandering in the streets or meandering in the old *suq* of Bar Dubai, one feels much closer to Bombay than Damascus, as indeed one is. The disequilibrium is usually not an open preoccupation: only when the power of non-citizens cuts too close to the bone of the most important of all Dubai realities, business, trade and money, does reaction set in. Dubai has seen several financial scandals in recent years; large as they were, they would probably have passed almost unnoticed during the halcyon 1970s. Even now, the Dabawanis do not like to talk about the crash of the Agra Group in 1984; two Indian financiers, brothers, left the country in a hurry, leaving debts of 300 million dirhams behind them.

Even this was paltry in comparison with the story of Abdul Wahab Galadari, banker, trader, the very prototype of the Dubai financier, who built the Hyatt Regency hotel and its attached Galleria complex. The bold architectural concept was not enough; by 1987 the only really lively spot in this frank temple of consumerism was the central indoor skating rink, much favoured by children and their nannies gossiping around the edges. When Abdul Wahab Galadari left for Europe, his debts were reckoned to amount to 1,000 million dirhams. But the real scandal was to whom the money was owed: much of it had been borrowed from banks in which, at the time, he himself held controlling interests. Banks are not legally permitted to lend more than 5 per cent of their declared capital to members of their own board; some of Galadari's loans are said to have been close to 300 per cent of the bank's paid up capital. An ad hoc committee set up by the Emirates' Central Bank froze assets whose face value was almost equal to the total amount of the debt – if buyers could be found for them, which was unlikely in the economic climate of the mid-1980s. With consummate bad luck, Galadari also found himself facing an American indictment on a drugs charge. The American charge was eventually revoked and he was able to recover his $10 million bail money, which was no doubt useful as he sat out his exile in Britain.

This tale would not be complete without one more detail. In Dubai there is not too much pointing of fingers at Galadari for his financial exploits on the fringes of legality; there, but for the grace of God, would go many others. Why then did the case become a *cause célèbre*, with the arm of justice swinging harder than it had ever done before? Inevitably, in the light of the subsequent American involvement, the thesis of a CIA conspiracy came up. But it can probably be rejected. It has been trotted out too often in the Middle East with myriad variations; in this case there were no serious indications that it applied, at least to actions taken before the drugs indictment which proved an embarrassing mistake, nor would there seem to have been any motivation. However, another element was involved – a latent 'racism' that hardly dares to speak its name. The Galadaris are the descendants of one of the Persian families which settled in Dubai in the 1920s. Everyone considered them perfectly assimilated and some family members had held high office in the emirate. However, when one Galadari unfortunately embroiled himself in a slightly murky affair, the opportunity was there to be exploited by a few jealous rivals who tried to make the whole clan, and, by insinuation, other 'Persians' totter on their pedestal. The manoeuvre, if it was one – and there are no more than rumours to support the thesis – was only partially successful. Other members of the Galadari family continue to play their usual role in the Dubai melting-pot without any visible problems.

Another good example of Dubai's spirit is the story of the

founding of Emirates Air, in direct competition to Gulf Air. Gulf Air is the joint national carrier and common property of Bahrain (where the operational centre is concentrated), Oman, Qatar and Abu Dhabi – not, as is commonly thought, of the UAE. On the other hand, Dubai is extremely proud of its airport, which, with over 200 landings and take-offs per day, is one of the busiest in the Middle East. When Dubai asked Abu Dhabi to 'nationalize' the company – i.e. turn its stake into that of the UAE – Abu Dhabi refused. To add insult to injury, Gulf Air then decided to reduce the number of its flights to and from Dubai while stubbornly rejecting any tariff concessions; until the end of the boom no one really examined prices in the Gulf and as a result the air fares were among the highest in the world. The Dubai Government thought all this a good enough reason to form its own airline, Emirates Air. Gulf Air first reacted to this rather as a gazelle reacts to a mosquito, but in Dubai it was no joke. Playing its cards carefully, Emirates began by securing traffic rights to destinations like Karachi and Amman, sure-fire winners even in a tighter market, and selling cut-price tickets, mostly to a market of migrant workers. After two years of activity Emirates had managed to go well beyond this limited service. In Dubai, the promoters are now loftily saying that if Abu Dhabi changes its mind and wants to share its part in Gulf Air, they would be ready to consider sharing a stake in their own 'national carrier'.

The rivalry between different emirates of the UAE in the domain of aviation goes further. The Federation includes not two, but six international airports. Besides Abu Dhabi and Dubai, Ras al-Khaimah and Sharjah (a small jewel for connoisseurs) are in regular, if unequal, service. Add to that Al Ain and Fujairah on the Indian Ocean coast and the UAE probably holds the world record for airport density.

Sharjah

Even though Abu Dhabi and Dubai together account for 70 per cent of the population, 80 per cent of the surface and an even larger percentage of the revenue, there are still five other states in the Federation. Financial analysts do not talk much about

Sharjah, Ajman, Umm al Qawain, Ras al-Khaimah and Fujairah. The five are often lumped together as 'the northern emirates' which sometimes – especially when the term is used in Abu Dhabi – can include Dubai. There can be few places on earth where so many complications of human and territorial geography are brought together in a limited space; even the imbrications of the Swiss cantons are simple in comparison. Oddly enough, the British cartographers and diplomats who put their stamp of approval on this impossible set of convoluted borders before they left the Trucial States were proud of it; at least that was the opinion of one member of the commission whom I met fifteen years after the event. As with most such aberrations, it was to prove far more difficult to correct afterwards than making sense of enclaves and salients at the time.

Of these five small states, Sharjah is the only one with any pretensions to political and economic autonomy, thanks to the discovery of important gas reserves and, probably even more, to the personality of its ruler, Sheikh Sultan Muhammad al-Qasimi.[13] Sheikh Sultan is the only one of the seven rulers of the Emirates who has had a modern education. He graduated from the University of Cairo as an agricultural engineer and then, much later, after he had become ruler of his little state, returned to his studies in Britain and became a passionate student of regional history. In 1986 he published the first volume of what he hopes will be a six-volume history of the Qasimi family: *The Myth of Arab Piracy in the Gulf*.[14] He devotes a considerable part of his fortune (which is tiny, admittedly, compared to that of Zayed, but not completely non-existent) to his library, where he likes to spend several early-morning hours before getting down to the job of governing his emirate.

Inevitably, Sultan is considered a maverick in the region. This has not kept him from trying, within the confines of his small state and modest means, to realize a workable synthesis of tradition and the realities of the modern world. Just as inevitably, he has enemies, both inside and outside his emirate. In the summer of 1987, while he was on one of his library-foraging journeys abroad, a small palace revolution broke out, and his brother Mohammed proclaimed himself the new Emir. Mohammed is considered closer to the usual style of the local traditional leader and perhaps also to the ruling princes of Abu Dhabi. After a few feverish days, everything returned to normal, with a new family agreement that gave Mohammed a slightly bigger say in government affairs. The outside world would probably never have been aware of this storm in a *stikkan* (the small glass in which tea is normally served) if it had not happened at a time when the Gulf was very much in the limelight. Some analysts even managed to find a relationship between the palace coup and Sultan's supposed links with the Iranian revolutionaries, largely predicated on the fact that the Emir has always encouraged trade from his harbours, including trade with Iran; the cross-Gulf car ferry link from Bandar Abbas lands in Sharjah and continued to do so during the war. That is hardly, in this world of pragmatic traders, proof of any particular affinity.

But then Sharjah has been rather special for several generations. In the 1930s, the sheikh of the time, Sultan bin Saqr, heard that Imperial Airways was looking for a landing field somewhere in the region and offered space. He was no doubt particularly interested in the 600 rupees of monthly rent, plus a personal grant of another 500 rupees.[15] Still, the very fact of being ready to accept such a durable foreign presence was remarkable. At the time, the other sheikhs of the Trucial Coast showed one of two reactions: either a blind xenophobia that brooked not the slightest discussion or, if they themselves were slightly more amenable, a marked fear of their own fiercely conservative tribesmen, some of whom were still subject to a good deal of Wahhabi influence. The sheikh's acceptance was all the more astonishing in that it defied more than a century of traditional Qasimi hostility towards all things British.

Sharjah's public schools have been taking in girls and boys for a quarter of a century and a direct consequence of this was an over-representation of Sharjans in the upper echelons of the Federation's administration. Was, because the wave crested rather quickly and a surprising number of disillusioned Sharjans returned to their home emirate, surprising, because Sharjah has not known a particularly brilliant economic situation, even before the big oil price drops of the mid-1980s. The Emirates' school system is largely decentralized and the Sharjah schools give an admirable image of the particular spirit of the place. The girls' secondary school looks very much like most of the schools in the Gulf: a large square central courtyard with classrooms giving onto wide covered galleries all round. But once inside the school, everything is changed. In the Common Room, there is an almost palpable sense of joy in living and learning and a real intellectual curiosity, not an over-plentiful commodity in the schools of the Gulf. The headmistress happens to be a member of the ruling family but she is in no way a dilettante. She has managed to communicate her enthusiasm to her pupils and remarkably well to her teachers. This is also the only school that I have ever seen in the Gulf – and I have visited dozens – where the omnipresent Egyptian teachers were absolutely radiating happiness in knowledge and joy in teaching. Furthermore, and this is also rare, they were all well groomed and carefully dressed. The contrast with so many other schools was too striking to be pure chance.

And what about the idea of a little emirate where the social event of the season is a book fair, held in a big tent and full of visitors from morning to night, both young people and those not so young? What about the local amateur dramatics group (another rare institution in the Gulf) which gives benefit performances for the school for handicapped children, whose hard-working director is another young sheikha who obtained her diploma in special education in California. Sharjah is also home to the Emirates' most independent paper; the astonishing *Al Khaleej* often sends the Abu Dhabi censors into a rage, but, federalism being what it is, they can do nothing about it.

Sharjah is not without its own problems and incoherences, beginning with the rather mad scale of urban building projects during the boom. 'Think big' seems to have been the motto behind the multi-layered motorways and not one but two huge new covered *suqs* that look like a Western architects' vision of Aladdin's cave. The second of them has had difficulty getting beyond the stage of an empty shell, while the shop-keepers in the first look hungrily at any passing prospective customer. Too many private and public hospitals are chasing patients and personnel and a whole street of banks stands oddly devoid of customers.

Sharjah has also tried attracting tourists. Some of the hotels are architectural marvels and the fine sandy beach leaves nothing to be desired except, perhaps, coconut palms, but parasols go a long way to fill that lack. The most spectacular hotel of the lot is built in the form of a huge pyramid whose main facade is of glass; it would be a masterpiece, were that wonderful glass sculpture not oriented directly to the south, which makes the interior courtyard practically unusable eight months out of the twelve, despite enormous air-conditioning bills. Sharjah was beginning to appear on the travel agents' circuit as the businessmen became scarcer, and the hotels were just getting used to the new clients when the tourist business suffered a severe blow. In October 1985, the Emir decreed that henceforth no more alcoholic beverages would be sold or served in his domain. It is a sad commentary on the *mores* of the West that, as soon as the European tour operators heard the news, they cancelled all their group reservations and the tourist business was nipped in the bud. The businessmen, many of whom used to stay in Sharjah, suddenly found the 15 kilometres commuting to Dubai too far. In Sharjah nobody will admit it, but in Dubai the story goes that Sheikh Sultan, who is himself a sober man and a quietly practising Muslim, was shocked into his decision by a prison visit. He is said to have found some of his relatives among the prisoners held for driving while intoxicated, and this was enough to make him try to tackle the modern evil head-on.

The other emirates

No such scruples prevail in the emirate of Ajman, five minutes from central Sharjah by car. It is difficult not to say simply 'Alas, poor Ajman' and leave it at that. Ajman has been singularly unlucky in its various attempts to find its own niche in the surrounding galaxy of wealth and well-being. It tried to become a regional tax haven, but since there was not really much to be gained compared to the rules elsewhere, this hardly seemed worthwhile to the businessmen whom the measure aimed to attract. Space was allocated to a regional stock exchange which never opened its doors. While housing was practically impossible to find in Dubai, Ajman tried to play the role of the dormitory suburb, but as soon as the crisis eased up a bit, whole blocks were abandoned and flats and office space remain empty, an unhappy prefiguration of what a ghost town could look like.

Then Ajman hoped to take over from Sharjah as a tourist destination. However, except for the fact that liquor is sold freely, it is difficult to discover its charms. There is a single slightly sleazy hotel on the shore and even the beaches are less attractive than those further down the coast. They have neither the completely virgin spaces that can still be found along the Indian Ocean coast nor are they as attractively equipped as in Sharjah.

The only real tourist card that Ajman holds is one that cannot be mentioned on any prospectus. In the beach hotel a discreet inquiry for the 'recreation room' elicits instructions to go round the outside to an outbuilding that looks like two portacabins glued together. No windows, or rather, all the windows are blocked and the interior is lit by particularly harsh neon lights. All round the walls, except for the space occupied by the bar, are rows of slot machines, rigged to take dirhams. I saw the place at lunch time when it is perhaps not at its best. The samples of human decrepitude hanging out there made me feel far more sympathy for the prohibition of alcohol (not to mention of gambling, equally as iniquitous in the eyes of the faithful) decided on by the sheikh next door. Slot machines and all-day bars are not the best ambassadors of Western culture.

Ajman, like the other small emirates, spent most of the 1970s getting used to Sheikh Zayed's handouts. Like Umm al-Qawain and the others, it does have something of its own personality, or at least tries more or less to show that it has one. But none is really viable independently, at least not on the scale and up to the standard to which Abu Dhabi's prosperity have accustomed them. Even tiny Umm al-Qawain (in point of fact, its territory is more than twice that of Ajman, but the eponymous town is considerably smaller) has a flavour slightly different from the others, probably the most rustic of all.

The biggest of the remaining northern emirates and the only one that had its moment in the limelight of history as centre of the Pirate Coast is Ras al-Khaimah, which stretches all the way up to the mountainous border with Oman. But old glories are unlikely to be revived by either the three cement factories belching their smoke into the blue mountain air or the huge quarry which was, for a time, supposed to take over where Gulf overproduction of cement had left off. The quarry was opened specially for the construction of the Bahrain causeway; nothing is left of it now but a gash in the mountain.

The seventh emirate, Fujairah, does not touch the Gulf, but only the Indian Ocean coast. It had its own micro-boom, which had little to do with the big one of the 1970s, which passed it by, and much to do with the conduct of the war between Iran and Iraq. Fujairah became a re-supply centre for the scores of ships, often more than a hundred at a time riding at anchor off-shore. The business began in 1984, when the risks of shipping inside the Gulf began to push up insurance premiums: after a time, the owners preferred to keep their tankers and cargoes waiting outside the war risk zone[16] until a firm contract appeared, and then send the ships with their well-paid volunteer crews on the final dash into the Gulf. Then came the trans-shipment business. First only tankers serving Kuwaiti and Saudi ports were involved, bringing oil to Khor Fakkan or more often Fujairah, for loading on to the long-distance vessels belonging to the international companies. At some moments during the war, cargoes were also being off-loaded in Fujairah and their contents, particularly containers, sent on by road to Dubai and beyond.

After 1986, Iran changed its tactics and the real sea war began, with attacks by small patrol-boats, rockets and helicopter gunships. A small hit on a passing tanker, especially if it did not kill too many neutral crewmen (which, unfortunately, seemed to happen more often as 1987 went on), was such a commonplace that the captains barely bothered to announce them. One of the better ways to keep up with what was happening was to drop in regularly on the Dubai shipyard, where many of the vessels showed up for repairs and the grapevine was fairly accurate.

Fujairah became a huge ship's chandlery specializing in long waits; sometimes ships spent months waiting for orders to steam towards Hormuz. There was never much difficulty in finding sailors ready to risk their lives for bonuses that could double or triple their normal pay. One of the reasons used to explain the construction of yet another international airport at Fujairah was to make swapping crews easier, as if the country had been getting ready for a thirty years' war.

A few ships anchored off Muscat, but they were a handful compared to the veritable flotillas further up the coast. Muscat is further away, of course; it also placed many more restrictions on the liberties of the men on the ships. There was little chance that Oman would give permission for bored sailors to come ashore, even for a few hours. Fujairah does allow this, but this does not mean that it has turned into an Arab Hamburg or Djibouti.

The UAE and the Iran–Iraq war

Active neutrality in the war – which nobody here liked to have labelled 'Gulf' – was the order of the day in the Emirates. This became even more true after the first direct Iranian missile attacks on Kuwait early in 1987 and it was paradoxically reinforced after the events in Mecca that summer. There were signs of a veritable realignment within the GCC, not always very well hidden behind the façade of political unity. The GCC summit in Riyadh at the end of December 1987 asked the Emirates to take charge of trying to continue contacts with Tehran when relations with Kuwait and Saudi Arabia were at their most tenuous. Since 1980 the UAE had pushed its neutrality to what might be called the extreme. It went through all the motions of Arab solidarity towards Iraq, including several hundred million dollars of subsidies or loans on conditions so soft that it was difficult to see them as anything other than disguised gifts. This did not immediately efface the healthy dose of suspicion towards the Arab brother; as late as 1982, Iraqi Ba'athist agents were trying to promote their ideas from a base in Ras al-Khaimah, and encouraging the last remnants of PFLOAG, the Popular Front for the Liberation of Oman and the Arab Gulf. Suspicions vis-à-vis the Iraqi regime were probably reinforced in Abu Dhabi by the presence of so many influential Iraqi exiles. On the other hand, Dubai and Sharjah, even more than Abu Dhabi, really do feel that Iran is a close neighbour, a long-standing trading partner with whom there have never been particular problems, and the one-time mother country of a considerable part of the citizenry – not all of whom suffered Abdul Wahhab Galadari's misfortunes. Iran never made any difficulties for the Emirates,[17] and as Kuwait and Saudi Arabia edged closer and closer to the Iraqi position (whether or not they shared its ideological concerns is another question) the Emirates became ever more deliberately neutral.

The attack on the Abu Bakouch oil platform off Abu Dhabi on 25 November 1986 in which over twenty people (all of them foreigners) were killed, was almost certainly an error on the part of the Iraqi air force.[18] It was never claimed by either belligerent; given the importance of the propaganda war on both sides, the omission is significant. For Iraq it would have been most embarrassing to admit to having attacked a generous, brotherly Arab country's oil installations, unless – which is not impossible in the convoluted thinking that underlay much of the war's action – the attack had been deliberate blackmail to ensure a continued flow of aid despite tightening budgets. On the other hand, if Iran had wanted to goad the Emirates, it would not have hesitated to crow about its success.

But Iran did not want to provoke the UAE. By the autumn of 1986, relations had returned sufficiently to normality for a new ambassador to take up his post in Abu Dhabi, where the Islamic Republic had been represented by a chargé d'affaires for five years. The hojatolislam's white turban was much in evidence on the diplomatic bench during the opening session of the sixth GCC summit later that year. Dubai, with or without the blessing of the central government in Abu Dhabi, had all along had its own 'ambassador', Ayatollah Khomeini's special representative.

When the Mubarak oil field, 45 kilometres offshore from Sharjah, was hit on 18 April 1988, during the war's first real naval battle fought, like the only other one in early July of the same year, between Iranian and American ships, the damage was extensive. Some of the installations were knocked out of commission for months; the British-registered storage ship, *York Marine*, and the American supply tanker *Willie Tide* were both badly damaged. The revenues from Mubarak are divided between Iran and four members of the UAE. The attack on the oil field, which went largely unrecorded in the smoke of the big shoot-out, provides a telling demonstration of the absurdity of the long Gulf war. While Iran continued to deny responsibility for the shelling of Mubarak, putting all the blame on the Americans, it offered to help indemnify the UAE for damage suffered in an attack which it explained as a tactical error. The offer was made by the Iranian Under-secretary for Foreign Affairs, Ali Mohammed Besharati, who flew to the Emirates for a three-day visit of conciliation 'in order to reinforce the traditional relations between the two countries.'[19]

Iran must indeed have been concerned to keep up good relations if, at a time when its own economy was buckling, it was ready to make such an offer to one of the richest countries in the world. The overriding concern was to keep the UAE from being tempted to follow Saudi Arabia in breaking off relations. The Under-secretary was evidently listened to by the President of the UAE. At the end of the visit, Sheikh Zayed stated 'The protection of the Gulf and the guarantees for its security and stability can only be assured by co-operation and understanding between all the countries of the region.'[20] In other words, Zayed was ready to forgive the mistake. It was not, perhaps, too difficult to persuade him, even though the incident was probably the Emirates' closest brush during the whole war.

Even during that last frantic year, the war on the doorstep was never seen as a mortal menace. Two years later, the invasion of Kuwait by the 'Arab brother' was far more keenly felt and desperately resented. In the UAE, which in terms of miles was very far away from the centre of the action, it was nevertheless a veritable stab in the back. The Emirates were prepared for the war: full mobilization with even the religious leaders donning uniform as an example. It does not really matter whether Iraq could or would have sent Scud missiles to Abu Dhabi or, had it been able to fulfil its boasts, marched on through eastern Saudi Arabia to take all the Peninsula. The damage was done. Whatever sentiment of Arabism had been whipped up in the decade before (whether by the Palestinian writers and journalists, or by politicians) was gone. The Emirates openly joined Oman in promoting the idea that Gulf cooperation should include both sides in the Gulf. The trials of 1990 and 1991 may even have helped to take some of the edge off the basic problems of unity and to override the fragility of the

Federation's internal structures.

The first generation, those who were just into adulthood when the Federation was founded, greeted it enthusiastically and threw themselves into the adventure with considerable idealism. It was fortunate that the foundation coincided with the period of enormous economic expansion. It was also fortunate that it came just when the notion of small states was becoming fashionable: the geo-political version of 'Small is beautiful'. Bursting onto the world as rich, fashionable little states had only one real drawback. To be adulated, fawned over, solicited to the point of obsequiousness that verged on and sometimes overstepped the fine line of honesty, was enough to turn the heads of states, their rulers, princes, and even simple citizens.

The question of the succession

And yet the idealism of the early years lived on, almost miraculously, as the adventure of trying to forge a state continued. Disillusion came very slowly and then not for strictly economic reasons. Sheikh Zayed of Abu Dhabi is getting on in years; Sheikh Rashid of Dubai, without whom the UAE could not have come into being, has been succeeded by his son, Sheikh Muhammad, a member of that generation which believed most strongly in the idea of the Federation. In a world where ruling is still a very personal thing, that can have long-term consequences, especially when the delicate moment of the succession of Sheikh Zayed comes.

Zayed has been the incarnation of the ideal of union and the Federation has rested in equal parts on his will to make it work and his generous financial support. Most of the schools and hospitals in Umm al-Qawain or Fujairah which brought the half-forgotten emirates almost up to the standards of Abu Dhabi or Dubai were gifts from Sheikh Zayed's privy purse. The drop in oil revenues has inevitably brought at least a lower level of generosity; in itself this is not so important because, as elsewhere in the Gulf, much of the infrastructure is already in place. I have already explained the peculiar relations that exist in South Arabia between a very rich sheikh and a poorer one, or the interaction between the sheikh, money and the ordinary citizen, with gifts that are not to be considered as bribes but as a mechanism for spreading the money through the tribe. For Sheikh Zayed, in that sense the whole of the Federation was his tribe; but not all the other sheikhs were ready to acknowledge that fact.

Doubt has begun to creep into the marrow of the emirates. Many people are wondering whether, when the day comes, Sheikh Zayed's successor will be able to instil the same enthusiasm into his direct and less direct subjects. There seems no one on the immediate horizon with the same mixture of real charisma, subsidies and native intelligence. When Zayed was a child, few sheikhs' sons had much formal schooling and Zayed was no exception; even today he reads with difficulty, but few people in the region can match him for an *ex tempore* speech.

What then? Are we on the way to a redistribution of the cards and eventually a redrawn regional map? One factor must be taken into account: the longer a state lasts, the more it becomes in itself, *ipso facto*, an element of institutional permanence. The Arabian peninsula has no rules like those of Africa saying that all borders inherited from before independence are untouchable, but practically speaking, new traditions can quickly make them look as though they were.[21] There are still interesting hypotheses to be examined. From Sharjah to Ras al-Khaimah a number of clear-thinking people are talking – always in speculative tones, it must be emphasized – of the possibility of a voluntary attachment to Oman in the eventuality that the Federation shows too many signs of weakness. One can, of course, find good historical precedents for such a move. In such a hypothetical situation, Dubai would probably be quite happy to think of itself as the Singapore of the Gulf (the second one, because Bahrain already sees itself in this role), directly integrated into the GCC but otherwise responsible for its own destiny. That leaves Abu Dhabi, more difficult to fit into such a puzzle. Two ideas have been suggested to me in all seriousness. The first is that Saudi Arabia, going back to before the Buraimi agreements of the 1950s, could once again extend its claims over an Abu Dhabi left more or less orphaned by the Federation. The other is that Abu Dhabi should join the smaller emirates in their approaches to Oman. Despite the fact that

Sheikh Zayed has in recent years taken to having himself photographed in an Omani *amama* or turban, almost as often as in a *keffiyah*, Abu Dhabi would be a harder morsel to digest than Sharjah, Fujairah or Ras al-Khaimah.

All this is, of course, pure speculation. Nevertheless, it is revealing of a state of mind which is seriously worried about the future, not so much in its economic aspects – the reserves should last for a while, at least in amounts high enough to allow for upkeep – as about the political future. The Federation is fragile and people know that it is fragile. Paradoxically, the fragility is another reason why the UAE, even more than the other members, counts on the GCC's support in case of possible internal tensions.

CHAPTER 9

Oman: A Special Case

Is Oman really a Gulf country? In terms of pure geography, Oman touches on the Gulf for only 40 rocky kilometres on the inside face of the Strait of Hormuz. The ochre cliffs fall sheer into the sea and it was only in 1981, when army engineers blasted a road out of the rock, that the isolated fishing villages along the shore could be reached other than by boat. Most of the country turns outwards to the Indian Ocean, cut off from the Arabian peninsula by a sea of sand, the Rub al-Khali, the Empty Quarter, on one side and high mountains on the other. Until the age of the aeroplane, Omanis went more naturally to Zanzibar or Gwadur than to Dubai.

Historically, Oman has only partially shared the destinies of its Gulf neighbours. After the Portuguese were driven out in the middle of the seventeenth century, Oman was never again a colony or a protectorate, of either the Ottomans or the British. The long-standing special relationship with Britain has been a voluntary, state-to-state arrangement confirmed by successive sultans since the end of the eighteenth century. Instead of being subject to an imperial power, Oman stood at the head of its own empire which stretched from East Africa to the Makram Coast. In the first half of the nineteenth century, the Sea of Oman really was an Omani sea.

This colonial history in reverse is one base of the extraordinary independence of the Omanis, manifested in a public and private self-assurance which can be disconcerting for their neighbours and GCC partners. In terms of pure petro-accounting, the Omanis are the Gulf's poor relations; the problem is that they refuse to act the part.

There has been some historical contact with the Gulf, not all of it happy. Archaeologists have discovered traces showing that Oman was involved in a triangular trade between the Indus valley and Bahrain – Dilmun as it then was – long before there were any written documents. Several millennia later, the Ibadhi form of Islam which has become one of the distinguishing features of Oman[1] was born in Basrah in southern Iraq and arrived in Oman through the Gulf. In the seventeenth and eighteenth centuries the Omanis pushed their conquests as far north as Bahrain and then, as the power of the Qawasim grew along what was then called the Pirate Coast, the Omani sultans and their unruly neighbours began a long period of alternate alliances and warfare. The decline began in the middle of the last century: problems in the African empire, competition from the Europeans with their metal-hulled ships and steam engines, and dynastic difficulties all contributed to the involution that led Oman to turn inwards upon itself for more than a century. During that time it had absolutely no interest in the Gulf.

Visually, too, Oman is different. It has large zones of traditional agriculture, spectacular mountain scenery and, in Dhofar, the only corner of Arabia where there is an annual monsoon. All around Salalah is a circle of mountains as green as the Jura for four months of the year; the people who live there speak a non-Arabic south Semitic language and are cattle-breeders like those of the Yemeni highlands. The Omanis, including the northern, Arab, Omanis, even look different. For one thing, their dress is distinctive. It requires a practised eye to distinguish between a *dishdasha* from Kuwait and one from Riyadh, or a Bahraini *keffiyah* and *guthra* from its Dabawani twin. But in any Gulf gathering, it is easy to spot the Omanis for they wear turbans. Few Omani women wear the black *abaya*; their costumes are as bright as hummingbirds and veils are very rare; in the desert, the bedouin women wear masks, but that is another matter. The Omanis are also physically different: they look more like Yemenis than like other Gulf people. More often small and wiry than sleek and plump, they are often quite brown but with 'Arab' rather than 'African' features, with the exception of descendants of the African slaves to be found here and there along the coast. In most places in the Peninsula, I have to moderate my walking pace to match that of my companions; in Oman, particularly in the interior, I have trouble keeping up.

And yet, today Oman is indubitably part of the political landscape of the Gulf. First, its geographical position gives it, along with Iran, joint guardianship of the key: the Strait of Hormuz. The vagaries of history left a strip of land wedged in between the Batinah coast and the Musandam Peninsula as territories belonging to Sharjah and Fujairah; the discontinuity, although between friendly states, complicates matters from schools and health services to roads and rights of passage even for civilian aircraft. But there is no question that the Musandam Peninsula, pointing due north into the Strait of Hormuz, is Omani. With it, Oman becomes a factor to be reckoned with for all the countries of the Gulf, including Iran and Iraq.

Oman's political organization differs more in detail than in essence from that of the other Gulf countries: like them, it is based on a paternalist absolute monarchy. Yet, perhaps more than for the others, the monarchy must found its legitimacy on tribal consensus which remains the only guarantee of stability. There is not the geographic contiguity, nor the possibility of largesse that exists in Kuwait or Qatar or even the UAE, nor the huge family network reinforced by both money and the religious factor of Saudi Arabia. The great Omani tribes, especially those of the Ibadhi interior, have a strong and quite recent tradition of independent action. Inevitably, as the country proceeds towards more modernization, the tribal base will look increasingly anachronistic. The search for a new equilibrium was one reason for establishing the Consultative Council. This institution bears little resemblance to a European parliament, nor is it supposed to. Its purpose is to give a voice to sectors of society which were excluded from the traditional system of consultation and consent, which was limited in practice to the tribal chiefs. Members of minor tribes and people entirely outside the traditional system had no way of making their opinions heard, however important their actual position might have become. Without tribal connections and therefore never completely integrated, these 'disenfranchised' groups included the urban merchants who arrived from the Indian subcontinent several centuries ago, the Baluchis and, for different reasons, the Dhofaris.

Finally, Oman shares with the other Gulf countries the luck, or the burden, of having an economy almost exclusively based on oil. True, the Omani oilfields are paltry compared to those of Abu Dhabi, Kuwait or Saudi Arabia. In 1987, average daily production was 500,000 barrels, while the Emirates were pumping 3.4 million and Saudi Arabia more than 4 million barrels a day. In compensation, Oman does have real possibilities of natural development beyond oil, from agriculture and in particular from fisheries. However, the near-panic that struck in 1986 when oil prices plummeted showed that the day when Oman can cheerfully say good-bye to oil is still far away. One might have thought that Oman was fairly safe from a post-oil shock simply because it had never been through the happy trauma of living with unlimited means. Yet the shock occurred.

With the passing of time, the question of whether or not Oman is really a Gulf country becomes increasingly irrelevant. When it joined the GCC, Oman decided that henceforth it would be part of the Gulf, in the same way as it was the Sultan's deliberate decision that his country should join the Arab League, the Islamic Conference Organization and the United Nations. What keeps Oman different is that, with no ex-colonial complex to cope with, it has refused – rightly or wrongly – to think of itself as involved in the normal scheme of North-South relations or even developing versus developed countries. There was certainly much condescension in Queen Victoria's relations with Sultan Said of Muscat, Oman and Zanzibar and, until very recently, many of the British expatriates working in Oman had at least occasional lapses when they forgot that the Raj was dead. But from the time of Sayyid Said[2] to that of Sultan Qaboos, Oman has known how to make the point, politely but firmly, that it is not to be treated as a dependency nor as a minor partner. This is precisely what sometimes throws Oman's partners and friends off balance.

Into the modern world

When Qaboos became Sultan in 1970, Oman was a complete anachronism in the twentieth century. His father, Said bin Taimur, had imposed his stringent rule in a desperate attempt to preserve the country and its people from the pernicious influences of the encroaching modern world; to his mind such evils were manifest everywhere, from the wearing of shoes or sunglasses to going to school. Inevitably, it was British advisers, the only outside friends of this strange man, who persuaded the young Qaboos to overthrow his father. By a near-miracle, the son had been sent to England to be educated while the other Omanis were kept as far as possible in almost total ignorance. Said sincerely thought that the outside world was wicked and that complete separation was the best way of preserving his subjects from corruption.

However, whether he liked it or not, the outside world was encroaching. After much persuasion, the old Sultan had given his consent to an oil concession and by 1969 the first wells were in production. For the strategists of the time, the Dhofar rebellion was an even more important factor; they saw in it a dangerous centre of Communist agitation whence revolt could spread to the whole Gulf and beyond. In this they were right; where they went wrong was in confusing the effects of expropriation, which gave the movement international importance, with the origins of the revolt. It began as a reaction to the complete neglect of the province as the Sultan's quasi-private domain. It would have been almost impossible to reintegrate Dhofar into the Sultanate under the old Sultan. The rebellion, however it was fuelled, was a fight for the basic minimum of a decent twentieth-century life, something that Said bin Taimur had always refused his people; the character of the Dhofaris, harder-edged than the northern Omanis, was as much a part of the revolt as the fact that their situation was objectively worse. The coup was inevitable. Afterwards, Qaboos continued to show an immense confidence in his British mentors and advisers, sometimes even more than they themselves might have wished.

Omanization had become a fashionable term even before the oil price crash of 1986. By mid-1987 only about 7,000 Britons remained out of 12,000 the previous year. In the course of 1986, 10 per cent of the British officers serving with the SOAF, the Sultan of Oman's Armed Forces, had gone home – the last of the budget expenses to be cut. About 200 seconded officers remain with 1,500 others on contract. The word 'mercenary' is never used.

Of course, not all the expatriates were Britons and the basic problems linked to immigrant labour are not very different from those of the other Gulf countries. They are perhaps less acute in Oman, which has, by Gulf standards, a fairly large native population. Of over one million inhabitants,[3] one can estimate that approximately 80 per cent are Omanis. This means that there are twice as many Omanis as native Kuwaitis. One consequence of this demographic situation is that Omanization is not a vain slogan, if it is carried out sensibly and in stages. The most intelligent Omanization will not obviate all need for foreign labour. Even in the dark years of poverty and oblivion there were always immigrant workers in Oman: specialists in date pollination for instance and, on the Batinah coast, circumcisors. And, in hard times, it was the Omanis who went abroad to look for work: before 1970, the dockers of Kuwait were practically a closed Omani corporation and 'Omani' in Kuwaiti dialect still means 'labourer'. Even now, several thousand Omanis, mostly from the villages of the interior, form the bulk of the army and police forces in Abu Dhabi and Dubai; the pay is higher than in Oman, although the perks are not as good.[4]

It will be a long time before Oman produces enough native doctors and nurses, teachers and architects or even gardeners and bank clerks to be able to dispense entirely with foreigners. Where real Omanization could come quickly is in the key posts of the administration and the nerve centres where basic decisions are made. The process is under way. The contracts of one quarter of the foreign non-military personnel were not renewed between 1986 and 1987. It was, in fact, high time; among educated Omanis, however pleasant they may be, signs of mild annoyance, of friction, were becoming detectable. The Omani administration was notable for its relative efficiency and, despite a few mishaps, basic honesty and absence of corruption. A few resounding scandals have come to light. They involved a great deal of money, but relatively few people; the ordinary, run-of-the-mill Omani functionary remains basically honest. This is one good sign for the future. Another is a professed and often real willingness to work, not only individually but for a collectivity: the family first of all, but beyond that, the country – a sentiment related to a feeling of national pride, of belonging to a nation and not just to a tribe. This is, in the Gulf, unique to Oman and in the Peninsula shared only with the Yemens.

The new Omani university, named after Sultan Qaboos of course, provides a whole constellation of examples for the study of what can be called Omani style. The idea was in the air even before 1980 and the formal decision was announced by the Sultan in 1982. One of the first questions to be resolved was: who was going to teach in the university? and linked to it: in what language? Besides the Sultan's unabashed anglophilia, one reason for the decision to adopt English as the main teaching language was the availability of good English-speaking lecturers. It is also a consequence of the reluctance to give over even more of the country's education system to Egyptians; they are indispensable because only they can provide the numerous teachers needed, but they are often disliked for their rapacity and mediocrity. Mediocrity was exactly what the Sultan wanted to avoid in his new university, and the appointment of Sheikh Amr al-Amiri as the first Vice-Chancellor was confirmation of this. Sheikh Amr is as much, or even more, at home in Western as in Arab culture; he had been an academic in Kenya before coming back, like many other 'Zanzibaris', to a homeland most had never seen. From the early planning stage onwards, Sheikh Amr and his colleagues, translating the wishes of the Sultan, insisted on building a real university with academic standards comparable to those of Europe, where students would be expected to work for their degrees, not just spend a few pleasant years in beautiful buildings. All courses, apart from Arabic literature and Islamic theology, are taught in English. As soon as the university opened in 1986, it became clear that most of the students required extra language tutoring, and a preparatory year made up mostly of intensive English courses was added to the curriculum.

As each Gulf country established its own university, the same questions were discussed. Most decided to teach in Arabic on ideological grounds and also so as not to make life too difficult for the students. The question of teaching staff was not easy to resolve whichever decision was taken, because the quality of the professors will largely determine how deep the academic soil will be ploughed. Egypt produces so many graduates at all levels that they have become a major export product – of varying quality. Like the other Gulf countries, Oman is in serious danger of Egyptianization of its language and its culture by sheer weight of numbers in the schools, the primary cultural vector in a country emerging from illiteracy. Finding Arab lecturers of a high standard might have been possible had no political considerations been involved, by leavening the Egyptian lump with Iraqis, Syrians, North Africans (a few Tunisians were already teaching in Omani schools) and, obviously, Palestinians. But, beyond the question of assuring the best possible quality of teaching, there was real hesitation at the idea of opening the country to a group of Arab intellectuals who would inevitably have been more or less politicized and politically active; that factor also weighed in the final balance.

The construction of the university campus outside Muscat at the very northern fringe of the 'Capital Area'[5] led to a completely different kind of controversy, one which barely missed giving rise to an international scandal. The affair went far enough in the British press to engender allusions to 'The Banana Sultanate' and mutterings about 'Oman, the most corrupt country in the Middle East' – in fact, sheer nonsense. What came close to a concerted campaign was based entirely on the way tenders were granted. The main contract went to Britain's Cementation Corporation in which, at the time, Mark Thatcher, the Prime Minister's son, held a major financial stake. Despite the British Government's vehement denials of undue influence, people in the Gulf would hardly consider it unusual, much less wrong, that some preference should be given to the company in which the son of such a good friend as the British Minister (quite regardless of who happens to be holding that office) was a major shareholder. An *ex post facto* verification of allegations that the construction cost 40 per cent more than it should have done – the figure that appeared in several British papers at the time[6] – is practically impossible. A large part of the overrun was said to have gone into the pockets of a small number of prominent people; rumour had it that they were mostly from the 'Salalah mafia', several members of whom were sacked from official appointments in 1986. Forty per cent is almost certainly an inflated figure. It is, however, likely that some large commissions were involved, which would help explain the 1986 sackings, but according to careful financial observers on the spot they were modest compared to what was considered normal for large contracts in other Gulf countries.

Arab solidarity?

Oman has long been a favourite whipping-boy for almost anyone with progressive pretensions, Arabs and non-Arabs, in the Gulf or beyond.[7] The first charge was often something along the lines of 'valet of the West', usually only a fig-leaf for unstated questions referring to the 'real Arabism' of Oman. Such remarks often smacked of the propaganda put out by the Popular Front for the Liberation of Oman and the Arab Gulf, which sailed under the unwieldy acronym PFLOAG,[8] and were heavily larded with vague accusations of not being firm enough supporters of the Arab cause. The first of these, the 'valet of the West' line, is now outdated, and can be largely discounted; other Gulf countries drew much closer to the West during the war and by its end the situation had completely changed. The PFLOAG line is more important and is worth looking at in some detail, particularly since a growing number of young Omanis are being sensitized to political thought and exposed to the favourite ideas of one or another Arab political camp when they go abroad – or listen to the radio. Oman is no longer isolated.

Even if Arab solidarity has as often been a catchword as a dynamic reality, the idea that Oman is somehow lacking in it is surprisingly widespread in the Gulf and indeed all over the Middle East. The insinuations take the form of a catalogue of 'sins' stretching over the whole of Qaboos' reign. The first is often a charge of a lack of filial piety,[9] a grave accusation in an Arab society. Then may come the support given to President Sadat at the time of the signing of the Egyptian peace treaty with

Israel. Then came the refusal to follow the majority of the Arab League in breaking off relations with Egypt.[10] The next 'sin' will usually be the Sultan's request to the Shah of Iran for help in settling the Dhofar rebellion, and finally – or perhaps especially – his long refusal to open the Sultanate to Palestinians.

Was that enough to make the Omanis 'bad Arabs' or, worse, 'traitors to the Arab cause'? Quite apart from the fact that practically all Omanis (to the extent that they are interested in such a discussion) would probably deny such allegations – and without going into the eternal debate of who or what is a good or bad Arab? or for that matter what is an Arab? – a few remarks would seem in order. When the Arab League was formed in 1945, Oman, as a sovereign state, would have been eligible for membership, but Said bin Taimur was not interested, any more than he was interested in the United Nations or anything beyond the borders of his beloved, backward country. After the accession of Qaboos, when Oman did present its candidature, it was immediately accepted by both organizations.[11] Even now, the Sultan dislikes summitry and avoids it when possible. He feels obliged to be present at the annual GCC meetings, but did not, for example, attend the Islamic summit in Kuwait in January 1987. Only when he feels that the agenda directly concerns himself or his country and that he can do something about it, will he overcome his hesitations. This was the case with the Arab summit in Amman in November 1987, when the two issues up for discussion were the war between Iran and Iraq and the position the Arabs were to take on Egypt's return to the fold. Following the same logic, the Sultan was present at the Casablanca summit in May 1989, when Egypt officially returned to the Arab League.

Oman refused to sign the resolutions condemning Egypt at the Baghdad summits of 1978 and 1979, after the conclusion of the Camp David agreement and the peace treaty with Israel. Ever since the Rabat summit of 1974 stated that the Arabs should seek a solution to the Arab-Israeli conflict by all possible peaceful means, Oman has interpreted the resolution in a broad sense, while considering that it is too far distant from the conflict to have a direct impact. This interpretation meant refusal to join in the chorus of invective against President Anwar as-Sadat of Egypt. 'In the absence of any sensible alternative, what else could we do?' explained the Omani Minister of State for Foreign Affairs.[12] The Omani position has not varied one inch, while the other Arab countries, particularly those of the Gulf, have spent months and years looking for an elegant way to reinstate Egypt. By the time of the Islamic summit in 1987, its exclusion had become a hypocritical anomaly; Egypt was quietly providing military assistance to a worried Gulf, training Kuwaiti security personnel, and passing military equipment on to Iraq itself. When the Amman summit adopted its hybrid recommendation leaving the League members free to restore relations with Egypt, Oman's five fellow-members of the GCC all did so within a fortnight.

Oman stays as far as possible from the turmoils of inter-Arab politics. The Indian Ocean is a long way from the tempests of the Levant, the country is not rich enough to play any significant role even when it comes to financial assistance,[13] nor is it much given to verbal hyperbole. Even during the period when relations were at their worst with South Yemen, there was never hysterical raving on the Omani side – only cold and nasty shudders.

To understand Oman's relations with its peninsular neighbours, a little psycho-sociology is in order. As the last of the Gulf countries to find oil and the last to join in the game of modernization, Oman is still considered by many people in the Gulf as the country bumpkin. Its extreme restrictions in granting visas until GCC rules forced a little relaxation did not help in dispelling its slightly sinister air of mystery. As late as 1985, when I said I was going on to Muscat, Kuwaiti friends would look at me with pity and only just refrain from giving me extra rations and a candle to speed me on my way. What particularly annoys the neighbours is that these poor relations do not act the part: instead, they keep talking about their long history, and worse still, their empire. They even have the gall to be proud of the fact that their sovereign is a sultan (i.e. a king and not simply an emir or prince), who is descended from a line of sultans that has reigned without interruption for almost two and a half centuries. Furthermore, being Ibadhis – not all, but a large enough majority to colour the politico-religious atmosphere – has kept the Omanis out of the religious turmoils of the last decade. All these factors combine to complicate relations between Oman and its Gulf partners: the deep patches of incomprehension can lead to frank disdain on both sides.

Independent foreign policy

Oman's foreign relations have been consistently marked by an independence that sometimes, in the eyes of others, has smacked of arrogance. In contrast to that of Saudi Arabia, which has traditionally been characterized by cautious reaction, Oman's foreign policy is marked by long waits, and then sometimes surprising, often disconcerting action taken after a decision that can be entirely heedless of the international ambience or the possible reactions of friends, neighbours or allies.

Examples abound. The Omani refusal to follow the majority of the Arab countries in their castigation of Egypt is only one among many. Another is the agreement on military and civilian co-operation that Oman signed with the United States in 1980. Many Arab countries, including those in the Gulf, expressed their disapproval with greater or lesser vehemence. The agreement gave the Americans access to four Omani air bases, Seeb (Muscat), Khasab (Musandam), Thamrait (Dhofar) and Masirah Island, while stipulating that permission must be sought in advance of the use of each. It did not grant either sovereignty rights or permission to station American troops in the Sultanate. In exchange, the Americans paid for upgrading the four bases (including the construction of a runway over 2 kilometres long at Khasab) and promised several purely civilian projects, such as the construction of dams along the Batinah coast. The Pentagon had some difficulty in persuading Congress to provide aid to a country whose per capita income was considerably higher than the usual ceiling; the promise of being able to use facilities, even surrounded by a fence of restrictions, in such an eminently strategic situation persuaded enough hesitant members for the bill to go through. The agreement was supposed to last five years. In 1985, when the time came to renegotiate, the Americans hoped to add a few more privileges. In particular they wanted free access to Omani ports with the possibility of allowing sailors to disembark plus, ideally, the right to station a few troops in the Sultanate.

Oman refused almost all these requests. The only real addition to the original agreement was the right to pre-position military equipment – in limited quantities and under direct Omani control. In the meantime, under pressure of the Gulf war, several Gulf countries had cobbled together arrangements with the Americans that went further than those contained in the original Omani agreement which had caused such an uproar in 1980. Saudi Arabia had accepted – or requested – the presence of small groups of American troops at key points in the Kingdom plus the much-publicized AWACS (Advance Warning Aircraft System) with their crews.

As a third example, it was almost ten years after the end of the Dhofar rebellion before formal relations were established between Oman and the Popular Democratic Republic of Yemen, South Yemen. Kuwait and the UAE had worked hard at mediating a rapprochement fraught with a stock of mutual distrust; the reconciliation was the biggest diplomatic success of the first years of the GCC. Even after formal recognition came in 1983, it was four more years before the two countries were ready to exchange ambassadors. In the meantime there was the murderous coup within the party structure in Aden in January 1986 (see Chapter 10).

While Riyadh and the other Gulf capitals hesitated as to what their reactions should be, Oman became South Yemen's chief advocate within the GCC, insisting that the revolt was a purely internal matter and that it should have no effect on the Council's relations with the PDRY – nor on the promised aid. The Omani Minister of Foreign Affairs, a Dhofari and a reformed rebel, was the first official foreign visitor to arrive in Aden after the tragic events and the South Yemenis have not forgotten this.

A fourth example: in September 1985, out of a clear blue sky, Oman suddenly announced that it was establishing diplomatic relations with the Soviet Union. Even British diplomats, still the best connoisseurs of the Sultanate, were surprised by what had long been considered the most anti-Soviet country in the Middle East. The Americans were more than surprised; they were furious.[14] They told the Omanis what they thought, warning them of all the dire consequences of a Soviet diplomatic offensive in the Gulf; the Omanis politely told them to mind their own business. It was the very beginning of the Gorbachev era. Two months later, the UAE followed the Omani example. Over the preceding years, the UAE had several times been on the verge of establishing relations with Moscow, but retreated each time in the face of Saudi displeasure. The Omani decision, which surprised the Saudis as much as everyone else except the Kuwaitis, who seem to have been privy to the discussions without having really served as mediators, may indeed have retarded the re-establishment of relations between the USSR and Saudi Arabia.[15] The Kingdom would hardly want to be seen as following an Omani lead. For Oman, the decision followed logically on the normalization of its relations with South Yemen, plus a new interpretation of the geo-political situation. It also probably provided a not unwelcome opportunity for showing, particularly within the GCC framework, its independence of Saudi Arabia.

One last example of the sometimes disconcerting Omani independence can be found in the relations with Iran, both before and after the revolution. The Sultan had asked the Shah, his imperial neighbour, for help in polishing off the Dhofar rebellion. By all accounts, not only did the Iranian troops behave quite badly, but the demand itself provoked a ferocious outcry from some of the northern Arabs: how could Qaboos have asked for help from a non-Arab?[16] The Iranian help was useful even if it did become one more item in the catalogue of grievances often used against the Sultan.

Then came the Islamic revolution and, the year after that, the war between Iran and Iraq. Oman, despite the old friendship with the Shah, managed to stay neutral, refusing to join in the condemnation of Iran by the Arab foreign ministers meeting in Tunis in September 1987. The inevitable result was, once again, that it was charged with lack of Arab fervour. Omani relations with Iran remained normal all through the war. In fact, as the years went by and Oman felt itself in a position to take more initiatives, direct contacts and official visits grew. Muscat also became the site for discreet meetings. In 1987 and 1988, the Omanis repeatedly found themselves using their good offices to repatriate injured or dead Iranians and prisoners captured by the Americans in successive engagements in and around the Strait of Hormuz.

Oman did sign the Amman summit resolution in November 1987, condemning Iran for not having responded to the Security Council's Resolution 598 asking for a cease-fire. But seven weeks later, at the GCC rulers' meeting, it was Oman and the UAE that advocated a far more conciliatory text asking for the opening of a dialogue.

Unlike the Emirates, Oman does not have a large population of Iranian origin. There is nothing like the network of family and commercial relations that exists between Dubai and Sharjah on the Arab side and Lingeh and Bandar Abbas on the other. The small boats that scuttle across the Strait of Hormuz from the Musandam ports hardly qualify as a cargo fleet; whatever goods they carry – contraband more often than not – are in minute quantities. From the spring of 1987 onwards, some trans-shipment for Iran was going through Muscat, but the volume remained very small compared to that in the UAE ports.

As the war years went by, Omani neutrality in the Gulf conflict began to annoy some of its neighbours. Kuwait, in particular, once it had become embroiled, saw it as a lack of solidarity. So did the Americans. In response to the Sultan's appeal for a dialogue with the Iranians at the time of the GCC summit in December 1987, there were bitter Kuwaiti remarks about people who could speak of dialogue while they were far from danger. The irony was perhaps misaimed; Oman is in fact the only Gulf state which has a common border with Iran. The Strait of Hormuz, at its narrowest, measures less than 24 miles across. Oman and Iran, like most coastal states, have declared a 12-mile limit for their territorial waters. In consequence there are no international waters between them and in fact they overlap slightly and for a few more miles beyond only the thinnest sliver of international seas separates them. The navigation schemes pass through Omani waters.[17]

Oddly, there was not the same degree of annoyance with the Emirates, as though it were more natural for them to maintain traditional close relations with Iran. Kuwait's confused disappointment is also probably linked to a diffuse sense of being let down by Oman, the only other counterweight to Saudi preponderance within the GCC, and just at the time when Kuwait was feeling itself increasingly hemmed in. The American reaction was more straightforward. Why should the Omanis, whom they considered their friends, and who were so close to the whole thing, stay neutral while they themselves were becoming more and more involved?

After the cease-fire, as the peace negotiations began, Sultan Qaboos again quietly tried to bring some influence to bear: on the Iraqis so that they would not lay down unreasonable demands, and on the Iranians, to show themselves more conciliatory in view of future relations in the Gulf. One month after the cease-fire went into effect, it was reported that Qaboos was working on a reconciliation between Iran and Saudi Arabia.[18] At the end of the year, the Sultan, who hates travelling, embarked on a campaign of personal visits to break the negotiating stalemate. He took on a difficult task, indeed.

Internal situation

In contrast to the extreme fragmentation of the Emirates or the long Saudi march towards internal unity, based, like the design on the Saudi flag, on the Koran and the sword, the Omani monarchy depends on a balance of power among the tribes: it is from them that the Sultan, as arbiter, must derive his legitimacy. In conformity with Ibadhi custom, power can only be legitimately conferred on him who merits it; and it can also be taken away. Oman has not always been easy to rule; the conflicting claims of the tribes were often stronger than the power of the reigning Sultan. Yet, somehow, an historical idea of Oman emerged and the tribes of the Ibadhi heartland – the oases on both sides of the Jebel Akhdar and down the Sharkiyya to Sur – learned to live with the people of the coast. Despite all the disputes and the violence which marked Omani history until less than a generation ago, they did manage to find a *modus vivendi* more often than they fought. At the time of the Dhofar rebellion, the possible loss of the South was the obvious problem. It masked another danger, that some tribal chiefs of the North, seeing the extreme weakness of the old Sultan's grip, might raise their own rebellion – a new edition, so to speak of the imamate revolt of 1954–6,[19] when three tribal chiefs from the interior heartland, aided and abetted first by Saudi Arabia and then by Nasser's Egypt, rose up in revolt against the Sultan. This time it captured little international attention: it had nothing to do with the possibility of Communist advance in South Arabia. With the accession of Qaboos and the end of the Dhofar rebellion, internal equilibrium was re-established on a new fulcrum which took account of the Dhofari tribes who had never figured in the equation before.

Qaboos was lucky. He came to power on a wave of enthusiasm and with an enormous capital of confidence, just when the oil fields began to go into production. In the following decade both government and the private sector grew so fast that they could absorb all the available talents and provide even the most ambitious with scope for action. Almost every big family was able to place at least one member in a position of power. Like the former Dhofar rebels, the tribal chiefs were integrated into the system and neutralized. A sheikh who has become His Excellency the Minister is less likely to start his own little tribal revolt; and if the minister happens to be a son or a nephew, the result is almost the same. The oil income was fairly well diffused among the tribes by a complicated system of subsidies to the sheikhs, and most of them were astute enough to let it trickle down further.

In the first years after Qaboos's accession, so much needed to be done that every mud dispensary, every power line, every classroom under the palm-fronds was greeted as a near-miracle. During these years of grace, Qaboos could do no wrong and the consensus was so near perfect that outsiders could hardly believe it was genuine. But it was. Since 1985, a few signs have appeared indicating that the honeymoon is over; but to talk about disaffection would be going too far. The critics' first target was the enormous amount spent to celebrate the fifteenth anniversary of the Sultan's reign which coincided with the first GCC summit meeting held in Muscat. The buildings and roads built for the occasion remain and some were indispensable; nevertheless, two years after the event, some perspicacious Omanis were with some bitterness talking about the Sultan's 'Persopolis' – all the while hoping it was not so.[20]

There was no global accounting of the expenditures, but one indication of the scale is given by the laser show with which the Sultan entertained his princely guests in the magic setting of Muscat bay – repeated once for the general population in Muttrah. It was lovely, but the bill was said by reliable sources to have been $7 million.

It was still a time of euphoria. In 1985 Oman had felt almost nothing of the turndown that had begun elsewhere in the Gulf as early as 1982. No one wanted to listen to the grumblings of a few sceptics. The people, it was loftily said, were delighted to have something to entertain them, to remember in a society where public distractions remain rare. Promises were made that the following year, the year after the great projects for the capital area were completed, there would be others for those parts of the country that had been rather neglected. It was bad luck that the next year, 1986, was the year of the great oil price collapse.

If up to then Oman had felt hardly any effects of the post-boom period, it was also because the great 1970s boom had never hit Oman with the same force. Its oil production was relatively modest; 283,000 barrels per day in 1980, and it looked at the time as though production would diminish from 1981 on. Spending was carefully controlled and choices weighed; possibilities and consequences were taken into account. The following years, when the signs of slow-down were already apparent elsewhere in the Gulf, were really the best in Oman. So much remained to be done just to get the basic infrastructure into place that there was hardly a hint of saturation; even the oil glut had few negative effects. On the contrary. Since Oman is not a member of OPEC, it was outside the quota system and free to sell all the oil it could pump.[21] The first reserves peaked, as expected, but new wells developed during the frenzied oil search of the 1970s came on stream. Instead of cutting production, Oman raised it to 500,000 barrels per day by the end of 1985. And Omani oil easily found buyers, thanks to the war; the Omani oil terminals are directly on the Indian Ocean coast and so were well outside the danger zones in the Gulf.

In 1985, the Omani economy was stimulated even further by the enormous expenses linked to the year-end festivities. People knew that the following year would see a slight slow-down, a reasonable time for drawing breath. The only problem was that nobody expected oil prices to plummet so sharply nor so quickly. By July 1986, the price was $8 a barrel; after OPEC put its house in a semblance of order, it temporarily reached $18 in December. At $8, there was no way even for lucky Oman to push its production far enough to avoid losses. For the first time, Oman really felt the pinch.[22]

The projects for the interior which had been shelved while the capital area was preening itself for the celebrations had to be postponed again. Paradoxically, what had already been done in the way of development had given the villagers just enough taste of the modern world to make them impatient. The basics were in place: schools, however rudimentary, had appeared in the most remote mountain villages and dispensaries were functioning in every desert settlement. With new roads that made getting to Muscat from almost anywhere a matter of hours, at most days, and no longer weeks, the contrasts were easy to see. The enormous personal loyalty that binds most Omanis to the Sultan saved the day, but after the first questions were asked in 1985, 1986 was the year when the chilling shadow of disenchantment fell on Oman.

It did not lead to catastrophe. Just as the Omanis were about to forget their good habits of husbanding resources they experienced a jolt, but not a fatal one. The most positive aspect was the discovery that everyone was in the same boat; even the SOAF, the Sultan's cherished armed forces, saw their budget slashed. Only two ministries, education and health (neither of which could be charged with reckless spending), remained unaffected. With very close links between private business and government spending (ubiquitous in the Gulf), the shock waves spread everywhere. They probably came at the last minute to prevent the Omanis from becoming spoiled children. Until 1985, Oman had seen relatively little prestige spending. Even some projects that looked particularly extravagant, such as the Nizwa police academy, had not been built without any accounting. The year 1985 did see a few follies, including the Bustan Palace Hotel, built for the GCC summit, and probably the most splendid hotel in the whole Middle East. Presumably it fulfilled its first function perfectly – to impress the rulers and their suites; it is now one of the best arguments for opening the country, albeit timidly, to tourists. The Development Council, which serves as both planning board and conscience, was revived; it had been rather neglected in the three years before 1985, and this was one of its first recommendations.

Rational development planning was for a long time applied only to northern Oman. Dhofar was given a special status, even after its integration into the Sultanate or, more accurately, because of the efforts made to integrate it into the Sultanate. The Dhofaris enjoyed particular marks of favour from the time Qaboos took power. The roots went even deeper than the campaign linked to the end of the rebellion, when development expenses were considered an integral part of military strategy. For several years during the 1970s, close to half the national budget was devoted to what is officially known as the Southern Region, which covers approximately one-third of the country but has only 15 per cent of the population. The Sultan has a real affection for Dhofar; his mother is Dhofari and he spends practically half the year in one of his Salalah palaces, from choice even more than for political motives. Still, something of these remains. As soon as the Sultan was informed of the South Yemeni insurrection in January 1986, he immediately left for Salalah to be physically close to the Dhofari tribes, some of whom straddle the border. In the event, the Adeni troubles never spread to Mahra province on the Yemeni side of the Dhofar border.

By 1980 the northern Omanis, usually polite and patient people, began to think, and sometimes to say, that the special treatment had lasted long enough. They were not entirely wrong, because the coddling of the Dhofaris, politically justified at first, was rapidly turning them into spoiled prima donnas.[23] Being spoiled is not the same thing as being disgruntled to the point of presenting problems of internal cohesion. To the Jeballis – Jeballi or 'mountaineer' is the generic term used for the non-Arabic-speaking mountain tribes – grumbling seems to be an art form. Similarly, all over the country there are people who think that Oman could go faster and further towards the construction of a society with more participation in the decision-making process. They are far from a majority or even a significant minority. Most Omanis are still far more concerned about simply having a decent standard of living than worrying about any fancy notions of modern political rights.

Oil-poor though it may be by Gulf standards, Oman is, again by Gulf standards, rich in other potential. The 1986 shock served, among other things, to remind the Omanis of all the money that had been spent in the previous ten years without any real concern for the long-term future. Agricultural development has been a shibboleth for at least a decade and precious little has been done about it, considering the potentially excellent land available on the Batinah coast north of Muscat, around the Jebel Akhdar, in the Sharkiyya and on the Salalah plain.

One of the most stubborn bottlenecks was finally tackled during the winter of 1986–7, when, at least partially in reaction to the oil price drop, rational marketing of agricultural products was taken seriously for the first time. It suddenly seemed more sensible to bring bananas to Muscat from the gardens 50 kilometres away rather than let them rot on the ground and import Chiquitas from Guatemala. A government marketing authority was set up, given a proper budget, real scope for action and, as a director, an experienced administrator who combines ability and clout.[24]

The marketing board is only one aspect, but it is a good omen for an ambitious programme to realize the country's agricultural potential. Since 1980 a series of low dams were being planned along the Batinah coast to hold the considerable amount of rainwater that almost every winter runs off straight into the sea;[25] meanwhile the sinking water table was increasingly bedevilled with salt water infiltration. Dam-building is expensive; that is why the Batinah dams were given priority among civil aid projects under the 1980 agreement with the United States. The first of them was finally built and commissioned in time for the 1987 winter rains. Unfortunately, the first rainfall revealed serious construction faults: the water disappeared before it could be properly dispersed for irrigation. After the long delay, the dam seems to have been built according to a model developed for the Arizona desert without taking into account local hydro-geological factors. It was bad luck that the dam was close enough to Muscat to have become the goal of

Friday outings; those who came to marvel after the rain saw nothing but a puddle of mud. Some even had the unpleasant impression that the Americans, who were supposed to be friends, had made fools of them.

In January 1992, the long-awaited *Majlis al-Shura* met for the first time, after a complicated selection process that was somewhere between the appointed consultative assembly and real elections. Its prerogatives, if all goes well, should also be somewhere in a middle ground between the very limited powers of the body established in 1980 and a working parliament. The Omani citizens are becoming more demanding and it remains to be seen whether the very limited participation offered them will satisfy their ambitions for long.

The future succession

Many foreigners, especially among those who love Oman, worry about the future of the Sultanate, or more explicitly about the question of the dynastic succession. More foreigners, probably, than Omanis; a recurrent topic of private discussion among well-meaning expatriates, the subject is never mentioned in public.[26] All the other Gulf rulers have a crown prince or an heir presumptive designated by a family council. Not so in Oman, or at least not so far as is public knowledge. Yet exaggerated worry about the succession seems a misguided object of anxiety. To begin with, the Sultan is still a relatively young man (he was born in 1940), and despite his white beard, the youngest of all the Gulf rulers. That is in itself a favourable factor because continuity counts in a country where the monarch rules as well as reigns. Admittedly, there can always be an unhappy accident and Qaboos has no son – but in the Arabian peninsula that is less of a problem than in monarchies which apply the Salic law or Persian dynastic practices. In the peninsula succession does not necessarily follow the rules of primogeniture or even of filiation. In Saudi Arabia, ever since the founder-king Abdul Aziz (Ibn Saud) was succeeded by his son Saud, the kingship has passed from brother to brother. The al-Sabah family of Kuwait worked out a complicated arrangement by which cousins are successively named emir in order to keep a balance between different branches of the family.

True, in Oman the title of Sultan has been handed down from father to son for more than a century. This still does not mean that such transmission is a *sine qua non* for the continuity of either the dynasty or the institution of the sultanate. At least two possible scenarios can be imagined for the day when the problem becomes acute. The first is that a private agreement exists within the family, which is a much smaller, and therefore presumably more manageable, ruling family than that of the other Gulf states. If this were the case, it would be characteristic of the Sultan to keep it quiet to avoid coteries being formed around one or the other person. A second possible scenario is that Qaboos has neither designated nor participated in the formal designation of a successor, considering that the country is stable enough for the choice to be left to the tribal chiefs when the time comes. This second scenario is more probable than the first, particularly since it conforms with Ibadhi tradition. One of the features of Ibadhism is that any just man may be chosen as the head of the community and that succession does not follow lineage. In the religious sense, the head of the community is the imam, and that title has been vacant since the death, in Saudi exile, of the last incumbent, Ghalib bin Ali. Qaboos, like his forefathers since the eighteenth century, has never sought to take the title of imam. Yet a transposition of the rules of the election of an imam to that of a sultan is not unimaginable.

References to Ibadhism have become increasingly frequent. They are one more way of marking Omani difference and independence. Ibadhism has also proved to be a good insurance against possible Islamist stirrings. Muscat was the only city in the eastern part of the Arabian peninsula that completely escaped the shock waves of the Iranian revolution, and where there was never a hint of demonstrations. There was, however, a politico-religious storm much later, sparked off by a declaration by the Grand Mufti of Saudi Arabia at a meeting of theologians in Riyadh in 1986 that Ibadhism did not conform to the spirit of Islam.[27] In reply, the Ibadhi Mufti of Muscat spoke for three hours, transmitted *in extenso* on Oman television, refuting the arguments point by point. It was more than a theological dispute. In Muscat, the Saudi sheikh's remarks were considered an intolerable meddling in the interior affairs of a neighbouring country. There is, after all, no separation between religion and politics in strict Islamic thought and no single political notion is taken as seriously as what Westerners would consider purely religious affairs. In Muscat, it took a long time before the furore caused by what many people saw as a demonstration of the Saudi penchant for hegemony simmered down. Religion is a very serious matter in the Arabian peninsula, and the Omanis are no more ready to accept imperious condescension in religious affairs, from whatever quarter it may come, than in any other.

CHAPTER 10

Conclusion: Times of Crisis

The end of the Iran-Iraq war in August 1988 brought an enormous feeling of relief to the Gulf. Military and psychological damage to the six member countries of the Gulf Cooperation Council (GCC) had been minimal and, as they thought, the two main protagonists of the eight-year-long conflict were sufficiently exhausted to be neutralized for some time to come. Oil prices had risen again well above the disastrous 1986 levels. The break-up of the Soviet empire was sufficiently advanced to reassure even Saudi Arabia. Far from being the end of history for the countries of the Gulf, it was a period of cautious euphoria and great hope: finally, they thought, they had some chance of realizing their ambition of combining extreme well-being with some sense of security. There was even talk of reducing the absurdly high defence budgets, although not those for the internal security services.

The Gulf Cooperation Council was beginning to bear fruit. Born of the uncertainties of the war between Iran and Iraq, it had had some difficulty in finding its equilibrium. Officially, the talk was simply of economic cooperation. The great euphoria could not last forever, and the more clairvoyant realized that sooner or later reforms would be needed in the artificial economic systems. The GCC plans quickly showed up the pitfalls that lay in the path of any real concertation beyond polite lip-service. Ambitions changed with circumstances. As long as the 1970s boom was in full spate, local pride knew no limits; every emir wanted his intercontinental airport, his steel plant and his dry-dock. By 1981–2 it seemed that the boom might indeed be finite, and the first effects of the war next door were felt – although the two phenomena were not necessarily in direct correlation.[1]

Even before the first preparatory reunion of the foreign ministers of the member states, Oman had circulated a white paper proposing that a system to coordinate external defence and internal security be studied. The document was rejected out of hand. The spring of 1981 was still a time of calm in the Gulf; there had been no coup attempt in Bahrain, no bombs in Kuwait. True, there was wariness beneath the calm; in all the cities of eastern Arabia except for Muscat, riots had broken out in the wake of the Islamic revolution in Iran. They had been quickly and not always tenderly crushed.

Officially, the GCC's original aims were purely economic. The emphasis on questions of 'security', a field where it was often easier to reach quasi-unanimity, came gradually. Everyone wanted to feel secure; not everyone was ready to admit restrictions that could touch individual or collective purses. There have been hints that that was, in fact, the point from the outset, but that it was camouflaged. I was in Muscat when the foreign ministers' conference drew up the articles of association in March 1981. I am quite convinced that the idea of defence and internal-security cooperation was deliberately minimized in the beginning. However, in the quest for security that flourished in subsequent years, the notion became an obsession. It was probably the natural reaction to the long war next door, but, sadly, it cast a shadow over all of Gulf life. Almost anything can become a matter for security, from protection of the rulers to agricultural policy, and all rational planning or cost-effectiveness can be subordinated to it.[2]

The genesis of the GCC goes back to discussions before the British retreat from the Gulf in 1971. The possibility was evoked then of a nine-member federation: the seven emirates of the UAE plus Qatar and Bahrain. Kuwait, independent for a decade, would not have become a member, but was pushing hard for the creation of the Federation. Saudi Arabia, just beginning to become aware of its weight in the regional balance, was not enthusiastic. The project was finally shattered by an excess of pride: too many prickly emiri sensitivities to be taken care of, and the euphoria of the 1970s made the idea easy to forget.

Ten years later the establishment of the GCC was much more a response to the war or, more precisely, to the ambitions of two powerful neighbours, Iraq and the brand-new Islamic Republic of Iran, than to the beginnings of economic difficulties. This fact contradicts the official doctrine and officials are reluctant to admit it. At first, the establishment of the GCC was an act of mutual reassurance and psychological defence: practical, physical defence measures came considerably later. When the GCC was founded, in the spring of 1981, the Gulf foreign ministries, like most experts elsewhere, still thought the war would be short. And, at the time, they were not at all unhappy about the war as such. In September 1980, just after the Iraqi invasion of Iran, a senior Omani diplomat told me: 'I hope this war continues forever.' However shocking such a statement may appear at first glance, the same idea was expressed, with greater or lesser frankness, throughout the Gulf states.

The idea of the GCC germinated during the winter of 1980–1. The first public hint came in a joint communiqué by the future member states at a meeting of the Islamic Conference Organization in February. A decision of principle was taken there, and the articles of association prepared in Muscat the following month. The GCC charter was ratified by the six rulers in Abu Dhabi in May. Eleven years later the GCC is still seeking a real role.

Even when it became clear that the sadly drawn-out *Blitzkrieg* was going to last far longer than anyone had counted on, the war was still not frightening to the Gulf countries. The general thinking was that if it had not spread in the first few months, why should it do so later? That is why the Omani white paper of spring 1981, suggesting a common GCC defence component, was not taken very seriously. At the time, some of the countries even thought it could be a maneouvre to bring the other countries into what was considered – at least officially – as an unholy alliance with the United States. Less than a year had gone by since Oman signed the American access agreements of

1980, and the violent criticism that signature attracted had not been forgotten. From an Omani (and Saudi) perspective, the real danger at the time was in Afghanistan, which the Soviet Army had entered in December 1979 and where it was not yet bogged down. All the commentators were busily exhuming the notion of the old Russian dream of access to the warm seas. These theories were fuelled by the restiveness of the Baluchis (in Iran, primarily, but also across the border in Pakistan); they were, it was said at the time, only waiting for a slightly better consolidation of the Soviet presence to rise up in revolt and proclaim an autonomous republic under Soviet influence.[3] The cause of the Afghan rebels continued to touch a highly vibrant chord in Saudi Arabia, where far more television space was devoted to the Afghan war than to the Palestinian *intifada*. By 1991 the Soviet Union had long withdrawn from Afghanistan and the United States cut off aid to the Mujaheddin groups who had nothing left to do but squabble among themselves; the Saudis still supported some of the most radical leaders whose hangers-on did not hesitate to bite the hand that fed them.[4]

At the time it invaded Iran, Iraq was not only an Arab brother, but also an ally of the Soviet Union. Saddam Hussein hardly bothered to hide his ambition to become the master of the Gulf once the Shah of Iran was out of the running. Iran was hostile to the creation of the GCC from the beginning, considering it an inimical alliance directed against itself. That was not the case in 1981, nor was it true ten years later. When it was founded, the GCC was hardly more than collective psychological armour, certainly not a military pact directed against either Iran or Iraq. It only became one when Iraq attacked one of its members.

The place of Saudi Arabia

At its foundation, many observers thought that the GCC was nothing more than a fig leaf to hide a Saudi scheme to dominate the Gulf. As a strong centre with minor satellites gravitating around the fringes it seemed to be setting up an Arabian version of the relationship between the Soviet Union and the countries of Eastern Europe. The choice of Riyadh for the headquarters reinforced the theory.

The symbolic force of place is far greater in the Arab world than in the West. This comes partly as a result of the survival of the laws of hospitality (strongly apparent in any meeting in the Gulf, whether it be public or private). The host, master of the house, automatically becomes the president of a meeting, and his ideas and opinions, and above all his style, will carry considerable weight in shaping the session.

The 'natural' place for the headquarters of the GCC would probably have been Bahrain. The centre of communications in the Gulf, Bahrain was trying to expand its service sector to give employment to its indigenous work force at a time when Riyadh was still immersed in a boom economy. Furthermore, if anyone had asked the future officials of the GCC where, outside their home countries, they would like to live, a very large percentage would have voted for Bahrain. But no one asked them, and Riyadh was chosen. As host country, Saudi Arabia gave the Council 126,000 square metres of land and then added, as a second gift, the Secretariat building which cost 237 million Saudi riyals to build.

Then came the surprise. Once the Secretariat was firmly ensconced in their capital, the Saudis began to show a surprising reserve, almost a reticence to push themselves forward. This reserve was consistent with the general trend of Saudi foreign policy in both the Arab and larger international contexts; but it was unexpected when applied to the Gulf. Even the other Gulf countries were happily surprised.

Next came the choice of a secretary-general. The post carries considerable influence, more than in other regional organizations where the post of secretary-general tends to be a high-echelon civil servant, mandated by the member countries but rarely an innovator. In the brand-new GCC, with no institutionalized tradition to build on, the secretary-general had a very wide scope for independent action. Especially in the early years, he could, and sometimes did, act almost like a seventh head of state.

There was never any hint, it was explained afterwards, that the post could go to a Saudi. The choice of Abdulla Ya'coub Bishara, a Kuwaiti diplomat, former permanent representative to the United Nations in New York, was a bit like appointing the chief poacher to the post of gamekeeper. In 1981 many people in the Gulf were afraid of the Kuwaitis, and considered them too clever by half, always ready to use their wiles and their ruses to get the better of anyone else. Abdulla Bishara began a third mandate in 1988. In his time, he has made his mark as a professional diplomat ready and able at the right moment to go well beyond the role of the spokesman, the go-between or simple executant, to become the stage manager, or even the hidden power. Abdulla Bishara looks as though he has just stepped out of an Italian Renaissance painting; he is the courtier par excellence as described by Machiavelli. To watch him in action, one cannot help but think that he must have read the choice portions of Machiavelli's writings, to play so perfectly his role of modern courtier to princes who have certainly not all read the master.

Beyond the questions of place and personalities, one of the first tests of the role that Saudi Arabia had chosen to play, came in the summer of 1982, when Iraq was for the first time seriously threatened by the advancing Iranian offensive. The Iranian reconquest of its territory had begun the autumn before, but it was only once Khorramshahr had been retaken that Iraq suffered its first real battlefield defeats. For a time, it looked like a rout: the Iranians said they had taken 19,000 prisoners in the battle of Khorramshahr; it was a military and psychological turning point in the war. For the first time, the Gulf States and particularly Saudi Arabia had to face the question of the very survival of Iraq, which sent pressing appeals for help to its Arab brothers in the Gulf. Coinciding with the diplomatic letters, a series of bombs exploded in Kuwait in August. They were meant to be attributed to Iran and their effect was intended to push a frightened Kuwait into the protective arms of its northern neighbour, with the underlying aim of encouraging more financial aid.

The six GCC foreign ministers met to consider what their response should be, and this meeting in itself was an amazing act only a year after the GCC's establishment. Saudi Arabia suggested that they should give Iraq more active support. I have never been able to determine with certainty whether at the time this meant openly and actively entering the war; I suspect not.

The other countries all opposed a more active role in the war and preferred to continue in an unquiet neutrality. They knew they were more vulnerable – but they were also more accustomed to living with Iran, whatever the nature of the regime on the other side of the Gulf.

This was a lesson in history and geography for Saudi Arabia. Traditionally, the Kingdom has been inward-looking. Its heart lies in the desert of the Nejd and even during the period of territorial consolidation, when the conquest of the Hijaz and the Holy Cities forced the Saudis to begin paying attention to the outside world, it did so with reluctance. For decades, the only window opened was on the Red Sea coast. Until 1984, all the embassies and the Ministry of Foreign Affairs were in Jeddah, not in the capital. The province of Al-Hasa, or Eastern province, on the Gulf coast, was until very recently a welcome source of revenues (most of the oil reserves are there), but it was barely integrated into the Kingdom.

The doctrine of neutrality

From 1982 until the summer of 1987 neutrality was the official doctrine of the GCC states. During that whole period, Saudi Arabia kept its sang-froid despite multiple provocations from both Iran and Iraq. The GCC as a collective body repeatedly tried to mediate between their warring neighbours. Several of its members, including Saudi Arabia, did this individually. Apart from incidents like the aerial duel, in June 1984, which opposed Saudi F-15s, guided by American AWACS, and Iranian Phantoms, direct confrontation was very rare until 1987. But the 'tanker war', with increasingly frequent attacks on ships belonging to the Gulf countries, was difficult to ignore; and the capture of the Faw peninsula sucked Kuwait dangerously close to the vortex. For Iraq, which had been trying to internationalize the war since 1981, this at least was a minor triumph.

It is possible to pinpoint exactly the moment when strict neutrality was no longer observed as official GCC doctrine, if not always unofficial practice. The violent riots in Mecca, on 31 July 1987, were as shocking to the populations of the GCC and their leaders as those of 1979 had been,[5] and the international implications far greater. Significantly, it was only after that bloody Friday of the 1987 pilgrimage that the abortive attacks of the year before were made public. Each *hajj* season since the Iranian revolution had been troubled, and year after year the Saudi authorities had done their best to contain and to minimize the problems. Whatever one may think of the stubborn opacity of many of the information systems in the Gulf, in this case the censorship was motivated by a decision not to throw more oil on the fires of intolerance. It was a logical consequence of the policy of necessary neighbourliness which Saudi Arabia's GCC partners continued to preach. It was possible to keep quiet about the arms discovered in the baggage of pilgrims from Libya and Iran in 1986; but the full-scale riots of 1987 were something else.

The reticence of the GCC countries continued even after UN Resolution 598 calling for a ceasefire between Iran and Iraq had been adopted by the Security Council on 20 July 1987. The text included a firm but careful demand to both parties to accept a ceasefire, with provisions for sanctions and an arms embargo against the side that refused. Iraq accepted the resolution immediately, but Iran waited almost a year before doing so; it wanted the commission on responsibility for starting the war set up as a prerequisite to negotiations. The Mecca riots came ten days after the vote on the resolution and at a time when Iran was feeling increasingly isolated. Could there have been a phenomenon of cause and effect? Probably not. The pilgrims had left Iran for Mecca well before the resolution was voted and with the multi-centric power systems of Iran, they were hardly likely to be getting orders from those who were most concerned with such unholy matters as the United Nations and international opinion.

The Mecca riots of 31 July pushed Saudi Arabia to the brink of open war and yet the break in diplomatic relations came only months later.[6] Oman and the UAE tried to keep up their policy of active neutrality. Oman was the intermediary in the repatriation of wounded and killed Iranian sailors after attacks in the Strait of Hormuz. Both Oman and the UAE continued to work at keeping the bridges open by organizing ministerial visits and taking messages back and forth.

On 21 October 1987 an Iranian missile hit Kuwait's main oil terminal at Mina al-Ahmadi, temporarily knocking it out of commission. Only then did the GCC foreign ministers publish their first joint condemnation of Iran. The declaration reminded Iran and any others who might require it, 'that any aggression against one member country of the council is an aggression directed against all the members.' The declaration was not followed by any action: Saudi Arabia would have liked to have seen all its partners sign its request to the United Nations to have sanctions voted against Iran. They declined to do so, just as they declined to follow suit when Saudi Arabia broke off diplomatic relations with Iran six months later.

It would, however, have been inconceivable for the Gulf countries not to join the unanimous condemnation of Iran for not accepting the ceasefire at the extraordinary Arab summit in Amman in November 1987; even Iran's only Arab ally, Syria, was persuaded to sign the communiqué (though almost certainly at a price). Even then, Oman and the UAE continued to skirt carefully away from any policy that could be construed as anti-Iranian, whoever defined it. As a result, the final declaration of the six GCC rulers in Riyadh at the end of December 1987 was even less alarming for Iran than the careful Amman text. Commercial relations between the ports on either side of the lower Gulf had never slackened. And by 1987, at least one third of all Iranian imports passed through Dubai, and even Muscat had become a transit point.

The participation of outside powers in naval operations within the Gulf was not greeted with complete satisfaction by all the GCC states, although the varying attitudes were somewhat ambiguous. Official GCC position was clear: there was to be freedom of navigation in the Gulf and no big-power presence, with the sole exception of the ships attached to the American mini-base that had existed in Bahrain since independence. By September 1987 Western fleets were beginning to jostle one another in the Gulf and in the Sea of Oman. When I questioned a senior GCC diplomat about who had invited them all, the immediate answer was: 'No one; they invited themselves. Except, of course, for the escorts for the Kuwaiti tankers.' He was sincere. At that moment it looked very much as though the war – which had for so long remained almost miraculously circumscribed, leaving the GCC countries practically untouched – could submerge the whole region. The hesitations, only natural in the face of what could have been a mortal danger, were also a sign of the extreme vulnerability of these countries. Golden armour had protected them for a dozen years and let them bask in heady clouds of illusion. That era was finished well before Iraq invaded Kuwait. Some Western analysts, particularly in America, were counting up the billions of dollars of disposable income and flattering the local rulers, their governments and particularly their armies in order to encourage purchases of expensive weaponry. There have been hints in the Arab world of the deliberate under-estimation of the capacity of the local armies by the West. The West was thought to have pushed the Gulf rulers into the arms of would-be protectors at the first hint of real trouble. Such rumours may well be one more example of the wide-spread Arab propensity to see plots in any troubled corner; but inevitably they resurfaced in 1990.

Speculations on the potential efficacity of one or other army, or even of the GCC rapid deployment force, became a favourite topic for debate in Western strategic studies institutes between 1984 and 1990. The establishment of the GCC force was a milestone in the affirmation of Saudi power within the Council. It was perfectly logical that the main base of the Gulf force be established at Hafr al-Batn in north-eastern Saudi Arabia, not very far from the Kuwaiti border. By then the perceived danger was in Iran. Once Hafr al-Batn had been decided upon, the choice of a Saudi commanding general was inevitable. It might be acceptable to have a Kuwaiti directing the political wheels of the organization, but, as a spokesman explained the decision at the GCC summit in Muscat in 1985, 'it is unimaginable even to think of a commander of another (non-Saudi) nationality, even though he might be from another Gulf country, as long as the base is on Saudi soil.'

The first joint exercises in 1984 showed up the difficulty of making the various communications and weapons systems work together. Indeed, such integration was simply impossible in several sectors. The reaction, characteristic of worried boom states, was to go out and buy more systems. Finally Oman, which can hardly be suspected of anti-militarism, warned its partners that being the prize customers in the world arms bazaar was not a panacea for all dangers. An embryonic joint force was formed, with Saudi, Kuwaiti and Emirati contingents. Oman played a role not unlike that of France within NATO: it was finally persuaded to send small troop units on rotation. Bahrain and Qatar were exempted from supplying troops, but contributed to the finances. Besides the units actually stationed at Hafr al-Batn, others in the home countries were marked for the Force and given special training.

It was quite evident from the beginning that the GCC Joint Force could not be regarded as a serious deterrent in any serious armed confrontation, but it was supposed to give a show of collective self-confidence and to prevent dangerous, desperate and unconsidered moves. Unfortunately, when the attack came, from a friend, the modicum of new self-confidence was not enough to defend Kuwait. Perhaps nothing could have been done, but many Kuwaitis continue to wonder just what an army was for since when it came to the crunch it did not even retard the invaders by a day. Their criticism is not of the GCC force, which never had a chance to come to their help, but of their own armed forces. Direct criticism of the minister of defence was even more virulent. Once the lightening invasion was complete, could the GCC states have done other than ask for help – or accept the help the Americans offered to Saudi Arabia when it saw its ally in what it looked like imminent danger? To understand the reactions of the Gulf states in 1990 in the face of the invasion and the build-up to the second Gulf war, we should look at the relations those states entertained with the rest of the world.

But first, it is important to consider the relations of the GCC member countries among themselves. The reticence of Saudi Arabia, reluctant to make use of its power to put overt pressure on the smaller countries, was all the more astonishing because long before Saudi Arabia became the regional power it now is, it hardly hesitated to throw its weight around. The example of the Buraimi affair,[8] has not been forgotten; its final act, the long negotiation to give the Saudis a corridor to the Gulf between Qatar and Abu Dhabi, dragged on until 1974. The desert border between Oman and Saudi Arabia was not recognized until 1990.

The smaller states will not overtly go against the wishes of the big neighbour; but Oman and Kuwait were known to have done so before the Iraqi invasion. One example was the very polite refusal of the Kuwaitis to ratify the security cooperation agreement which would have given Saudi Arabia the right of hot pursuit across the Kuwaiti border and included a clause imposing automatic extradition of suspects wanted for a long list of possible crimes. Kuwait considered the agreement in breech of both its constitution and its long tradition of hospitality. The Saudi officials could hardly remain insensitive to the second of these arguments: Kuwait had given refuge to the founder of the Kingdom, the future King Abdul Aziz, and his father at the turn of the century. It was from Kuwait that Abdul Aziz set out to reconquer his lands. The proposal of the right of pursuit is generally applicable within the GCC, but it so happens that Kuwait only has borders with Saudi Arabia.

From the summer of 1987, the character of the GCC began to change. Kuwait, feeling ever more threatened by the terrorist elements discovered inside the country and the continuing war on its borders, moved closer to the Saudi position. When Saudi Arabia broke its diplomatic relations with Iran in April 1988, it was widely expected that Kuwait would follow, particularly in the wake of the long hijacking of the Kuwait Airlines Airbus almost certainly attributable to Iran. But Kuwait did not do so: one more sign of the efforts made to keep relations with Iran at least at a minimum level of civility, despite all the difficulties and complications of the war.

Concurrently, Oman and the UAE were taking a quite different stance in their attitude to Iran. Their insistence on maintaining normal contacts, and continuing dialogue, considerably annoyed the Saudis and, later, the Kuwaitis. Both regarded the behaviour of Oman and the UAE as indicative of a lack of solidarity with those of their partners who had had real trouble with Iran. This difference in perspective carried an echo of the old upper Gulf–lower Gulf dichotomy. Qatar was inclined to go along with the UAE: Bahrain said nothing, but would do nothing to antagonize Saudi Arabia.

The existence of the GCC was in itself reassuring to the smaller members. They were full-fledged members of an organization whose scale is such that their influence is multiplied by the multiple skeins of family and historical ties that criss-cross the Gulf. The influence of Qatar or Bahrain in the United Nations or even within the Arab League was minimal. Within the GCC their ideas were listened to, and they could even become the instigators, the champions or the spokesmen of an important policy decision.

However paradoxical it may seem, being a member of the GCC gave even the smallest among them a certain guarantee against the possible 'Saudi hegemony' which many observers thought was the whole point behind the Council. On this point one must be careful to distinguish clearly between influence and an attack on sovereignty. Saudi influence has indeed become stronger and may well become even more so. The new situation after the second Gulf war goes beyond strategic and military concerns. There is a good deal of pressure, led by Saudi Arabia, to prepare and apply uniform civil and penal law; such codes would inevitably be marked by Saudi influence, and it is not at all certain that Oman, to take one example, would be ready to adopt it. The Omani case is particularly strong because it can invoke Ibadhi practice which would not necessarily be compatible with the Hanafite Sunni interpretations of other jurists.

Saudi influence could be felt in other Gulf states in the revisions of laws and practices in the name of harmonization. With few exceptions, they have assumed a stricter interpretation. 'Harmonization' of information policy and censorship has, for example, meant a new interpretation of the injunction against translations of the Koran, with the result that several classic translations into English and French have been taken out of bookshops in Muscat and Bahrain.[9]

Official explanations that such modifications are in response to interior pressures, and that 'the people' want to return to their traditions, are not good enough. The other Gulf countries do not need the constant re-legitimation of adherence to the outward forms of religion necessary to the Saudi system. On the other hand, and here is the real paradox, the fact that the small countries are equal to the giant Kingdom in their membership of the organization – even if that egality is more formal than real – gives them the assurance that they will be able to guard at least nominal independence. It is almost impossible to imagine that the King of Saudi Arabia could announce that he has decided to annex the domain of his brother and fellow-ruler, the emir of Bahrain. There would, in fact, be little reason for him to do so; the GCC neutralizes most of the temptations of open opposition and, for the most independent of the rulers, provides a framework for polite dissension while reassuring the Kingdom that its marches are secure.

The GCC has special importance for the United Arab Emirates, with its problems of internal cohesion. External policy has been a cementing factor between the individual emirates, and membership of the GCC has played an important role. Within the GCC, the Emirates speak and are listened to as one voice, which is not necessarily the case for the federal government when it comes to domestic policy. The GCC can play the role of lightning rod, as it were. Over the next few years, an increasing number of inevitably unpopular measures will have to be decided: taxation or charges for services like water or electricity that have so far been given for free. Being able to present unpleasant news as the consequence of decisions not by the local government, or worse, the Federation, but by a common accord within the GCC, could make such changes far more palatable.

The GCC is indeed beginning to take common decisions, including in the field of foreign affairs. There again, it can be of more service to the smaller states than the larger ones. When any question is up for consideration – for example, the relations of the GCC with the European Community or the European Free Trade Association for reciprocal free trading rights – the early stages of the work can be done by the Secretariat, which can also put together the basic documents and do the background research. For small countries which suffer from a chronic shortage of specialized native personnel, this is of enormous benefit. It is probably too early to think about common diplomatic missions abroad, though they may become possible one day.

The strange tale of Ficht al-Dibl has long thrown a tiny spanner into the works of good neighbourliness between Qatar and Bahrain. The dispute for the possession of two sand spits – one of them, Hawwar, covered by water at high tide – would be laughable if it were not, at the same time, an excellent demonstration of the difficulties the GCC has in playing the role of regional arbitrator and of the limits of King Fahd's authority in playing Solomon for his neighbours. The dispute has lasted for decades, from well before independence, but the most recent crisis erupted when a Dutch technical crew arrived on Ficht al-Dibl from Bahrain to put up a radar and what was presumably some basic infrastructure that could be used for future oil exploration. Their mission ended with the hurried evacuation of the island after shots from the Qatari mainland.

Even the personal interventions of King Fahd brought no solution. After a last attempt, it was announced in late 1987 that the case would be taken to the International Court of Justice in the Hague. The decision was announced in Riyadh by King Fahd himself. In that last face-saving gesture, he could present what was really an avowal of failure as a Saudi initiative. Seeing the difficulties involved in solving this tiny dispute did not help the GCC's standing with the local population. They did not miss the point either that Saudi Arabia, not the GCC, was the official mediator. To argue that the dispute far predated the Council and that Saudi Arabia had a long-established legitimate interest did not quite suffice to explain why the Council was kept completely out of the matter.

The invasion of Kuwait and the immediate call for international protection can, from an intra-Gulf perspective, be understood in two ways. Either it went very far in showing up the weakness of the member countries, individually and collectively, despite their enormous preoccupation with security and their arms expenditures, or it was the first test for common action in foreign affairs. Both of these facts are true. In the aftermath of the war, the Damascus declaration[10] could have been a milestone in tackling together the difficult problem of future relations with the poorer parts of the Arab world. Two difficulties wrecked the agreement. The first was Kuwait's reluctance, born of fear, to accept the presence of so many Arab troops from Egypt and Syria; the second, was the difficulty in finding a unanimously acceptable definition of relations with Iran.

Relations with the outside world

It is very difficult to gauge just how far the GCC countries really want commonality in their foreign relations, and at what point, whatever the public declarations, they will insist on making their own decisions. In the case of the Iraqi invasion of Kuwait, the old animosity towards that revolutionary troublemaker facilitated the decision for immediate common action. That decision in itself influenced the future course of affairs in a military and, more importantly, in a political sense. The relationship with Iran has already been dealt with. Further afield, it is important to look at positions in relation to four key areas: the United States, the former Soviet Union, the other Arabs and Europe. Besides those four areas, two more require at least a mention: one is the Islamic world, as such – beyond the Arab world – and the other is the Indian sub-continent.

Relations between the Gulf countries and each of these areas are more complex than is often recognized. The most complicated of all are relations with the United States, and these have become even more so since the Iraqi invasion of Kuwait and the subsequent crisis and war. So many considerations must be taken into account, many of them contradictory, that the final result is a tangled web in which I think at least three main strands must be distinguished. The first is the desire for what are regarded as the benefits enjoyed by Western societies, from a common belief in the virtues of free enterprise, to the attraction exercised by high technology and all the comforts of a society of consumers of which the United States has become the arch-model. The second is a function of the traditional American alliance with Israel. The third is a complex geo-strategic relationship involving America's role in a one-superpower world, coupled with the gnawing remembrance of American abandonment of its ally, the Shah of Iran. The Iran-Contra affair did not help matters, and memories are long in the Middle East.

Any analysis in this field is complicated because each element, taken separately, contains the germ of its opposite. There is a genuine desire to acquire every technological marvel, to send young people to the best American universities, to become fervent partisans of Wendy's. At the same time, and in almost the same breath, the Middle Eastern patrons of a Kentucky Fried Chicken shop will castigate the West for its lack of moral values, its permissiveness and the crisis of the family. America is deprecated for its villainy and depravity at the same time that it is considered the guarantor of territorial integrity and of the institutional status quo, accepted by the great majority of local citizens. Europeans are not entirely exempt from criticism, but in general criticism of them will be far less virulent than towards the United States. Those who criticise a consumer society are often cheerful practitioners of its ways, and few would question the absolute values of capitalism and of free enterprise. The collapse of the Soviet empire has not simplified feelings, nor has the enormous role played by the United States in the Gulf war. The ferocity of Saudi anti-communist sentiments explains how President Reagan was able to persuade King Fahd to contribute US$32m to the Nicaraguan Contras' war chest.[11] Without communism to fear, cynics say there is no more motivation for the American friendship.

Money, or rather oil, is used as explanation for the prompt action of the Americans in 1990 and 1991. The Gulf Arabs cannot imagine that the United States and President Bush acted in good faith and that the basic American streak of decency and the rule of law (perhaps a bit tardy in manifesting itself) also played a role. Gratitude for having saved them from the Iraqi scourge is united with suspicion; it could only have been a Kuwaiti who said: 'What a pity that we can't move the whole country westward and become a 51st state.'[12] Even that heartfelt exclamation may not be valid for long.

The object of love and hate at the same time, even after the second Gulf war, the United States remains the habitual scapegoat for the innumerable contradictions arising from the pitfalls that await societies trying to preserve their traditions even while they enter the modern age. On that point in any case, the Sunni majority in the Gulf has been influenced by the

Iranian revolutionary propaganda and one of the difficult tasks of the GCC states and their allies during the Gulf crisis was to counter the notion of America as the arch-enemy of Islam.[13] Psychiatrists are familiar with individual love-hate relationships, with attraction and repulsion consuming one another in bitter internal struggle. Here such a phenomenon appears as an element of the collective consciousness.

The anti-American stands were not simply a direct consequence of the American-Israeli alliance, as was the case in some parts of the Arab world. Despite the important role Palestinians long played as opinion makers in the Gulf, as advisers, editorialists and broadcasters, there the question of Palestine never became the unique focus of political life it was in the Levant. The Gulf countries were generous in their support of the PLO and, just as they had continued to support Chairman Yasser Arafat in the dark days of 1982–3, they were among the first to recognize the creation of a Palestinian state after the Palestinian National Council in Algiers in November 1988.

Such support was not always a foregone conclusion. In late 1983, when Arafat seemed close to the end of his tenuous hold on the Palestinian movement, Syria made insistent requests to the Gulf States to stop supporting him. Had they done so, it would certainly have contributed to the establishment of a new PLO more or less under Syrian auspices. The GCC considered the situation in a ministerial meeting and, in one of its first common policy statements, decided to continue its support to Arafat. At the time, a high official of one of the Gulf countries who insisted on anonymity said, 'Actually, we were not entirely happy with the situation. But after much reflection we decided we would rather deal with the devil we know than with one we don't.'[14] Besides moral, diplomatic and financial support, the Gulf countries furnished the Palestinians with a place, or places, where tens and hundreds of thousands of them lived and worked. Some did very well and the Palestinian millionaires of the Gulf in turn helped the PLO. The Palestinians also provided the indispensable skilled manpower to build the host countries. Under the circumstances of the time, the result was a symbiosis from which the Gulf countries benefited immensely.

As often in the Gulf, Oman was a special case. As long as old

Sultan Said bin Taimur ruled the country, his general distrust of anything new, and his xenophobia which brooked of no exceptions except a few trusted Englishmen, extended, as one might expect, to the Palestinians. After Qaboos took over, his own misgivings concerning anyone and any movement even faintly suspect of being tinged in pink were firmly encouraged by his British advisers. Many of them had been active in the fight against the Front for the Liberation of South Yemen (FLOSY), and for them the Dhofar war was simply a continuation of what they had known in Aden. Qaboos did not require much encouragement to keep out people who kept talking about revolution and who, at the time, openly engaged in terrorism. 1970, the year of Qaboos's accession, was also the year of the triple hijacking to Zarqa. The first Palestinian hijacking of an El Al flight to Algeria had taken place in 1968. The ban continued until after the Palestinian National Council in Algiers in November 1988 and the proclamation of the Palestinian State and the renunciation of terrorism. More than a decade after the end of the Dhofar war, and after the formal renunciation of terrorism in 'neutral territory' in the Cairo declaration of 1985, the Omani attitude had become an anachronism which was only doing harm to its image in the Arab world. But as usual, Oman did not worry much about that.

Saudi Arabia long held something of the same reasoning. It would only permit a Fatah office, not one of the PLO as such, because of the Marxist factions among the membership. That also changed only with the recognition of the Palestinian state after the Algiers meeting. In practice, the Saudi distinction made little difference because the immense majority of politically-active Palestinians were members of Fatah which, besides, had a quasi-monopoly on furnishing PLO offices abroad.

It is against that background that Gulf reaction to the Palestinian support and Yasser Arafat's explicit endorsement of Saddam Hussein's invasion of Kuwait must be seen. Quite aside from the actions of some individual Palestinians in Kuwait, the overall position of the PLO and its leaders[15] was considered pure treachery, a stab in the back, to be neither forgiven nor soon forgotten.

The American-Israeli friendship was more of a hindrance by its indirect fall-out than in any direct sense. It was mostly the successes of the pro-Israel lobby in Washington in blocking arms sales to the Gulf countries that made the friendship felt. Arms sales, whatever the moral issues involved, are a fairly accurate barometer of international relations. The hue and cry raised in America in March 1988 with the announcement of the Saudi purchase of Chinse C(SS)–2 missiles is an example. But it represented more than that: it was a clear signal that the United States was no longer in complete control of a market it thought captive. Kuwait had gone the same way in 1986. When the American Congress refused to authorize the sale of Stinger ground-to-air rockets at a time when the Iran–Iraq war was getting uncomfortably close, Kuwait turned to the Soviet Union and bought SAM-8s. Two years later, Kuwait again asked the Americans to sell it forty F-18 fighter planes. That request was granted with some minor reservations because by this time, after practically breaking with Iran (through no wish of its own), Kuwait had been granted the status of a minor ally, at least in American official opinion. This status was not enshrined in any formal treaty, as the unfortunate Ambassador Glaspie accurately told Saddam Hussein in their fateful conversation just before the invasion of Kuwait. The cynics are quick to point out that the brilliant performance of American arms was the century's greatest sales pitch, but in fact, it was neither necessary nor in the strictest sense conclusive.

The Gulf crisis changed Gulf perceptions. Even before Israel was dragged to the peace table in Madrid in October 1991, there was a subtle shift of opinion even in Saudi Arabia, paradoxically thanks to Saddam Hussein and the Iraqi Scud missiles. It is difficult to be on the receiving end of the same missile launchers and not feel some sympathy with the other victims. Suddenly Saudi newspapers dropped 'the Zionist entity', and started simply printing 'Israel'; Tel Aviv became a dateline like any other. It was not, by a long way, friendship or even recognition but the first breech in what had seemed an impenetrable barrier. The shifts in the American position towards Israel, the end of the unquestioning, unreasoning support for Tel Aviv, did not come about overnight, nor were they equally felt in all quarters. However, even the subtlest changes were noted, and welcomed, in the Gulf.

The United States has long had difficulties in being accepted as it would wish to be seen: real friends of the good, disinterested in anything but the help it can dispense. Even more than other major powers, the US is perceived very much as a fair-weather friend, or at least as one who is there only when it serves its own purposes. Honour, friendship and keeping one's word remain absolute values in the Gulf and they are intertwined into an indivisible whole. Neither the American ships sent to the Gulf in 1987 nor even the enormous effort of the Gulf crisis and the liberation of Kuwait have entirely dispelled the lingering doubts engendered by the abandonment of the Shah.

The last Shah of Iran was not much loved in the Gulf countries, not even in Oman, despite the help he had given the Sultan in finishing off the Dhofar rebellion. The idea that there would be a natural affinity between autocratic monarchies does not hold up under the weight of old rivalries, of differences in mental structure and of historical divergences between Arabs and Persians. Mohammed Reza Pahlavi Shah was also disliked for his barely disguised ambition to dominate the Gulf under cover of being its protector, a natural consequence of his avowed aim of making Iran the world's fifth most powerful country and the first in the Middle East. He formally renounced his claims to sovereignty over Bahrain only under much British pressure in 1970. He still claimed the islands of Abu Musa and the Greater and Lesser Tumbs near the Strait of Hormuz which British cartographers had, at some point, attributed to Sharjah and Ras al-Khaimah. These islands played a large part in Iraqi propaganda at the beginning of the Iran–Iraq war (Saddam claimed to be defending Arab lands wherever they were), and later became bases for the Iranian Revolutionary Guards.

And yet, neither the Gulf monarchs nor their people forgot that when it came to the crunch, the Americans abandoned their friend and protégé. The rest of the sorry tale hardly needs retelling. The handling of the embassy hostage crisis, the failure of the Tabas rescue mission and the subsequent paralysis of the giant did nothing to restore American prestige in the area.

Then, with the war that dragged on, the people were just beginning to think about the possibility of America playing a positive role again (especially after diplomatic relations were restored with Baghdad in 1985), when the Iran-Contra affair came to light. The Gulf looked on bemused as the extraordinary sequence of events was unveiled: the Americans were selling arms to Iran in the hope of getting the American hostages in Lebanon freed while under the terms of 'Operation Staunch'[16] claiming to do no such thing. The arms went through Israel, or Brazil, or Portugal, plus a few other channels, and the drama unfolded like an overloaded stage plot: scandals and lies, defiance of justice and of the American law, criminal incomprehension and incompetence up to even the highest level of government. Even the ludicrous aspects of the story – such as the extraordinary idea of sending American emissaries to Iran armed with a chocolate cake (bought in the best *patisserie* in Tel Aviv) and a Bible inscribed by President Reagan himself to Ayatollah Khomeini – showed such a flagrant incomprehension of the situation that they could only elicit painful wincing, not even a good laugh.

For the United States, the issue was complex. Its constant policy had been that of 'containing' the Soviet Union; any disinterested act of protecting small, vulnerable countries was subordinate. By early 1987, the thaw between the two superpowers had begun, though the first major disarmament agreements had not yet been signed. Officially, of course, the explanation was that the United States was there to ensure freedom of navigation in the Gulf; that was true, but this bit of the strategic policy puzzle fitted into others. American declarations and, in particular, American actions made the point clear. When Kuwait first approached the United States in the early winter of 1986–7 about the possibility of re-registering part of its fleet under the American flag, it was turned down flat. Kuwait then turned to the Soviet Union, which without fanfare immediately suggested chartering three ships to Kuwait. At that point, Kuwait turned back to the Americans, who agreed the second time around.

In the five years between 1985 and the invasion of Kuwait, the Soviet Union's role in the Gulf had been completely transformed. After the invasion of Afghanistan, the Gulf states worried less about Iran than about a possible Soviet drive through Baluchistan to the warm seas just beyond the Strait of Hormuz. The turning point came in September 1985. Oman, whose prickly anti-Sovietism had its roots in the Marxist help to the Dhofar rebellion, surprised everyone by announcing the establishment of normal relations with the Soviet Union. The UAE followed two months later. Then Hisham Nazer, after his new appointment as Saudi Minister of Oil replacing the long-serving Ahmed Zaki Yamani, at the end of October 1986, announced that his first visit abroad was to Moscow.

Even before the collapse of the Soviet Union, the situation had changed radically. One after another, the Gulf states established diplomatic relations with the country that had renounced its official atheism – a very important point. In the months leading up to the Gulf war, the Soviet Union joined the United Nations embargo and, although voting for the Security Council resolutions, tried until the last minute to avert the war. But then, to the obvious astonishment of Saddam Hussein, the Soviet Union acquiesced to the use of force to end the crisis. Neither Saddam nor anyone else knew how close the USSR was to collapse. With the crumbling of the once-feared empire began the process of building new relationships with the Central Asian republics. Saudi Arabia had been active in Azerbaijan, Tadjikistan and parts of Uzbekistan several years earlier, sending Korans and gifts for mosque construction. Despite this, the Saudi government has not really entered the competition for influence in the area opposing the Turkish and Iranian models of society.

Relations between the Gulf countries (including the GCC as a group) and Europe remain far short of what the former would like. The European Community has difficulty taking this financial giant for anything but a political gnat. The USA has disappointed the Gulf by some of its acts of commission; the countries of Western Europe, individually and collectively, continue to disappoint by acts of omission. Iran still complains about occult British influence, but otherwise the last vestige of anti-colonial resentment is fast receding. In its place are links of real affection, particularly towards Britain. England, and to a lesser extent Scotland and even Ireland remain points of reference all over the smaller Gulf states. Britain is regarded as a friend, but when it disappoints is considered with that much more bitterness. In Qatar, and to a lesser extent in Kuwait, there is a small côterie of influential francophiles. There is almost nothing political about this, and the emotional francophilia easily embraces the French-speaking part of Switzerland where many of them have summer houses – sometimes in addition to those on the French Riviera.

The GCC states remain highly sensitive to whatever is said and done in Europe. The European Community is a point of reference; the GCC regards it as a model, but also as a consolation since it is evidence of the difficulties that even highly developed countries face in attempting to advance together rationally. The GCC is particularly attracted by the idea that Europe could come to represent an alternative to superpower dependence, especially with only one remaining superpower. That is also why the GCC is so anxious to establish better institutional links to the European Community and concurrently with the European Free Trade Association. Petro-chemicals are only part of the story. For the GCC, the negotiations have had a value worth more than even the most brilliant commercial success: they have bestowed on the Council, at least in its own eyes, legitimacy as a fully-fledged interlocutor with international stature.

Without exception, the individual Gulf countries are looking for the same thing. Their experience of Europe as a protecting force may have given them an exaggerated idea of the importance of Europe and its freedom of political or economic manoeuvre. The Gulf countries are constantly asking Europeans to be more active on the political scene of the Middle East and the enormous discrepancies of military might deployed in 1990 by the Americans and the European members of the coalition shook their confidence in Europe less than one might have imagined.[17]

The scene seems set for Europe once again to become the preponderant outside partner for reasons entirely different from before. Can it be done? I am not quite sure that the Europeans, despite the courtesy shown in the discussions with the

Community and more recently with EFTA, are quite ready to accept the countries of the Gulf, and the GCC as such, as equal negotiating partners. To do so, the Europeans will need to overcome their prismatic view of the Gulf countries as rich, slightly naïve, and useful in carefully limited fields: as spoiled adolescents to be flattered, as possible lenders or investors to be guided and contained as necessary, as providers of oil, and as excellent consumers of arms and other goods that Europe continues to turn out better than the Japanese.

When the GCC was established it aroused a great deal of suspicion in many of the Arab countries, and in the Arab League itself. It was accused of separatism, of opting out of the Arab mainstream, of going its own way and striking another blow at the grand design of Arab unity, which had already by then lost much of its aura.[18] Gamal Abdel Nasser had been dead for over a decade; the squabbles of Iraqi and Syrian Ba'athists were hardly an inspiration for unity; Colonel Moammar Qaddafi's version of pan-arabism frightened almost everyone but himself. The aims of the Arab League, deprived of its Egyptian centre of gravity, had been reduced to the most basic level: opposition to Israel and, when things were going well, a defence of the Arab language and culture.

By 1985, the perspective had changed. The GCC, which had never talked about union, fusion, or even federation – all words that had become the laughing-stock of the Arab peoples and of the outside world – suddenly found itself being regarded in a different light. Among Arab intellectuals and at the Arab League headquarters, the GCC was suddenly hailed as a model of what the future could hold for the Arab world.

It became fashionable to plan regional organizations based on the GCC model. Even in an ideal and idealized future, not all of them could have the positive attributes of the GCC. In particular, they lacked the considerable homogeneity in political structure and philosophy, plus the social structures which help to overcome the differences in size and in riches. Still, the GCC was openly presented as a model, first of all for the Greater Maghreb.

The Arab Maghreb Union (usually referred to by its French acronym, the UMA) was declared in February 1989, only days after the rather more surprising Arab Cooperation Council which, at the outset, included Iraq, Jordan, Egypt and North Yemen. The UMA has shown surprising resilience to the strains that tore asunder the newly resurgent Arab League in 1990 and 1991; the Arab Cooperation Council shattered when Egypt refused to follow Iraq and became a key member of the military coalition against Saddam.

In the Gulf and in the whole Arabian Peninsula Islam is so much a part of life itself that it is not even a point for discussion. Saudi Arabia does have a deliberate policy to further Islam, but for the other states the affinity with the rest of the Islamic world is as much emotional as political or institutionalized. The Islamic Conference Organization, with strong links to the Saudi establishment, is still seeking a new equilibrium after the shocks caused by the Iranian Revolution. The stormy relations culminated in Iran's refusal to attend the Islamic Summit in Kuwait in 1987; after that, the Organization seemed to become the de facto standard-bearer of Sunni Islam and a symbol of the reassuring face of Islam[19] to the outside world. When an Iranian delegation showed up at the ICO ministerial meeting in Amman in March 1988 to negotiate the number of Iranian pilgrims[20] that were to be given visas to go on the next pilgrimage, the discussions almost inevitably turned to politics and the Iranians walked out. Over the next two years, relations see-sawed until the restoration of normal relations between Iran and Saudi Arabia in early summer 1991. It is the very naturalness of the Peninsula's relation to Islam, as natural as the very air its people breathe, that gave rise to so much anger when Saddam – that atheist, as they saw him – tried to play the card of Islam against them.

Oddly, the relations between the Gulf countries and the Indian subcontinent are so uneventful as barely to merit discussion. That situation could conceivably be only a temporary lull in a long history of regional geo-political interaction. Beginning in Basrah, which in normal times is already a Gulf port, on down to Dubai and Muscat, one can increasingly sense the proximity of the subcontinent. A Saudi from Jeddah probably feels less at home in Dubai than a Gujarati from Bombay. Some of the affinities are quasi-anecdotal: the realm of the curries begins in the spice market in Basrah (not Baghdad); from Abu Dhabi on down, the men wear a *wizara* (a longhi or sarong) under their *dishdasha*,[21] or on its own (particularly as a working garment).

Other manifestations of the closeness could, some day, become far more significant. The most important of these is the interpenetration of the populations. Some groups originally from the subcontinent, like the *Luwatiyya* of Muscat who came from Hyderabad (now in Pakistan) several centuries ago, are closely integrated into their country of adoption. Although they have retained a good deal of their specificity, the community is now one of the important breeding grounds for high-echelon Omani civil servants. Such integration is a continuing process; in 1987, Dubai adopted new rules that permitted far wider groups of immigrant workers to bring their families with them, inevitably a first step toward a permanent installation.

When Abdulla Bishara, the GCC Secretary-General, worries about the difficulties of being a small, rich and thinly-populated island in a part of the world that is basically poor and overpopulated, he is thinking specifically of the nearby subcontinent. For the time being, the relationships are still modelled, and distorted, by economic realities. For at least a few more years, the Gulf countries will be able to call the tune; the bizarre relationship that has developed between Pakistan and Abu Dhabi, in which Sheikh Zayed alone injects almost as much money into the economy as the whole American government, is a striking example of the oddities that can develop. Interestingly, during the war between Iran and Iraq it seems that no one ever thought seriously of asking either India or Pakistan to intervene, to help in lowering tension or even to do patrol duty in the Gulf. Pakistan contributed a contingent of 2,000 troops to the coalition against Saddam after the invasion of Kuwait; India allowed American planes to re-fuel on its territory until an enormous outcry brought the practice to a halt.

The future of the Peninsula

The last important point is that of the future relations between the GCC states and their immediate neighbours. From the time of the foundation of the Council there was speculation on the subject. In some Kuwaiti circles where a lingering pan-arabism still held sway, it was suggested that Iraq should become a member once its war with Iran was over. There are a clutch of organizations, most of them dating from before the foundation of the GCC, which carry the 'Gulf' label and did in fact include Iraq (the health ministers' conference and the Gulf Organization for Industrial Consulting, with offices in Doha, are two examples). Iraq participated financially in the Gulf University in Bahrain, or was supposed to do so, and sent a token number of students there. Still, the idea of including Iraq in the GCC never had many advocates apart from a handful of Kuwaiti intellectuals – and of course the Iraqi government.

The Iran-Iraq war finished with something close to an Iraqi victory, with a good deal of help by the international community and particularly by the Gulf states. Iraq made much of the fact that it was fighting to defend them all,[22] even though it is impossible to know what would have happened had the war never started. Having, in his own view, defended the Arabs from the Persian horde, Saddam Hussein felt that he had finally earned the right to be considered officially as the protector of the Gulf, as he had proclaimed himself at the beginning of the war, when the Gulf states wanted none of it. This was also the main argument used to support Iraq's desire to become the seventh member of the GCC.

Seen from the Gulf, things were a bit different. Iraq has a population larger than that of all the Gulf states (including Saudi Arabia) put together and, even at the end of the Iran-Iraq war its economic, agricultural and industrial infrastructure was incomparably more developed. As we have seen, it was and still is possible within the GCC to work together (even with the presence of Saudi Arabia) because the basic options have been the same: the institutions of the monarchy, liberal (and sometimes licentious) capitalism combined with a wide-spread welfare system for the citizens, and basically similar social and religious structures.

With Iraq there is little of that. Even though Iraqi Ba'athism in its newest incarnation had lost much of its socialist tinge, it was still quite distinct from the paternalist monarchies of its neighbours. The demands of the war and the rivalries with Iran pushed the official Iraqi image to include many more Islamic references, but the Ba'athist secular state nevertheless remained very different from the Saudi Islamic Kingdom, and its relationship with Islam quite unlike the less structured but naturally close relationship with Islamic values that obtains in the other Gulf States. As long as the war lasted, Iraq had to tow the line because it badly needed the help of the Gulf states. But only a few months after the cease-fire, long before any official peace treaty was signed, Iraq was showing its mettle, and the Gulf states, without saying so, were getting nervous.

Before the Iraqi invasion of Kuwait there was a good deal of talk in the Arabian Peninsula about the nature of the relations to be established between the GCC countries and the Yemen, the only non-member country of the Peninsula. The two halves of Yemen, the former Popular Democratic Republic of Yemen (or South Yemen) and the former Arab Republic of Yemen (North Yemen) had finally put aside their incessant quarrels and, in the wake of the collapse of the Soviet empire, declared their union in May 1990. This new Yemen occupies the south-west of the Arabian peninsula of which it is both the poorest and the most populous country with 12.5 million inhabitants and one of the world's highest birth-rates. It would dearly like to become a member of the GCC, but the chances are slim in the near future. After the Iran-Iraq war, Yemen was still divided and it was easier for the GCC to exclude all new-comers – and thus to exclude Iraq which it feared even more than the by-then enfeebled South Yemen. After the second Gulf war, too much anger was generated by what was seen as Yemeni support of Iraq. Purely economic arguments are not cited and are probably not the most relevant. Both Yemens were prime recipients of GCC aid money, most of which has dried up.

Yemen may not always be so poor. With unification, oil exploration has developed enormously. By early 1992, the sadly run-down port of Aden was one of the very few in the world where more oil rigs were coming in than going out. Despite the experience of a quarter of a century of Marxist ideology in the South and of prickly military republicanism (and multiple *coups d'etat* and assassinations in the North), Yemen is still recognizably a southern Arabian society. Even the vicious civil war in Aden in January 1986 can only be understood in that light; 10,000 people were killed in ten days and over 50,000 eventually fled, mostly to the North. No attempt to explain the events of 1986 as the result of doctrinal differences has managed to stand up to serious scrutiny. The only explanations that make sense must take tribal loyalties and geographic origins into account as much or more than any ideological basis. The most committed hard-line communists were killed in the fighting, not because of their ideas but simply because most of them were on the wrong side of the firing at any given moment; they fled to the North.

Soviet and US interests first developed the oil fields along the former border between the two countries; the fact that most of them may be part of one huge structure was a not unimportant factor in pushing for unification. Unity had been a 'national aspiration' for decades, but hardly a natural outcome. All Yemen had never been under a single political leadership, unless one counts that of two legendary queens, Bilqis (King Solomon's friend, the Queen of Sheba) in the 9th century B.C. and Arwa, two thousand years later.

Less than three months after Yemeni unity was proclaimed came the Iraqi invasion of Kuwait. Yemen was in a difficult situation. Today Yemenis are quick to point out that their country was the first to condemn the Iraqi invasion. But the really hard decisions were still to come. Yemen, along with Iraq, Jordan and Egypt, was a member of the ill-fated Arab Cooperation Council; the ACC was important to it as a means of countering Saudi Arabia and maintaining self-esteem since the Gulf Cooperation Council had spurned it. Many Yemenis genuinely like Iraq and even admire Saddam Hussein. Even before the revolution of 1956, Iraqi agents were at work in Yemen and many of the revolutionary heroes were Iraqi-trained; the 'experts' are still there. Expatriate Yemenis generally found work in Saudi Arabia, Kuwait or the UAE; few had the Egyptians' direct experience of life under Saddam. Until the Sana'a papers were freed of censorship late in 1991 and ran the stories, most Yemenis had never heard of Kurds being gassed, Shi'a holy cities bombarded or mass executions. They still had difficulty believing that Saddam did not win the war after all that footage of British or American planes coming down in flames (on the fuzzy Yemeni television, Spitfires and Tornados are hard to tell apart) and a triumphant Saddam holding on. Pictures of Saddam decorated walls a year after his defeat – especially in the former North Yemen, but less so in the South where the last quarter of a century had provided a more realistic political education.

Yemen's predicament was compounded by two factors: the ancestral distrust of Saudi Arabia and the fact that Yemen was the only Arab member of the UN Security Council in 1990 and 1991. There it was admirably served by Ambassador Abdulla al-Ashtal, a brilliant diplomat (from the former South) – but even he could not save a situation where Yemen was seen again and again as defending Iraq (in the sole company of Cuba). Yemen regarded its responses as an attempt to hold a neutral and sensible line.

Retribution was swift. Saudi Arabia sent 800,000 Yemenis packing. Yemenis were the only foreigners in Saudi Arabia who needed neither visa nor sponsor. When the rules changed so that like other migrant workers they needed both, most were forced to return home. Saudi Arabia probably in any case wanted to reduce the number of Yemenis in the Kingdom over the next few years; what made the reabsorption difficult was its suddenness and the sad fact that those who returned were the least qualified and enterprising. Many others quietly arranged matters with Saudi friends or officials. The Saudis were particularly accommodating for Hadramis, natives of the relatively rich and pious Wadi Hadramaut in former South Yemen.

Yemeni unity would probably have been impossible without the introduction of a democratic process; its survival depends largely on how well that process can be mastered. The trappings are there: a surprisingly liberal constitution (accepted by a large majority in a referendum last May, despite the opposition of the Islamic groups), a flowering of political parties and a genuinely free press. At last count there were 44 political parties, including offshoots of every shading of political theory that ever existed in the Arab world and a few local originals, including one that purports to represent 'the Yemeni minorities' (i.e. the Africans of the Tihama and the Jews).

That same democracy will make integration with its Gulf neighbours that much more difficult. If Saudi Arabia distrusts Kuwait's limited parliamentary experiment, it regards Yemens' budding but real democratic experience as anathema.

While Yemen's relations with Saudi Arabia – the neighbour who really counts – remain dreadful, at least one old problem is about to disappear with the demarcation of the Omani border. Oman and its old enemy the PDRY established diplomatic relations in 1985, but the border question, punctuated by a skirmish or two, remained. Sultan Qaboos has decided that giving away a few kilometres of desert is an easy price to pay for peace and simplicity, and a signature is expected imminently. The Mahra tribesmen along the desert border long ago stopped paying attention to the border when they discovered the Omani health and social services. Where the border counted was near the sea, scene of bitter mountain fighting during the Dhofar rebellion. Many Yemenis look with yearning towards Oman, wistfully considering it a model for what their country could become.

The aftermath of the 1991 Gulf war, which could have been liberating to both the GCC and its individual societies, does not seem to be quite that. While Oman and the UAE plead for a new regional constellation in which Iran would have its place – but not an overwhelming one – Saudi Arabia and Kuwait remain transfixed by the spectre of Iraq. Nothing, they say, can be done, nothing can go forward, so long as Saddam Hussein remains the master. The period of liberation, self-esteem and self-confidence that seemed to be in the making just before the invasion, has been temporarily put into abeyance; and the opening-up of society has become more fitful. This period could be quite short-lived; signs of *détente* can be discerned here and there, even in Saudi Arabia. It is almost impossible, a year after the end of the Gulf war, to know which group has the more credible vision: those who look to an increasingly close relationship with the United States and the West, liberated from most of the constraints that once inflected such a policy, or those who seriously hope that the Gulf states, in an ideal regional arrangement which must necessarily include Iran in some form, will be able to make independent decisions. This difference corresponds once more to the old and newly revived split between the upper and lower Gulf. Since the general thinking is that the Gulf has no future unless it somehow holds itself together – not necessarily in opposition to Iraq or anyone else – both these attitudes are probably true. Arabic is a subtle and difficult language where one word can have many meanings, including the primary one linked directly to its root and another signifying the opposite. In much the same way, the Gulf, where almost every facet of reality carries within itself the germ of its opposite, remains a place of rich paradox.

Notes

Chapter One: Introduction

1 There was, of course, a time when a British resident watched over both sides of the Gulf from his vantage point first at Bushire on the Persian side, and then, until 1971, in Bahrain.
2 For a long time, Arab geographers called the Red Sea 'Al Khalij al-Arab' which translates as 'the Arab Gulf', with slightly more justification, even though the southern third of the African shore has never been Arabized.
3 There was a tiny population living on Greater Tumb and Abu Musa. It would be difficult to know just how to catalogue them: they speak a dialect made up of almost equal parts of Arabic, Farsi and Urdu (like the few hundred inhabitants of Kumsar, the isolated port at the tip of the Musandam peninsula). Without reflecting on whether or not they are Arabs, they considered themselves subjects of the Qasimi sheikhs, and herdsmen from the Trucial Coast – as it then was – sometimes brought over a few goats for winter grazing. Little Tumb was uninhabited.
4 Or Persian. The two words are not absolute synonyms. The Persians are the Farsi-speaking majority in a larger area called Iran, whose name is derived from the same root as 'aryan'.
5 C. Niebuhr, *Entdeckung im Orient. Reise nach Arabien und anderen Ländern – 1761–1767.* (Copenhagen, K. Moeller, 1773).
6 Exactly like the road used during the Iran-Iraq war once the shelling of Basrah had become serious in 1982.
7 Salem al-Jabir as-Sabah, *Les Emirats du Golfe* (Paris, Fayard, 1980) p. 110.
8 In *The Myth of Arab Piracy in the Gulf* (London, Croom Helm, 1986).
9 Qawasim is the plural of Qasim which, as an adjective, became the family name of the sheikhs of both Ras al-Khaimah and Sharjah: al-Qasimi.
10 This paradox is set out with some force by Dr Muhammad Rumaihi, a Bahraini sociologist living in Kuwait, in *Beyond Oil* (London, Al Saqi Books, 1983) esp. chapter 2.
11 As-Sabah, *Les Emirats du Golfe*. I am indebted to Dr Salem as-Sabah for this information; the re-translation from French into English is mine.
12 Information given at the GCC summit in Riyadh in December 1987.
13 Its full name is the Co-operation Council of the Arab States of the Gulf and not '... of the Arabian Gulf'.

14 Ibadhism is a particular form of Islam, neither Sunni nor Shi'a. See p.287 note 27.

15 This word has been used more in recent French writing on revolutionary Islam than in English but it seems useful and more accurate than 'fundamentalist' or 'integrist' or even, as has been written occasionally, 'ultramontane'. The best discussion on the subject is in Bruno Etienne, *L'Islamisme radicale* (Paris, Hachette, 1987).

16 The Qatar Ministry of Health began charging fees in February 1989, but only to non-resident women patients at the new women's hospital. Fees were approved by the GCC Ministers of Health at a conference in Kuwait at the end of 1988. *Gulf Times*, Doha, 8 January 1989.

17 These figures are taken from the statistical bulletins of the countries themselves and should all be treated with caution. They are nevertheless useful to give an idea of the general proportions.

18 Bruno Etienne's analysis, in *L'Islamisme radicale*, pp. 52–3 was tremendously useful to me in helping to formulate ideas that I had been ruminating for a long time.

19 The Egyptian fellahin, islamized for 1400 years, still think and basically function according to the ancient Egyptian calendar rather than the movable Islamic one.

Chapter Two: Iraq

1 The border touches the river 25 kms further downstream just above Abadan.

2 See Amin Ma'alouf, *Les Croisades vues par les Arabes* (Paris, Jean-Claude Lattès, 1983; paperback: J'ai lu, 1985), chapters 4 and 5 and passim.

3 The recent bibliography on Iraq is very thin indeed, even considering the serious long articles in papers and journals. Among the rare books is that of Marion Farouk-Sluglett and Peter Sluglett, *Iraq since 1958 – from Revolution to Dictatorship* (London, I.B. Tauris, 1990) or in French, Paul Balta, *Iran-Irak, la Guerre de 5,000 ans*, Paris, Editions Anthropos, 1987). It is true that doing any serious research on the spot is extremely difficult; it was so before the war and became even more difficult during the fighting.

4 See also one of the most interesting studies of Iraq – Samir al-Khalil, *Republic of Fear: Saddam's Iraq* (London, Hutchinson Radius, 1990).

5 For simplification, I shall use 'Gulf states' or 'Gulf countries' when I mean the six members of the Gulf Co-operation Council, 'Arab countries touching the Gulf' when Iraq is to be included, and 'Gulf riverine states' when that is what is meant, i.e. all the above plus Iran.

6 Cf. L. Graz, *L'Irak au présent*, (Lausanne, Les Trois Continents, 1979) pp. 216 ff.

7 Quoted in *The Economist*, 6 February 1988.

8 I would also venture that Yemen qualifies as a nation (both Yemens together, although there the current political separation does pose a problem) and arguably, Oman.

9 Shahram Chubin and Charles Tripp, *Iran and Iraq: Society and Politics 1980–86*. (Geneva, Institut universaire des Hautes études internationales, 1986) p. 19.

10 The only possible sources of such material because official figures on religion were never made public, even before the war. They are probably not even known with certainty, because the question was not included in census forms. In any case, the Planning Ministry, responsible for all statistics, has not published any since 1981. Everything, from small animal censuses on, was considered strategic material. Careful observers think that if anyone has the information on religion, it is probably the police, or one of the branches of the political police, but such material may not be centralized. They give as evidence the particularly careful scrutiny of Shi'a, particularly in the early years of the conflict with Iran. The scrutiny existed, but it may have depended more on local knowledge than on any formal registers.

11 For more details, see L. Graz, 'Die Turkei und ihre asiatischen Nachbarn', *Europa-Archiv*, 23:42, 10 December 1987, p. 692.

12 There were, during the war years and afterwards, reports of several aborted coups and assassination attempts against the president; but they were all tightly circumscribed and not popular uprisings.

13 There were also instances of Iranian Kurdish tribal leaders and individuals rallying to Baghdad, but they were far fewer.

14 Cf. Graz, 'Die Turkei und ihre asiatischen Nachbarn'.

15 *Le Monde*, 24 March 1988.

16 The first official complaint was in an Iranian letter to the UN Secretary-General dated 3 November 1983.

17 I was able to visit the camps alone, without an official guide.

18 The term, which means fighter, is used here to denote specifically the Iraqi Kurdish guerrilla. In the autumn of 1988, the Turks were using it as a generic term for all the Kurds who had fled to Turkey, including women and children.

19 *Chemical Weapons Use in Kurdistan: Iraq's Final Offensive*, A Staff Report to the Senate Committee on Foreign Relations, 21 September 1988.

20 Oral confirmation from a Western diplomat in Baghdad, October 1988.

21 The largest Kurdish community of all, some 8 to 9 million.

22 Officially, the Iraqi Kurds were never called refugees. Turkey had signed the international conventions on asylum with a reserve saying that it would accept refugees only from East European countries. The Iraqis were 'temporary guests for humanitarian reasons.'

23 Personal interview at the Turkish Foreign Ministry, Ankara, October 1988.

24 With the exception of Palestinians according to the reasoning – which is not unique to Iraq – that if Palestinians had been absorbed, there would no longer have been a Palestinian cause.

25 Michel Aflak lived in Baghdad from the break between the Syrian and Iraqi branches of Ba'athism, until his death in 1989; even in retirement he was always given the first role in party protocol. Salah Eddine Bittar was

assassinated in Paris on 21 July 1980. He was buried in Baghdad, and Iraq accused Syrian secret police agents of his murder.

26 Only Oman, Somalia and Sudan did not break off relations with Egypt. Several other countries, including Saudi Arabia, apparently hesitated until the last minute – probably because they were aware of the manoeuvre – but the anti-Israel reflex was too strong to make them go against the general tide.

27 After the outbreak of the war, the Iranians argued that the production of the film could be considered proof of Iraqi premeditation well before the battles actually started. Why otherwise, ran the argument, have devoted $7 m to a film whose obvious purpose was to prepare the population for the next battle of Qadissiya.

28 The establishment of a commission to settle the question of responsibility is clearly invoked in point 8 of UN resolution 598, which is the basis of the cease-fire and of the peace negotiations.

29 For almost day-to-day details of that September, one can consult Balta, *Iran-Irak*, pp. 130 ff.

30 *La Guerre Irak-Iran. Islam et nationalismes* (Paris, Albatros, 1985).

31 It became a treaty in Baghdad later that year but has, in international law, retained its Algiers label.

32 The five members of the murder squad were arrested by the French police. The head of the commandos, Anis Naccache, was sentenced to life imprisonment. He became far better known to the public when his freedom became a prime demand of a group calling itself the Solidarity Committee for Arab and Middle Eastern Political Prisoners and which had links not only with the takers of hostages in Lebanon but also with the spate of terrorist attacks in Paris in the autumn of 1986.

33 Arnold Hottinger, in *7 Mal Näher Osten*, (Munich, Piper, 4th edn) p. 256, writes in fairly enigmatic terms of the American secret services. Hottinger is known as one of the best-informed analysts in the Middle East.

34 An attempt to rescue the hostages in a daring commando raid failed completely. The operation was plagued by a combination of bad luck – a desert sandstorm – and, according to foreign military analysts, bad planning and even worse co-ordination. The failure was perceived by the Iranians as a 'miracle' and it became a further source of humiliation for the Americans, after that of the hostages themselves.

35 In time, the propaganda also probably became less effective for purely technical reasons. Iraqis liked to watch Iranian television and listen to the Iranian radio before the war: the films were more interesting and the music more up-to-date. After the revolution, the cross-border audience dropped precipitously; the interest in what Iraqi friends called 'Mollahvision' was very limited. The same phenomenon could be seen in Bahrain.

36 The conference was transferred to New Delhi, but the inscription in the dedication stone at the entrance to the centre may confound future archaeologists, with its ambiguous wording, honouring Saddam Hussein as master of the non-aligned conference of that year.

37 During 1987 and 1988 the official exchange rate was four to five times the

black-market rate.

38 The RCC remains the organ of decision, in economic as well as political and even military affairs; the government's job is to execute orders given by the RCC.

39 See, inter alia, the 'Declaration of the Iraqi Minister of Foreign Affairs, Sa'adoun Hammoudi, before the Security Council of the United Nations published in Baghdad by the Ministry of Foreign Affairs in 1981 and B. Porat and U. Dan, *Operation Babylon*, (Paris, edition Balland, 1986).

40 'Report of Specialists named by the Secretary General to Investigate Allegations by the Islamic Republic of Iran concerning the Use of Chemical Weapons', New York, Security Council Document s/16433 26, March 1984 and ff. See especially the report published on 1 August 1988 by Eric Dahlgren and Manuel Dominguez.

41 Quoted in *Le Monde*, 24 March 1988.

42 The fuss made in early 1989 around the Libyan chemical weapons/ pharmaceutical plant at Rabta provides another example.

43 Despite the war, Iraq hardly qualifies as a poor country.

44 Quoted in *Middle East International*, 10 October 1987.

45 Hottinger, *7 Mal Näher Osten*, p. 267.

46 It would have been unthinkable to circulate jokes about Saddam Hussein in Iraq while it was routine to hear amusing Ayatollah Khomeini stories in Tehran. When I told an Iraqi friend that, he literally gasped.

47 Al-Takriti is also the family name of the president. Family or clan names, practically abolished in Iraq for over a decade, began to reappear at the end of the war.

48 MEI, 14 September 1990, p. 6.

49 IHT, 15–16 September 1990.

50 *The New Yorker*, 1 October 1990.

51 By the US Senate Foreign Relations Committee, 20 March 1991. Until then Glaspie had been 'kept on ice' by the State Department to some embarrassment on the part of her colleagues.

52 MEI, op. cit.

53 In a paper given at a symposium organized in Paris in June 1988 by the Institut français de rélations internationales.

Chapter Three: Iran

1 Among those who have used it at one time or another were the group around Habib Dahaoui in Tunisia, the Qutbists in Egypt, a small group in Djibouti and of course, those in Lebanon. See A. Tehari, *Holy Terror*, (London, Sphere Books, 1987) pp. 174, 178 and 186 ff.

2 This theme, in an elaborate framework, is one of the underlying premises of *L'Orient Imaginaire* by Thierry Hentsch (Paris, Edition du Minuit, 1988).

3 Gary Sick, 'Iran's Quest for Superpower Status', *Foreign Affairs*, vol. 65, no 4, Spring 1987, p. 699.

4 Cf. Jean Gueyras, 'La longue bataille du president Saddam Hussein pour

l'internationalisation du conflit', *Le Monde*, 20 August 1987.

5 Respectively, as of 1 January 1988, 167.4 and 92.86 bn bbl. (*Arab Oil and Gas Directory*, 1988).

6 See A. Kapeliouk, 'Comment Israel tire parti d'une guerre prolongée', in *Le Monde Diplomatique*, October 1987.

7 *The Economist*, 20 August 1988.

8 *The Military Balance, 1988–89*, (London, International Institute for Strategic Studies).

9 *Arab Oil and Gas Directory*, 1987, 1988.

10 Jose Garçon, 'La France et le Conflit Iran/Irak', *Politique étrangère*, 2, 1987.

11 It first made the headlines before the war, in 1979, when the then Saudi oil minister, Sheikh Ahmed Zaki Yamani, scared all of Europe and America with a remark about 'Palestinian extremists who could sink a redundant tanker' across the Strait and cut off the traffic.

12 At the end of May 1988, the commander of the US fleet in the Gulf, Admiral George Crist, was widely quoted when he warned of 'new Chinese missile batteries that were capable of firing all the way across the Strait'. (AP dispatches, 30 May 1988).

13 Oral communication from Soviet Foreign Office official, Moscow, April, 1989.

14 Private communication, 1986.

15 See Graz, 'Die Turkei und ihre asiatischen Nachbarn'.

16 See Etienne, *L'Islamisme radicale*, pp. 157 ff.

17 S. Chubin, *Iran and its Neighbours*, (London, The Centre for Security and Conflict Studies, 1987) p. 5.

18 Particular tribute should be paid here to the diplomatic skill of the Iraqi ambassador in Washington at the time, Nizar Hamdoun, who was the chief architect of the turn-around in Iraqi-American relations from the complete break dating from the time of the 1967 war to what practically amounted to co-belligerency.

19 The French aircraft carrier *Clemenceau*, which arrived in the Sea of Oman in August 1987, never entered the Gulf; its presence has more to do with showing the flag after the break in diplomatic relations than with any strategic goals.

20 AMAL is the acronym for al-Mouaj al-Mouqawma al-Lubnania, 'The waves of the Lebanese resistance'; in Arabic, the word means hope.

21 One of the reasons was probably the desire of the Americans to play a role in the abortive Lebanese presidential elections in August-September 1988. But even US-Syrian intervention could not bring the Lebanese parliament to a valid election.

22 UN Security Council Report, Doc. S/20147, 24 August 1988.

23 At the time of the cease-fire, the ICRC had registered 50,182 Iraqi prisoners in Iran and 19,284 Iranians in Iraq. It knows it has not seen all the prisoners on either side. The Iraqis claimed that Iran held 75,000 prisoners and the ICRC estimate was not much lower. In Iraq the total, even with a fairly large number of new prisoners taken in the final weeks of

the fighting, was approximately 30,000. *Middle East International*, 26 August 1988.

24 Personal interviews with the desk officer at UNHCR in Geneva in April and September 1988.

25 In early 1990 Saudi Arabia was still missing from the list.

26 The Foreign Office in particular was trying to break out of the international isolation. In December 1989 much was made of the visit of the Romanian president Nicolae Ceausescu – a European, of whatever stripe – even as security forces were firing on demonstrators in his own country. A week later, Ceausescu had been executed in his own country, and embarrassed statements were being issued in Tehran.

27 Iran, for ideological reasons, has repaid almost its entire foreign debt since the revolution and came out of the war with practically no long-term debt. European bankers, particularly German ones, were ready with proposals for financial schemes that did not transgress the no-interest strictures.

28 *Midnight's Children* and *Shame* which are, respectively, highly disrespectful of India at the time of partition and Pakistan from Zulfikar Ali Bhutto to Zia ul-Haq.

29 Imam Abdullah al-Ahdal was a Saudi national closely linked with the World Muslim League and his assistant and librarian was a Tunisian, Salim Bahri. They were shot at close range in Imam al-Ahdal's office at the Brussels mosque. The Imam had received several threatening messages after he had made what were considered fairly modifying statements, saying that while Rushdie's book was insulting, unnecessary, tendentious and blasphemous, the leader of Shi'a Islam's condemnation of the author to death was wrong. (Reuters dispatches, 30 March 1989 and *Le Monde*, 31 March 1989).

30 These included not only the wearing of make-up or letting a lock of hair stray out from under the headscarf, but also the act of smiling at a man in public; any of these could bring a citation in front of a 'court of morality' and, besides public humiliation, dismissal for working women.

Chapter Four: Kuwait

1 Certainly not, as some foreign sources reported, the Shi'a; the Shi'a community included some very rich businessmen and some less rich as well as immigrants who were not rich at all – just as in the non-Shi'a population.

2 There are no income tax returns to consult because there was no income tax. There was however the 'Palestinian tax', a levy on official salaries – more or less voluntarily given too by employees of many private businesses – that was handed over to the PLO. This was usually 5 per cent of the gross salary, and paid by all Kuwaitis as well as Palestinians. In addition, the Palestinians contributed another 5 per cent or in some cases 10 per cent of their incomes to Palestinian funds.

3 The US $1 million monthly Kuwaiti contribution to Makassed was its main source of income. When it stopped coming in August 1990, there was

immediate alarm at the hospital which was also the most important place for the treatment of Palestinians from the West Bank.

4 When the Iraqis formed their puppet 'Free Kuwaiti' government for the few days before they annexed Kuwait as the '19th Province', they named as President, 'Colonel' Ala' Hussein Ali, who was indeed a Kuwaiti. Before being 'promoted' to that high office, he was a clerk in a cardboard carton factory. His employer, the former minister for public works, Mr Abdullah Dakhil, later said, almost wistfully: 'When I saw his face on television, presented as our president, I could only think "Poor fellow, he was just used. He was only 30 years old, and he was always so polite." ' Such a government could in no sense be described as representing Kuwait.

5 Basrah and Baghdad were associated in the first mandate agreement of 1920. Mossul was only added in 1925, after the treaty of Lausanne. Until then it had been left in a legal limbo.

6 On this whole period, innumerable details can be found in Ahmad Mustafa Abu-Hakima, *The Modern History of Kuwait: 1750–1965*, (London, Luzac & Co Ltd, 1983).

7 Abdul-Reda Assiri, *Kuwait's Foreign Policy*, (Boulder, San Francisco & London, Westview Press, 1990.) p. 3.

8 Al Hasa became one of the centres of military action once the hostilities against Iraq broke out in 1991.

9 Abdul-Karim Qassem: statement in Baghdad press conference, 25 June 1961.

10 United Nations Security Council Records, S/4844 (New York: 16th Year, Supplement for July, August and September 1961.) p. 3.

11 Interview with the Lebanese magazines *Al-Sayyad* and *Al-Nahar*; reported in Foreign Broadcast Information Service: Near East and Asia (FBIS: April 4, 1973).

12 Umm Qasr, the Iraqi military port, was put out of commission in the first months of the Iran–Iraq war by the Iranian blockade. Basra, the merchant port one hundred kilometres upstream from the mouth of the Shatt al-Arab, was useless. Besides the fact that Iran controlled the east bank for most of that distance, the river was blocked by wrecks and mines and the silt piling up without the usual dredging.

13 Billion in British usage, i.e. million millions.

14 Personal interviews.

15 Personal interviews with Ambassador Nizar Hamdoun, Under-secretary in the Ministry of Foreign Affairs.

16 During the 1990–1 Gulf crisis, keeping people waiting became a hallmark of Iraq's arrogance towards high-ranking emissaries; the special representative of French President Mitterand, Michel Vauzelle, UN Secretary-General Javier Perez de Cuellar and the president of the International Committee of the Red Cross were all submitted to the treatment.

17 Report of Professor A. Kaelin, UN Commision on Human rights, 1992.

18 In Baghdad, just as some shortages were beginning to be felt in late August, the market was, for a short time, flooded with Heineken's beer.

The Iraqis told some naïve journalists that this had been brought from Kuwait, and the journalists duly reported this. This could not have been true; even if an occasional carton of beer was smuggled into Kuwait, there could never have been enough to make a dent in the Baghdad market.

19 The desalination plants were considered one of the weakest links in the Iraqi occupation plans. Such plants require constant maintenance (usually provided by expatriate engineers) and frequent replacement of parts. Stocks were not likely to hold out long against an embargo. The deliberate oil spills of the first weeks of the war could only worsen matters.

20 Kuwait was a major investor in the tourism industry.

21 Some of these figures are taken from MEI, 14 September 1990, p. 19: Anthony McDermott, 'Iraq and Kuwait – two vulnerable economies'. McDermott also puts Iraq's debts at between US$70bn and US$80bn, of which, according to the Bank for International Settlements, US$13.6bn were owed to Western lenders.

22 They were not, then, in any way 'seized' as the Iraqis claimed on 19 September, when, in reprisal, they themselves did seize whatever assets they could lay their hands on in all the countries that had frozen Iraqi and Kuwaiti funds and other assets.

23 At the liberation, Lt Gen. Charles Horner, one of the commanders of the US Air Force, wrote a letter of appreciation to the resistance movement, addressed to Maj. Gen. Khalid Uday.

24 The rationale being that since Kuwait was now a province of Iraq there was no need of separate embassies.

25 For example, the Kuwait Fund, the Kuwait Investment Authority or the Kuwait Petrol Company, including the Q-8 distribution network.

26 Amnesty International estimates that there were about 50 political prisoners in the largest sense – including hijackers and other convicted terrorists. Membership and suspected membership of *Al-Dawa* automatically carried the death penalty in Iraq. Two of the original 17 hijackers had been freed after completing their sentence.

27 In Iraq, all university libraries had been deprived of periodical subscriptions and foreign books. The excuse for this was the shortage of foreign exchange since the early part of the Iran–Iraq war.

28 So far, we have had no serious evidence of forced enrolment in the Iraqi army, although there have been rumours.

29 To protect the family of the young woman I have not given her name.

30 Saudi Arabia, which is rarely cited as a model of democracy, has long been much fairer on that score; it is not easy to attain Saudi citizenship (although easier than in Kuwait) but once done there are not the same distinctions or classes.

Chapter Five: Saudi Arabia

1 The official figure was 402 dead; the toll may have been even higher.

2 *Majlis* means literally 'a sitting' and is used both for the place and the occasion of a formal sit-down meeting. All officials or high-ranking people

in the peninsula have a *majlis* (called *diwaniyya* in Kuwait); a king's is simply grander than that of a village sheikh which may be simply a flat space under a tree.

3 The French weekly magazine *Jeune Afrique* had a long-running argument with the authorities of the Kingdom over the name. *Jeune Afrique*, which has strong links with the Maghrebi countries, refused to acknowledge that an individual country could use the word 'Arabia' and consistently referred to the Kingdom simply as 'Saudia'.

4 Without getting involved in a theological quarrel, having to do with the fact that all Muslims consider that they believe in the unity of God, i.e. the first pillar of Islam – as proclaimed on the Saudi banner – I will, for the sake of simplicity, continue to use the better-known term of Wahhabites.

5 Not unique to Islam, cf. the Old Testament, Lev. 26, 1 and Deut. 5, 8.

6 Kerbala reappeared in the news when its name was given to a long series of Iranian offensives in the war against Iraq; it is the site of the tombs of Hussein and Hassan, the venerated Shi'a martyrs, grandsons of the Prophet Mohammed.

7 This may change again. In a system where political and religious actions are so closely entwined, the ostracism to which Egypt was subject after the signing of the Camp David Agreement and the Peace Treaty with Israel rubbed off even on Al Azhar, particularly among relatively unsophisticated people. With the 'rehabilitation' of Egypt, Al Azhar is expected to regain all its former lustre.

8 Etienne, *L'Islamisme radicale*, p. 271.

9 For example, Surat LX, The Woman Tested

O Believers, take not My enemy and your enemy
for friends, offering them love, though they
have disbelieved in the truth that has come to
you, expelling the Messenger and you because
you believe in God and your Lord. ...

Translation Arberry, *The Koran Interpreted*, Vol. 2, p. 271.

10 In the whole Peninsula there are very few indigenous non-Muslims; a few hundred Jews remained in the mountains of Yemen after the 1951 exodus and a handful of Bahraini Jews continue to live discreetly in Manama. As far as I know, these are the only examples of heterodoxy in the native populations, with one possible exception: Arnold Hottinger in *7 mal Näher Osten*, p. 275, refers rather tantalizingly to corners of the Kingdom where Islam has never penetrated. When I asked the author about this point, he admitted that he had little documented information but was personally convinced that it was so.

11 The essay, 'Arabs and Western Civilization' in *Arabian Essays* by Ghazi A. Algosaibi (London, KPI, 1982) is a particularly interesting example, because it was written from the inside. Mr Algosaibi was a minister until he was relieved of his post, probably at his own request; one does not quit a ministerial post in Saudi Arabia. He then became the Kingdom's ambassador to Bahrain.

12 Letter published in *Le Monde*, 20 August 1987.

13 Churches are allowed to function in all the other Gulf countries with the exception of Qatar; in some of them either the land or the church buildings were gifts from the ruler to the Christian community.

14 In English, among others: D. Holden and R. Johns, *The House of Saud*, (London, Sidgwick & Jackson, 1981) and, in slightly more racy language, R. Lacey, *The Kingdom* (New York, Harcourt Brace Jovanovich, 1981).

15 On the very day the attack began, a crowd burnt down the American embassy in Islamabad in response to rumours saying that the Great Mosque had been defiled as the result of an American conspiracy.

16 At the beginning of the Islamic revolution in Iran, some Shi'a claimed that Ayatollah Khomeini was the *mahdi*, but he himself squashed the suppositions.

17 Sadiq al-Mahdi, the former Sudanese prime minister, is the great grandson of Muhammed Ahmed.

18 Not all did; some were taken hostage and killed later during the siege.

19 After 1975, the various militia groups had been reorganized and re-equipped with the help of American advisers; the contract had originally been budgeted at $330m. One of the contractors who had been given the job of instructing four of the twenty battalions that made up the national guard was the Vinnell Corporation. This arrangement is supposed to have been instrumental in facilitating the entry into the Kingdom of CIA agents. cf. Holden and Johns, *The House of Saud*, p. 360.

20 Groupe d'intervention de la Gendarmerie nationale; the French SAS.

21 This figure is very conservative. Census figures, for obvious reasons, do not give details and would, in any case, be hopelessly out of date.

22 Aramco is the acronym of the Arabian American Oil Company which had been progressively nationalized between 1974 and 1979 but was still responsible for field operations. The members of the consortium were Exxon, Socal (Standard Oil of California), Texaco and Mobil.

23 Hottinger, *7 mal Näher Osten*, p. 305.

24 After supporting Iran at the beginning of the war, South Yemen had shifted to a strict neutrality when Iran refused to follow all the resolutions calling for a cease-fire and/or negotiation.

25 Tunisia was in a particularly high-risk situation three months before the deposition of President Habib Bourguiba with the tensions between the government and the growing Mouvement de la Tendance Islamique (MTI) near flash point.

26 This is not the place for a long discussion of the role of the state in 'sending' pilgrims or allocating permits to go on the pilgrimage, which involves the question of Islam and the civil society. Suffice it to say that in many – but not all – Muslim countries, it is the sending state that gives permission to its own citizens to go on the *hajj* and often allocates funds not only for the individuals' expenses but also for accompanying personnel.

27 'A View of Education', in *Arabian Essays*, pp 6ff.

28 Alas, the influx of many Egyptian teachers has not been an unmixed blessing. Despite the undeniable quality of some, too many others are not courageous enough to stand up to their students – and their parents – and

too often let sloppiness go and give unmerited grades, with or without small gifts.

29 The literal meaning of Islam is 'submission'.

30 Curiosity has not always been well thought of in the West either. cf. the French proverb 'La curiosité est un vilain défaut' – curiosity is a nasty failing.

31 The punishment for adultery can be carried out if four male eyewitnesses serve as 'proof'. The unfortunate killing of the Princess Misha'al (*Death of a Princess*), which was abundantly commented on in Europe, did not take place because of proven adultery but as a punishment for disobedience within the royal family.

32 Lacey, *The Kingdom*, pp. 380–1.

33 Anonymous spokesman of the organization quoted in the French magazine *Jeune Afrique*, 25 January 1984.

34 cf. similar prohibitions in the medieval Catholic church against 'usury'. Interpreted with varying strictness, they complicated the banking careers of Catholics for centuries and assured that of Jews and later Protestants. The Florentines managed fairly early to find an arrangement with heaven, probably analogous to that of many Arab bankers, no less pious Muslims for all that.

35 *The Economist*, 19 March 1988.

36 Sheikh Salah al-Hajelani, lawyer and president of the Supreme Council for Arbitration of the Euro-Arab Chambers of Commerce, developed this idea in a lecture he gave in Geneva in March 1988.

37 *The Military Balance, 1988–9*, p. 95.

38 Saudi Press Agency, quoted by *Middle East Economic Digest*, 9 January 1988.

39 There is none now on personal income in any of the Gulf States. There has been some talk of it in the UAE, but no decision has been announced.

40 According to the list of major budget allocations for 1988, only four departments have not had major budget slashes: pensions, the wheat board, the arms industry (where no figures at all had been divulged for 1987) and Saudia, the national airline. (*Middle East Economic Digest*, 9 January 1988).

41 IISS, *The Military Balance, 1987–88*, p. 110 and 1988–89, p. 112.

42 G. Corm, *Le Prochei-Orient éclaté* (Paris, 1983) p. 85.

43 Saudi Arabia is responsible for the amount that is to be pumped and for the pricing policy, but most technical operations are assumed by Aramco according to operating contracts. This type of arrangement is practically the norm in most oil-producing countries. Algeria and Iraq are exceptions among major exporters in assuming the whole chain of technical operations.

44 A few days after the public announcement of C(SS)-2 acquisitions, a British paper revealed that Israel had been in discussion with China for two years about the possibilities of military co-operation, particularly for an advanced radar system that had originally been designed for the Lavi fighter-bomber which was abandoned in 1987 (*Sunday Times*, 10 April 1988).

45 A group of Indian workers went on strike in Kuwait in the spring of 1989; it was an almost unknown phenomenon and their protest was against the shady labour brokers who were responsible for bringing them to Kuwait under particularly wretched conditions rather than for political motives.

Chapter Six: Qatar

1 The International Institute for Strategic Studies (London), gives 385,000 including some 300,000 expatriates. *The Military Balance, 1988–89*, p. 111. The figure may be a little high.
2 The statistics vary from source to source and year to year. Some years, the UAE shows a higher income-per-capita figure, but the distribution is far more unequal, even among UAE citizens, than among Qataris.
3 *Arab Oil and Gas Directory*, 1988, p. 333.
4 The 'Federation of Nine' would have included the seven emirates of the present UAE plus Qatar and Bahrain.
5 The last available figure is Qatar Riyals 604 m ($165.94 m) for 1983/4 given by *The Military Balance, 1988–89*, p. 111.

Chapter Seven: Bahrain

1 An offshore bank – or for that matter any offshore business – is one domiciled in a country, but accepting (in the case of banks) funds only from non-residents.
2 The 'Country reports on Human Rights Practices' published in Washington annually.
3 The other presumed – and self-proclaimed – organizer *in absentia* was Medhi Hashemi, who was subsequently executed by firing squad in Tehran, on 28 September 1987.
4 One can fairly talk of a middle class in Bahrain, but practically nowhere else in the Gulf.
5 The most violent and bloody practices have long been forbidden in Bahrain where the self-flagellations and self-mutilations common in Iran (and, before the war, in the Shi'a holy cities of southern Iraq) are much attenuated.

Chapter Eight: United Arab Emirates

1 The first two of these happen to have been French, the third English. All were published between 1973 and 1980. They were all lent to me at various times on my travels but I can find no trace of any of them in serious libraries. But they did (or do) exist.
2 The story that he kept the banknotes under his bed is probably apocryphal. It is almost certain that a traditional tribal chief like Shakhbout would sleep in the traditional way, on a pallet on the ground.

3 He died in early 1989.
4 W. Thesiger, *Arabian Sands* (London, Longman, Green, 1959) reprinted by Penguin Books, 1976.
5 For exchange rate see Appendix I.
6 In 1976 I remember having been struck by the fact that the only place in the whole of Abu Dhabi where in the course of a fairly long visit I had heard birds twitter was in the garden surrounding the palace of Sheikha Fatima, Sheikh Zayed's wife.
7 In any Arab meeting, it is practically an automatic reaction that the host becomes chairman.
8 The title is used not only for the rulers and the male members of their family, but also for the head of any tribe or sub-tribe. It can also be given as a courtesy title to respected prayer leaders, or preachers of Friday sermons as well as to any learned man, particularly if he is also respected for his piety.
9 Elsewhere many imported imams are Pakistani.
10 For more details, see F. Heard-Bey, *From Trucial States to United Arab Emirates* (London, Longman, 1982) pp. 238 ff.
11 The Qawasim of Ras al-Khaimah had accepted Wahhabism, but that is still a particular form of Sunni Islam.
12 Only 7.6 per cent of the labour force was made up of Emirati citizens according to a report published by the Ministry of Labour and Social Affairs in 1984.
13 Sultan can be a given name and as such should not be confused with sultan used as a title, as used by Sultan Qaboos of Oman. Malek or king, the title used by the kings of Saudi Arabia, Jordan and Morocco, is also quite commonly found as a name.
14 London, Croom Helm, 1986.
15 Heard-Bey, *From Trucial States to United Arab Emirates*, p. 299.
16 The exact definition varied several times, but was usually put at anything north of 25′ 30″ N, which made the line pass just north of Fujairah and Khor Fakkan, the Sharjah port on the Indian Ocean.
17 There were a few incidents in the naval war that remain unexplained, but they seem really to have occurred without deliberate intent to cause either physical or diplomatic harm.
18 The person who affirmed this was very well placed to know what he was talking about, but specifically asked to remain anonymous.
19 *Arab Oil and Gas Directory*, 16 May 1988.
20 Ibid.
21 The exception being the border between the two Yemens.

Chapter Nine: Oman

1 Ibadhism is a sect of Islam particularly identified with Oman and found, otherwise, only in a few places in southern Tunisia and in the Mzab (or Heptopolis) of Algeria. Cf. L. Graz, *The Omanis* (London, Longman,

1982) pp. 61 ff or, for more detail, H. Laoust, *Les sectes de l'Islam* (Paris, Payot, 1965, 1977).

2 Until the middle of the nineteenth century the sultans were more often called Sayyid. It is a complicated and confusing nomenclature. For more detail see Graz, *The Omanis*, p. 2.

3 There has never been a census. According to weighted estimates of health and education authorities plus the local representatives of UNDP and other UN agencies, the 1987 population can be estimated at 1.25 million, still below the 1.5 million used in official publications 'for planning purposes'.

4 The joke about the Emirates' 'Five-day army' is at least partially substantiated by the stream of cars pouring through Buraimi every weekend.

5 Muscat proper is a very small part of a long string of built-up areas interspersed with mountains and strung like beads along 40 km of coastal road.

6 The London *Observer* was particularly active in whipping up the froth during the summer of 1982.

7 Among the precursors, especially among non-Arabs, was Professor Fred Halliday with *Arabia Without Sultans* (London, Penguin, 1974) reprinted in paperback, 1979.

8 PFLOAG was the final incarnation of the Dhofar rebellion's last holdouts. It finally disappeared even in its last refuge, Aden. I looked for it there in September 1987 and found the sign on a store-front office that was permanently closed.

9 In the course of the palace revolution which brought Qaboos to power, one slave was killed and the old Sultan shot himself in the foot as he was taking his pistol out of his desk drawer. Said bin Taimur was flown to Bahrain, where he was treated in the British army hospital, then to London, where he died a natural death two years later. Anti-Qaboos propaganda has been so strong that I have more than once heard him accused of being responsible for his father's death.

10 Arab League rules still (in early 1990) call for a consensus in all decisions and do not allow for majority voting.

11 There were a few Saudi objections left over from the Buraimi crisis and warmed up by the fact that the last imam was still living in exile in Saudi Arabia. cf. Graz, *The Omanis*, p. 16.

12 Ibid. p. 171 (personal interview with the then Minister Qais Abdul Moneim Zawawi in 1980).

13 Characteristically, it has been giving some aid to Zanzibar, its former colony (which threw out the Arabs in a fiercely bloody revolution in 1964), where a fairly modest amount of money can go a long way.

14 Private communication from a diplomat in Muscat who wishes to remain anonymous, November 1985.

15 Re-establishment, because the Soviet Union and Saudi Arabia maintained normal relations from 1927 to 1938.

16 He had also got help from King Hussein of Jordan who sent officers and

troops. Ever since then and for a number of reasons, Hussein has certainly been the Arab leader to whom Qaboos feels closest, both politically and personally. For the Iranian expedition, see also Graz, *The Omanis*, pp. 41 ff.

17 One of the most bitterly disputed points at the beginning of the peace negotiations between Iran and Iraq in the late summer of 1988 turned on the Iranian demand – during a cease-fire that was not yet a peace – to inspect Iraqi ships going through the Strait of Hormuz to be sure they were not carrying war materials, a demand that was rejected by the Iraqis. The Iranian foreign minister, Ali Akbar Velayati, stated during an interview in Geneva that Iran had never stopped or threatened to stop a ship in Omani waters (confirmed by Omani sources); this means either that the Iraqis were going through on the Iranian side to test Iranian reactions – difficult for a big tanker but perfectly possible for a smaller vessel – or that they were being stopped in international waters, which the Iranians denied having done.

18 *Foreign Report*, 14 September 1988.

19 Cf. Graz, *The Omanis*, pp. 17–18.

20 The 1985 GCC summit was held two weeks before the 15th anniversary celebrations. The Omanis were particularly keen to show the other Gulf sovereigns – several of whom had never visited Oman – and their suites and even the journalists that Muscat was no longer the backward place many of them imagined.

21 It does, however, generally abide by OPEC prices.

22 Omani oil is expensive to produce. It cost an average of $7 per barrel to get to the coastal terminals in 1988 as compared with $1.50 for Kuwaiti or Saudi oil.

23 To give one example: the mobile health teams were expected, by the population, to provide a door-to-door service; bringing children to a central village vaccination point was considered tedious. The amazing thing is that the teams, made up almost entirely of foreign health workers, were given the order to go from hut to hut in the mountains, an enormous waste of time and energy.

24 Said Nasser al-Khusaibi, the first director, was the former *naib wali* of Dhofar, the executive officer under the wali or governor.

25 It rarely rains in Oman, but almost every winter there are one or two very hard rains at least in the mountains. Falling on a sun-baked soil, most of the water runs off without any possibility of absorption.

26 In general, in the Gulf, it is considered bad taste to talk about the private life of the rulers or their immediate family; in countries where the family is very large, there will inevitably be more occasion for gossip. Putting anything of the sort in writing is almost everywhere considered literally a crime of lèse-majesté. I hope the Sultan will forgive this discussion which I have included to dispel the misconceptions of many non-Omanis.

27 The theological differences between Ibadhism and Sunni Islam can become quite subtle. In general, Ibadhism is a strict, puritanical and fiercely egalitarian form of Islam which is, at least in practice, very rigorous

for its observers and fairly tolerant of others. One of the few easily accessible works on the subject is: Laoust, *Les sectes de l'Islam*.

Chapter Ten: Conclusion

1 After the first sharp rises in oil prices in 1979, the market stabilized and then slumped. No amount of tension in the ensuing years ever brought another shock of rising prices.
2 See, for example, the heavily subsidized wheat surpluses that Saudi Arabia sold to the European Community in 1987 (*The Economist*, 24 October 1987).
3 Though it was not much talked about, this idea was particularly frightening to Oman with its large population of Baluchi origin.
4 It was Saudi money that financed the training camps for the young hotheads coming from Algeria or Yemen for 'the defence of Islam'; those same young men, returning to their home countries after a few years in Afghanistan, joined the hard-line movements that spent much of their time denouncing the Gulf monarchies.
5 November 1979 was the date of the Mecca uprising of Juhaiman bin Muhammad al-Otaibi and his companions.
6 Iran and Iraq did not formally break off diplomatic relations until September 1987; for seven years one or two unfortunate low-level diplomats had been bottled up in their respective embassies in the enemy capital.
7 Personal notes of a press conference.
8 Cf. L. Graz., *The Omanis*, p. 17. For a more detailed account, see J.B. Kelly, *Eastern Arabian Frontiers*, London 1964, passim.
9 An 'authorized version' in English is now being prepared at the Islamic University in Medina.
10 See Chapter 4 on Kuwait.
11 The figure is given by Elizabeth Drew in her Washington Letter in *The New Yorker*, 31 August 1987. It is hardly a large sum on the Saudi scale. A comparison could be made with the two billion dollars that were reportedly promised to Syria's President Hafez el-Assad at the time of the Amman Summit in November 1987. (*Le Monde*, 11 November, 1987.)
12 The quotation is authentic, heard in 1991.
13 It is only fair to say that certain currents in America do support such thinking. In this respect, see, *inter alia*, the article by Hani A. Faris in Arab Studies Quarterly, Vol 9, No. 2, pp. 149 ff.
14 Notes of an off-the-record conversation in Doha, at the time of the GCC summit, November 1983.
15 With one notable exception: Salah Khalif (Abu Iyad), a long-time resident of Kuwait, refused to join the chorus. He was assassinated in Tunis on the eve of the war, almost certainly either directly by the Iraqis or on their orders.
16 'Operation Staunch' was the name given to an American policy decision to impose economic sanctions and an arms boycott on Iran, while trying to

persuade its friends and allies to do the same.

17 By 15 January 1991, the USA had 495,000 men in the Gulf (officially 65 per cent of the allied ground forces), Britain and France one armoured division each, plus assorted air and naval forces, and the other European countries considerably fewer. Much was subsequently made of the fact that the British had proportionately the highest number of casualties. This was considered as a sign of sacrifice and heroism rather than incompetence.

18 See Fouad Ajami *The Arab Predicament* (New York, 1981).

19 See Bruno Etienne, *l'Islamisme radical*, p. 267 ff.

20 After the Mecca riots of the previous pilgrimage season, Saudi Arabia had said that it wanted to impose quotas on all the Muslim countries and Iran had already objected.

21 In the upper Gulf, the *dishdasha* is worn over a pair of long drawers in winter, and in summer often simply with a modern pair of underpants.

22 That is also why Iraq will probably never be pushed too hard to repay the billions of dollars of 'loans' supplied by its Gulf supporters.

APPENDIX I

Regional Statistics

Saudi Arabia

Area: 2,240,000 sq km.
Population: 8-11,000,000 (of whom >5m are expatriates)
GNP:1986: SAR 286.69 bn ($77.415 bn)
1987: SAR 278.1 bn ($74.259 bn)
Currency: Saudi Riyal SAR:SAR 1 = $0.267
Oil production (1987): 4.25 m barrels/day (including neutral zone)
Oil revenue (1987): $21.2 bn

Bahrain

Area: 669 sq km
Population: 420,000
GNP: 1986: BD 1.495 bn; (1987: −±4%)
Currency: Bahraini Dinar BD: BD 1 = $2.65 (1988)
Oil production (1987): 43,200 b/d
Oil revenue (1987): BD 230m (est.)

United Arab Emirates

Area: 83,657 sq km
Population: 1,400,000 (>1 m expatriates)
GNP: 1987: Dh 85.0 bn (1986: −22%; 1987: −8%)
Currency: Dirham Dh: Dh 1=$0.272
Oil production 1987: 1,427,500 b/d (including condensates)
Oil revenue (1987): $9 bn

Iraq

Area: 438,466 sq km
Population: 16,200,000
GNP: 1986: ID 11,350 bn ($36,507 bn)
Currency: Iraqi Dinar ID: ID 1=$3.218 (official rate)
Oil production 1987: 2.35 m b/d
Oil revenue (1987): $11 bn

Iran

Area: 1,448,000 sq km
Population: 50,000,000
GNP: 1985/86 RI 15.306 bn ($174.46 bn)
Iranian Ryial RI: RI 1=$0.0140
Oil production: 2.3m b/d
Oil revenue (1987): $10 bn

Kuwait

Area: 16,918 sq km
Population: 1,600,000 (±1 m expatriates)
GNP: 1986/87 KD 5,250 bn
Currency: Kuwaiti Dinar KD: KD 1=$3.65
Oil production 1987: 1,095,800 b/d
Oil revenue (1987): $8.15 bn

Oman

Area: 212,380 sq km
Population: 1,300,000 m (±18% expatriates)
GNP: 1987: OR 2.4 bn
Currency: Omani Riyal OR: 1 OR = $2.6
Oil production 1987: 565,000 b/d
Oil revenue 1987: $2.8 bn

Qatar

Area: 10,240 sq km
Population: 350,000 (>250,000 expatriates)
GNP: QR 17,500 bn
Currency: Qatari Riyal QR: QR 1=$0.2747
Oil production 1987: 293,000 b/d
Oil revenue (1987): $1.8 bn

North Yemen

Area: 195,000 sq km
Population: 9,300,000 m
GNP: 1986: YR 29,870 bn
Currency: Yemeni Riyal YR: 1 YR=$0.104
Oil production mid-1988: 100,000 b/d

South Yemen

Area: 290,273 sq km
Population: 2,300,000
GNP: 1984: YD 378.2 m
Currency: Yemeni Dinar YD: 1 YD=$2.928

Exchange rates: official mid-1989 (in both Iran and Iraq there were significant differences with black-market rates)

Note: All these figures (except oil production and most of the exchange rates) should be treated with great caution and read with the utmost scepticism. Many are nothing more than estimates, others have been deliberately swollen or shrunk for reasons of internal policy.

Sources: *The Military Balance*, (London, International Institute for Strategic Studies, 1988–9); *Arab Oil and Gas Directory*, 1988; official statistics of the countries concerned.

APPENDIX II

Notes on the Bazoft Affair

By sheer chance, I was in Baghdad in September 1989 when the Iranian-born, British-based journalist Farzad Bazoft was arrested for alleged spying. This was the beginning of a protracted crisis in Iraqi-British (and ultimately Iraqi-European) relations that was exacerbated by Bazoft's execution by hanging in March 1990. I had never met Farzad Bazoft before but he told me his story in public the day before he was arrested. Since I happened to be at the airport when he was arrested and knew the people involved, I alerted both the British Embassy and the *Observer* office in London. Below is the unedited text of the memo I wrote to the Editor of the *Observer* at his request, immediately after the events described.

22 September 1989

Memo To:
Donald Trelford, The Observer

From: Liesl Graz

As Martin [Martin Huckerby, foreign editor of the *Observer*] asked me to do, I have put on paper the salient points of what I know about Farzad Bazoft's unhappy adventure in Iraq.

On Thursday, 14 September, Farzad – whom I had met very briefly, once [in Baghdad during the same visit, two or three days previously] – saw me in the hall of the Meridien Hotel (oops, ex-Meridien, now Palestine), where we were both staying, and asked me whether he could speak to me, quietly. He told me that he had gone to the site of the 17 August explosion presumed to be in an arms factory – you saw the ridiculous explanation of the Iraqi Embassy. I had heard from a Dutch journalist friend who also tried to go to there under his own steam that the taxi he had hired had, once he was in the outskirts of Al Hilla (the modern town nearest ancient Babylon) and been asked to go to the site, refused to continue and returned at speed to Baghdad. The suburb of Hilla in fact practically a separate town – called Iskanderiyya is a generally closed area at all times, thought to be a main centre of arms manufacturing in Iraq. When I asked Farzad whether he had gone in a taxi, he said no; he had been in a hospital car (How? answer: I have connections[1]) posing as an Indian doctor. He had photographs, he told me, and a sketch map of the site, as well as a damaged shoe and earth samples that he had collected there. He told me that he had arranged to have the shoe and samples sent out by the diplomatic bag (to my question of which one, he replied British) and then analysed by MOD laboratories.

Knowing that I was spending the weekend on Cyprus, he asked me whether eventually I would take his story and fax it from Nicosia. Quite honestly, I wasn't happy about the idea, but confraternal solidarity won out and I said that eventually I would[2]. Then he told me that he had the feeling that he was constantly being checked on, telephone calls were made to his hotel room to see whether he was there – no message, no voice, once he picked up the phone. With the telephone system what it is in Baghdad, and the general disorganisation of a hotel that a fortnight before had chucked out all its management on an hour's notice, that can happen. (It has happened to me, too, but I took it simply as an accident; I have been lucky in my recent trips to Baghdad to be able to come and go absolutely on my own, no minder, no official watchdogs.)

At that point he was wondering whether he should stay another day or two, especially since the Ministry of Information had been vaguely talking about another journalists' junket to Kurdistan for the following day. My instinct, and what I told him, was to get out of the country as quickly as possible. He told me that he was meeting James Tanzy, first secretary (I think that is his title) of the British Embassy that afternoon to ask his opinion. We arranged to meet at 8 o'clock, just before I was to go out for dinner, but he was not there.

The next day, Friday, when I came down to leave the hotel for my plane to Larnaca, I saw Farzad and an Arab journalist whom I did not know about to leave for Saddam Airport in a Ministry of Information car with an official minder, sorry accompagnator. The minder asked whether I wanted a lift. I had been taking taxis hailed on the street everywhere but this time there was no need for discretion. In fact, with my tandy, [portable computer] I was rather happy to have a Ministry of Information official there to help me through the multiple police and security checks, if necessary. Farzad seemed extremely nervous, and when I asked him whether he had seen James Tanzy and what the advice had been, he only said that it had been the same as mine. He was on his way to the 11.30 Iraqi Airways plane to London, and told me he was going straight to the *Observer* office from Heathrow. I was quite sure that you knew all about what he was doing in Iraq and were waiting with baited breath for his story.

As luck would have it, we had a puncture on the motorway leading to the airport. Farzad – even more nervous than before – climbed over the barrier to stand in the shade of a tree; so did I. After less than 30 seconds, first one, then two and finally three men who ostentatiously acted like self-important security men – no uniforms, but that is common – came and ordered us to return to the other side of the barrier. Farzad rather truculently, in English, told them. 'What's wrong? Are those generals' houses or something? …' I simply told them, in Arabic, that it was hot in the sun and we wanted to wait in the shade until the car was fixed. They hung around, but left us alone. I don't think this incident had anything to do with what happened later, but it did show Farzad's frame of mind.

When we arrived at the airport, Farzad and Ma'alouf (a Libyan exile freelance journalist for Arab magazines in London, also with British travel documents) went with the Ministry of Information minder to check in for the London flight (due to leave at 11.30) and I went to the other side of the hall to the Larnaca check-in counter. We met again at the police barrier, where I told Farzad and Ma'alouf to go along in front of me since their plane was a half-hour earlier than mine. Farzad's travel document elicited a slight delay in the booth – but again no more than is perfectly common and normal in Iraq. When my turn – next after Farzad – came, and after I had pushed my (Swiss) passport through the window, I was told to go to another booth: the computer was down. (By that time, the Ministry of Information official had disappeared as far as I could see.)

Ten minutes later, after having gone through another queue and security checks, I emerged into the transit lounge. Very empty, because there were only the two planes to London and Larnaca in the next three to four hours. I saw Ma'alouf, alone, and he asked 'Have you seen Farzad?' 'No; I thought he went with you …' and explained my mishap with the computer. Then Ma'alouf, without being particularly upset about it, said that 'They came to take him again, here.' I posted myself in a place where I could watch the doors; Ma'alouf left, I stayed until my plane was called. Then, as late as possible, I rang the British embassy and was able to get the duty officer, who as it happened was James Tanzy. I told him the story quickly, adding that Farzad might have been taken to the plane by another route.

You know the rest.

Iraqi interrogation prisons are not, according to all reports, pleasant places to be. Iraq is still technically at war with Iran, and exiles' travel documents must not really mean a great deal to the Iraqi *Mukhabarat*, the secret police, who know what double and triple agents can be like.

When Martin told me, on Saturday, that Farzad had been released, it seemed to me almost unheard of good news. When he did not show up, it was ominous, and gets to be more so every day.

Footnotes:

1. The 'connections' referred to turned out to be Ms Daphne Parish, a British nurse working for an Irish-run private hospital in Baghdad. She was arrested four days after Bazoft and convicted to fifteen years' imprisonment as an accomplice.
2. Making it clear that I would take if necessary only the text of a story, not sketches or other material.

Bibliography

Summary Bibliography

This is not a complete bibliography of the Gulf. Although there are not a great many recent books on the subject, the Gulf war spawned a large number of articles, particularly on strategic issues. Three main criteria have been used in deciding what to include: books and articles that seemed particularly interesting or important; books and articles which are quoted in this book; and when possible, works that are reasonably available to the interested reader.

BOOKS

Ajami, Fouad, *The Arab Predicament*, New York: Cambridge University Press, 1981.

Al-Khalil, Samir, *Republic of Fear: Saddam's Iraq*, London: Hutchinson Radius, 1990.

Al Qasimi, Sultan Muhammad, *The Myth of Arab Piracy*, London: Croom Helm, 1986.

Algosaibi, Ghazi A., *Arabian Essays*, London: KPI, 1982.

Arab Oil and Gas Directory, published annually (under the direction of Nicolas Sarkis), Paris: 1987 and 1988.

Arberry, Arthur J., *The Koran Interpreted*, London: George Allen & Unwin, 1953; one-volume edition, 1980.

As-Sabah, Salem al-Jabir, *Les Emirats du Golfe*, Paris: Fayard, 1980.

Bakhash, Shaul, *The Reign of the Ayatollahs*, New York: Basic Books, 1984; London: I.B. Tauris, 1985, and Counterpoint, 1986.

Balta, Paul, *Iran-Irak, Une guerre de 5000 ans*, Paris: Editions Anthropos, 1987.

Braun, Ursula, *Der Kooperationsrat arabischer Staaten am Golf: Eine neue Kraft*, Baden-Baden: Nomos Verlagsgesellschaft, 1986.

Chubin, Sharam and Charles Tripp, *Iran and Iraq at War*, London: I.B. Tauris, 1988.

Chubin, Shahram and Charles Tripp, *Iran and Iraq: War, Society and Politics, 1980–1986*, Geneva: IUHEI, 1986.

Chubin, Shahram, *Iran and its Neighbours, The Impact of the Gulf War*, London: Centre for Security and Conflict Studies, 1987.

Cordesman, Anthony, *Iran–Iraq and Western Security*: 1984–87, London: Jane's, 1987.
Corm, Georges, *Le Proche-orient éclaté*, Paris: La Découverte, 1983.
De Lage, Olivier, and G. Grzybek, *Le Jeu des six familles*, Paris: Autrement, 1985.
Djalili, Mohammad-Reza, *Diplomatie Islamique: Stratégie Internationale du Khomeynisme*, Paris: Presses Universitaires de France, 1989
Etienne, Bruno, *L'Islamisme radical*, Paris: Hachette, 1987.
Farouk-Sluglett, M. and P. Sluglett, *Iraq since 1958 – from Revolution to Dictatorship*, London: I.B. Tauris, 1991.
Graz, Liesl, *L'Irak au présent*, Lausanne: Les Trois Continents, 1979.
Graz, Liesl, *The Omanis: Sentinels of the Gulf*, London: Longman, 1982.
Halliday, Fred, *Arabia Without Sultans*, London: Penguin, 1979.
Heard-Bey, F., *From Trucial States to United Arab Emirates*, London: Longman, 1982.
Hentsch, Thierry, *L'Orient imaginaire*, Paris: Les Editions de Minuit, 1988.
Holden, D. and R. Johns, *The House of Saud*, London: Sidgwick & Jackson, 1981.
Hottinger, Arnold, *7 Mal Näher Osten*, 4th edition, Munich/Zurich: Piper, 1988.
International Institute for Strategic Studies, London: *The Military Balance*, annual, 1987/88 and 1988/89.
Khadduri, Majid, *The Gulf War: The Origins and Implications of the Iraq-Iran Conflict*, New York and Oxford: Oxford University Press, 1988.
King, Ralph, *The Iran-Iraq War: The Political Implications*, Adelphi Paper 219, London: IISS, 1987.
Lacey, R., *The Kingdom*, New York: Harcourt Brace Jovanovich, 1981.
Le Coran, trans. D. Masson, Paris: La Pléiade 1967: paper: édition Folio, 1980–86.
McDermott, Anthony, *Egypt From Nasser to Mubarak*, London: Croom Helm, 1988.
Mackey, Sandra, *The Saudis: Inside The Desert Kingdom*, New York: Houghton Mifflin, 1987 and New American Library, 1988.
Niebuhr, Carsten, *Reisebeschreibung nach Arabien und andern umliegenden Ländern*, Copenhagen: J. Mueller, 1773.
People for a Just Peace, *The Proliferation of Chemical Warfare: The Holocaust at Halabja*. Washington DC: People for a Just Peace, 1988.
Rumaihi, Muhammad, *Beyond Oil*, London: Al Saqi Books, 1983.
Said, Edward W., *Orientalism*, London: Routledge & Kegan Paul, 1978.
Sandwick, J.A., (ed.), *The Gulf Co-operation Council: Moderation and Stability in an Interdependent World*, Boulder, CO.: Westview, 1987.
Simpson, John, *Behind Iranian Lines*, London: Robson Books Ltd. 1988 and revised edn, Fontana Paperbacks, 1989.
Taryam, Abdullah Omran, *The Establishment of the United Arab Emirates 1950–85*, London: Croom Helm, 1987.
Thesiger, Wilfred, *Arabian Sands*, London: Longmans Green, 1959.

Zemzemi, Abdel-Magid, *La Guerre Irak-Iran*, Paris: Albatross, 1985.

ARTICLES

Ajami, Fouad, 'La crise d'identité culturelle du monde arabe', *Politique étrangère*, Summer, 1987.

Braun, Ursula, 'The Iran-Iraq War: its regional and international dynamics', *Orient*, 27, No. 4 (Dec. 1986: publ. June 1987).

Cable, James, 'Outside Navies in the Gulf', *International Relations*, Vol. IX, No. 3, May 1988.

Chubin, Shahram, 'La conduite des opérations militaires dans le conflit Iran-Irak', *Politique étrangère*, Summer 1987.

Corm, Georges, 'La Balkanisation du Proche-Orient entre le mythe et la réalité', *Le Monde diplomatique*, January 1983.

Graz, Liesl, 'Die Turkei und ihre asiatische Nachbarn', *Europa-Archiv*, 23:24, 10 December 1987.

Graz, Liesl, 'The End of the Era of Confrontation: The Soviet Union and the Middle East', *Le Monde diplomatique*, Arabic edn., May/June 1989.

Graz, Liesl, 'The Soviets and the Middle East', *Swiss Review of World Affairs*, Vol XXXIX, No 5, August 1989.

Gresh, Alain and Olivier Da Lage, 'L'Arabie saoudite, gardienne d'un ordre menacé', *Le Monde diplomatique*, October 1987.

Gresh, Alain, 'Périlleux dilemmes pour la politique soviétique', *Le Monde diplomatique*, October 1987.

Kapeliouk, Amnon, 'Comment Israël tire parti d'une guerre prolongée', *Le Monde diplomatique*, October 1987.

Kechichian, Joseph A., 'The Gulf Co-operation Council: Search for Security'., *Third World Quarterly*, Vol. 7, No 4 (Oct. 1985)

Salamé, Ghassan, 'Islam in South Arabia', *Arab Studies Quarterly*, Summer 1987.

Salamé, Ghassan, 'Les Pétromonarchies du Golfe et la guerre du Chatt el-Arab', *Politique étrangère*, Summer 1987.

Salamé, Ghassan, 'Perceived threats and perceived loyalties', Paper of Exeter University Symposium, *The Gulf and the Arab World*, Exeter, 1986.

Schloesser, J., 'US Policy in the Persian Gulf', *Department of State Bulletin*, Vol. 87, No. 2127, Washington DC, October 1987.

Sick, Gary, 'Iran's Quest for Superpower Status', *Foreign Affairs*, 64'4, Spring 1987.

Swire, Adrian, 'Merchant Shipping and the Gulf War', *Naval Forces*, Vol. VIII, No. III. 1987.

The following publications have been used repeatedly:

Al Qabas: esp. international edition (Kuwait and London)
Arab Times (Kuwait)
The Economist (London)
Gulf Times (Qatar)

Middle East Economic Digest (MEED)
Middle East International (London)
Le Monde, (Paris)
Le Pétrole et le gaz arabes (Arab Oil and Gas; Paris)

Index

Note: Major references are indicated by bold page numbers.